MANAGING FURTHER EDUCATION:
LEARNING ENTERPRISE

Educational Management: Research and Practice

Series Editor: Tony Bush

Managing People in Education
Edited by Tony Bush and David Middlewood

Strategic Management in Schools and Colleges
Edited by David Middlewood and Jacky Lumby

Managing External Relations in Schools and Colleges
Edited by Jacky Lumby and Nick Foskett

Practitioner Research in Education: Making a Difference
David Middlewood, Marianne Coleman and Jacky Lumby

Managing Finance and Resources in Education
Edited by Marianne Coleman and Lesley Anderson

Managing Further Education: Learning Enterprise
Jacky Lumby

This book, *Managing Further Education: Learning Enterprise*, is recommended for students in post-compulsory education taking the MBA in educational management offered by the EMDU, University of Leicester.

The modules in this course are:
Leadership and Strategic Management in Education
Managing Finance and External Relations
Human Resource Management in Schools and Colleges
Managing the Curriculum
Research Methods in Educational Management

For further information about the MBA in Educational Management, please contact the EMDU at emdu@le.ac.uk. For further information about the books associated with the course, contact Paul Chapman Publishing at www.paulchapmanpublishing.co.uk.

EM
DU
EDUCATIONAL
MANAGEMENT
DEVELOPMENT
UNIT

 University of Leicester

MANAGING FURTHER EDUCATION
EDUCATION
Learning Enterprise

Jacky Lumby

P·C·P
Paul Chapman
Publishing

Paul Chapman Publishing
A SAGE Publications Company
6 Bonhill Street
London EC2A 4PU

SAGE Publications Inc
2455 Teller Road
Thousand Oaks, California 91320

SAGE Publications India Pvt Ltd
32, M-Block Market
Greater Kailash - 1
New Delhi 110 048

British Library Cataloguing in Publication data

A catalogue record for this book is available from the
British Library

ISBN 0 7619 6558 0
ISBN 0 7619 6559 9 (pbk)

Library of Congress Control Number available

Typeset by Dorwyn Ltd, Rowlands Castle, Hants.
Printed in Great Britain by Athenaeum Press, Gateshead

CONTENTS

FIGURES

TABLES

SERIES EDITOR'S FOREWORD

Further education has often been regarded as the 'Cinderella' service. Sandwiched between the schools, whose requirements are often politically sensitive, and the more glamorous university sector, colleges have sometimes struggled to attract sufficient attention for their particular needs. Because further education provides such a diverse range of courses and caters for many different types of clients, it has not developed a clear identity or sense of purpose. Its very responsiveness, although a vital aspect of the sector, makes it difficult to demonstrate a distinctive mission.

The emergence of self-governing schools and colleges at the end of the twentieth century has led to major restructuring of the educational system in many countries. The incorporation of colleges in England in 1993 provides a clear example of the challenges facing managers when major structural change is imposed on educational organizations. The independence from local education authorities, and the imposition of a national funding regime, initially via the Further Education Funding Council, required major changes in management which inevitably disturbed previous arrangements.

There is a significant body of published research on the impact of self-management on schools, in the United Kingdom and many other countries, but a paucity of writing on the effects of incorporation on colleges. Because further education in England provides a particularly stark example of the genre, the research reported by Jacky Lumby is valuable both in giving the first detailed picture of the sector since independence and in showing how major structural change effects those who have to implement it.

The development of effective managers in education requires the support of literature which presents the major issues in clear, intelligible language while drawing on the best of theory and research. The purpose of this series is to examine the management of schools and colleges, drawing on empirical evidence. The approach is analytical rather than descriptive and generates conclusions about the most appropriate ways of managing schools and colleges on the basis of research evidence.

The aim of this series, and of this volume, is to develop a body of literature with the following characteristics:

- Directly relevant to school and college management.
- Prepared by authors with national and international reputations.
- An analytical approach based on empirical evidence but couched in intelligible language.
- Integrating the best of theory, research and practice.

Managing Further Education: Learning Enterprise is the sixth volume in the series and Jacky Lumby presents a fascinating account of the ways in which incorporation has changed the working lives of middle and senior managers. While the impact on management processes is faithfully documented, she also demonstrates the extent to which management styles and organizational culture have changed to accommodate externally imposed political imperatives. The book also shows how managers are not simply the prisoners of events, however powerful they may be. The educational leaders featured in this volume have responded to the external and internal pressures by developing an approach to management which recognizes that students' learning remains their central concern even when funding issues appear to be paramount. Jacky Lumby shows how good managers can succeed even in unpromising circumstances.

Tony Bush
University of Leicester
May 2000

PREFACE

The period since the incorporation of colleges in England in 1993 has been one of tempestuous change. Managers in the sector have been exhorted, lambasted, directed and, much less frequently, praised for their work. What has been less in evidence is listening to their view of events and their experience of managing. Specifically, the systematic and careful exploration of their experience though research has been limited. Working in the Educational Management Development Unit at the University of Leicester with many MBA students from further education, it has been a frequent frustration that when students ask where they can find research on aspects of management in the sector, there is so little to which they can be directed. The origin of this book was a wish to make a contribution to research in the field and particularly to give a voice to managers in the sector, providing evidence and analysis which would lead to a better understanding of the pressures to which they have been subject and the ways they have chosen to respond. The managers who contributed to this book by providing interviews shared this aim. Given the years of near political invisibility within the sector, there remains a passionate commitment to furthering people's understanding of the work of colleges and, as part of a deep commitment to learning, to sharing experience with their peers. Consequently, this book was predicated on a wish, by both the writer and those providing data, to communicate what it means to manage in a further education college, and how such experience has changed and developed since incorporation.

The decision to focus on management reflects my own central interest. It does not imply in any way that the perspective of others who work in the sector, lecturers, administrators, technicians and estates staff is of less importance or of less interest. The choice to devote a full volume to management was based on the desire to have the space to explore in depth the perspective and activity of managers.

The first chapter sets the scene of the context in which colleges have worked since 1993 and explains the rationale and methodology for the research which underpins the book. Subsequent chapters go on to explore the major areas of management which are undertaken in colleges. Chapter 2 analyses how far the leadership of both senior and middle managers may have evolved in response to the different environment. Chapter 3 provides an overview of the management of staff and the efforts to overcome the very difficult conditions in which colleges have had to try to retain commitment and enthusiasm. Chapter 4 explores the views of finance managers on the pressures to which they have been subject and details the methods of allocating funds internally, linking this to culture change. Chapter 5 considers the different conceptions of marketing in colleges and how these have been operationalized. Chapter 6 reviews the different theoretical approaches to quality and explores how quality managers have tried to encourage all staff to contribute to improving quality. Chapter 7 describes the extent of restructuring within the sector and explores how far there is a typical structure or not. Chapter 8 analyses the difficulties colleges have in managing information and communication given their size and fragmentation, and provides examples of how managers are approaching the issues. Chapter 9 focuses on the major changes in managing teaching and learning, defining what the change to being 'learner-centred' may mean in reality, and exploring the internal political currents which underpin curriculum change. Chapter 10 retains a focus on teaching and learning, turning to working with employers as the centre of attention, concluding that relations between colleges and employers are not yet sufficiently good and that the resolution may lie in planning and structural issues. Chapter 11 begins the process of pulling together the themes in the book and presents an argument that the culture of further education has indeed changed, presenting frameworks for how the change might be analysed and understood. Finally, Chapter 12 describes colleges' own view of the future and concludes that the sector justifies the epithet, which is the second part of the title of this book, 'learning enterprise'.

Covering such a wide range of management areas is an ambitious undertaking, and it is acknowledged that there is no way that every aspect of each area could be incorporated. Themes such as leadership, culture, human resource management, etc. merit a full volume in their own right. However, the aim was to give an overview of management activity and as such, choices have had to be made throughout to focus on particular aspects and to omit others. This has, hopefully, allowed a sufficiently broad view to support the summary in Chapters 11 and 12 dealing with culture change and the future, which assesses how far the management of the sector has developed and what its future challenges may be.

The structure of the book is therefore sequential and cumulative, allowing the reader to work from start to finish as a logical sequence and argument. However, recognizing that many people are more likely to dip into specific chapters according to their interests, each chapter can be read in isolation. It would, however, be helpful to the reader to glance at the opening chapter first to learn how the research was undertaken and how it is presented in the book.

Thanks are due to many people. First, this book would not have been possible had not many college managers given very generously of their time. Not only did they make time to give an interview or complete a survey questionnaire, but they were also very generous in their openness in describing their experience, not just the successes, but also the problems and failures. Their astuteness in summarizing their experience of management underpins this book. Tony Bush, Marianne Coleman and Ann Briggs gave detailed and insightful comments on drafts, and were consistently encouraging. Thanks are also due to Ann and my daughter Esther for each drawing one of the figures. I am grateful to Pip Murray and Jane Randal for administering the survey, to Rob Dixon for analysis of the latter and production of graphs and figures, to Carolyn Marriott for transcribing the interview tapes, to Christopher Bowring-Carr for producing the index and helpful comments, and to Diane Atkinson who provided administrative support. Thanks, finally, are due to my family for cheerfully putting up with my preoccupation for over a year.

In common with the managers I interviewed, I believe that further education has a vital role to play which merits much greater recognition and support. I hope this book provides a contribution to achieving that goal.

Jacky Lumby
May 2000

GLOSSARY OF TERMS

CMIS	Central Management Information System
DES	Department of Education and Science
DfEE	Department for Education and Employment
FE	further education
FEDA	Further Education Development Agency
FEFC	Further Education Funding Council
FEU	Further Education Unit
GNVQ	General National Vocational Qualification
HE	higher education
HRM	human resource management
ICT	information and communication technology
ISR	individualized student record
IT	information technology
LEA	local education authority
LMI	labour market information
MIS	management information system
NVQ	National Vocational Qualification
OECD	Organization for Economic Co-operation and Development
QA	quality assurance
SME	small to medium-sized enterprise
SMT	senior management team
TEC	Training and Enterprise Council
TQM	total quality management
UK	United Kingdom
UfI	University for Industry

1

THE DIVERSE SECTOR

THE WIDER CONTEXT

When asked in 1999 if someone walking round his college would see much that had changed since five years ago, a Director of Curriculum replied 'yes' and 'no'. There has been a massive amount of change in the further education (FE) sector in the UK leading to jokes like that of Tierney (1998, p. 2) that the only thing that has not changed is that 'Parking is still in short supply'. Despite the turbulent change, walking around any college, a visitor would see some continuity with what has gone before, classes being taught, workshops, meetings. On the other hand, as the Director indicated, there would be differences:

> The whole ambience of the place is different . . . The college now is not characterized by long corridors with doors with little glass windows and the teacher standing at the front. We have larger areas where there is more comfortable sitting, where there are carpets on the floor, where there are computers in the corner, where there are different sorts of activities in the same room, where in a computer suite you might have four groups who are doing different sorts of things. I think that makes it different and that's a reflection of the way in which the curriculum style and delivery has changed. . . . So, yes, I think it probably will be different.

The core of further education has always been, and remains, students and staff coming together to achieve learning and that provides continuity. However, the belief in change is justified, because as well as seeing familiar patterns of learning, the visitor would also see much that was new: resource-based learning centres, a wider range of staff working with students, less group-based teaching and more individually paced work, and so on. Perhaps the most fundamental change is the degree of interest shown in what colleges do. After decades of near invisibility in political terms, the activities and achievements of colleges have moved, if not quite centre stage, certainly to a position where, along with schools and higher education, they are scrutinized because of a belief in their importance.

Internationally, there is greater significance vested in the role of vocational education. As King (1993, p. 210) predicts, 'the once lowly status of vocational and technical schools especially in OECD [Organization for Economic Co-operation and Development] countries' is 'increasingly likely to alter' because of rapid changes in the organization of work. It is no longer feasible to assume that a proportion of the population is adequately educated by compulsory schooling alone. The recognition of the need to aim at post-compulsory education for all has been acknowledged (Imrie, 1995; Kennedy, H., 1997; Young, 1993). In South Africa, colleges are attempting expansion and reorganization to educate the previously excluded black majority (Lumby, 2000a). In China, vocational schools and colleges face the need to become more responsive as previously strictly state-controlled entry is breaking down in the face of market forces (Lumby and Li, 1998). In Hong Kong, the Vocational Training Council has embarked on a fundamental reshaping of vocational education in response to the shifting economic base (Lumby, 2000b). In the UK, King (1993) cites a report reviewing Scottish education in 1992, suggesting that no less than 70 per cent of each age cohort should be following a vocational track. Further education's time has arrived. However, alongside a strengthened commitment to vocational education, governments have also concluded that funding the required expansion is problematic. Public services vie for a bigger slice of the budget while politicians are reluctant to raise taxes to increase the overall size of the cake. Internationally, therefore, vocational education is subject to two trends: an increasing demand for ever greater efficiency in the use of the available funds, and encouragement to enter into partnerships to share the responsibility for investment (King, 1993).

The further education colleges of England, which are the focus of this book, sit within this wider context but are also very local. As Hall (1994) points out, every town of any size has one and sometimes more than one. Cities may have a number, competing or collaborating: 'Further education colleges are not standard, bureaucratically defined institutions but rather each is a product of its own history, the policies of its previous governing bodies and local education authority, and the local demand from employers and communities' (Hall, 1994, p. 9). Each college will have grown pragmatically in response to local need and be a unique product of its history. In total, the further education sector is of great significance, educating and training 3.8 million students in 1998–99 (FEFC, 2000). Despite its ubiquity and the large number of people who have had contact with the sector, it is still nebulous in the public eye (Robson, 1998). Its very diversity makes it difficult to pin down. Colleges have students from compulsory school-age 15- and 16-

year-olds to those who may be studying with the University of the Third Age in their eighties. The curriculum spans not only study and qualifications which are uniquely offered in colleges, but also those offered in parallel in school and in higher education. Consequently, locating further education in a distinctive position between school and universities is not easy. Defining it has eluded the state (Hall, 1994). Although colleges would disavow the attempt to be all things to all people, in some sense that is exactly what they are. Further education is the place where all can go, where no one is excluded because of age, largely the case with schools, or ability, largely the case with universities. Its very diversity and comprehensiveness allows colleges to offer an environment which is less intimidating and more empowering than many other educational settings. As one manager interviewed for this book put it, 'The beauty of FE for me is that it is comprehensive'. The comprehensiveness of the sector is its great strength and its Achilles heel. Colleges provide for all including, amongst much else, a safe haven for many people whose experience of education has not previously been very satisfactory. Thus its comprehensiveness is a great strength. At the same time, the diversity of provision robs the sector of neat visual images and sound bites to communicate in a simple, memorable way what it is and what it does. Some have argued that, in attempting too much for too many by chasing new markets, the sector has lost its way (Elliott, 1996). One theme the book will address is how far the sense of mission is clear in the mind of those who manage within colleges.

A further aspect of the UK context is the recent history of criticism of the sector. The 1980s and 1990s have seen repeated attacks on the achievement of colleges, both in attracting an appropriate range of students and then in providing an appropriate quality of education and training (DES, 1991; Edwards, 1993; Employment Department Group, 1993; Young, 1993). The White Paper *Learning to Succeed* (DfEE, 1999), despite a decade of change, reprised the same theme: 'The system fails a significant section of the community . . . There are too many providers where quality is not up to scratch . . . [There are] fundamental weaknesses in the current system' (DfEE, 1999, p. 5). Despite inspection evidence that poor standards are limited to a small number of colleges (ten colleges responsible for 70 per cent of unsatisfactory provision [Waterhouse, 1999]), attacks persist and the speed of introduction of new measures designed to achieve improvement continues unabated, the move from the Further Education Funding Council (FEFC) to a new Learning and Skills Council marking the start of the new millennium.

The experience of working within further education is framed by a pace of change which was described by one manager interviewed for this book as 'not just turbulent. It's frenetic all the time'. The combination of a negative press and successive changes has tested the sector to breaking point. Additionally, the results of change are welcomed by some and deplored by others, leading to allegations that the profession is in 'a state of crisis' (Robson, 1998, p. 585).

Managers within the sector have borne the heavy responsibility of implementing change, often imposed, while continuing their fundamental role of trying to achieve the best for students and for staff.

THE 'NEW' MANAGER?

As well as the sector as a whole, further education managers have been subject to persistent criticism. As senior managers they are placed at the uncomfortable interface between state executive bodies such as the FEFC, and staff within their own institution. Within colleges, middle managers have a parallel dichotomous position in relating both to senior managers and to lecturers and other staff. Something of a campaign has been waged in the literature alleging the rise of 'a new breed of academic managers' labelled 'managerialist' (Randle and Brady, 1997a, p. 126), who have 'set aside professional values' (ibid., p. 137) and whose role is 'to balance the budget, increase student numbers, generate income and satisfy the quality specifications of the FEFC' (ibid., p. 137). Lecturers are often portrayed as keeping alight the flame of educational and professional values in the face of oppression by the new strain of manager (Elliott and Crossley, 1997; Hartley, 1997; Randle and Brady, 1997a, 1997b). Further education is grossly under-researched (Hughes, Taylor and Tight, 1996) and what is lacking to evaluate the managerialist debate is more evidence on the experience of people who work in the sector. This book aims to make a contribution by giving a voice to managers in order to better understand their experience across the range of activities with which they are involved. It seeks to appreciate what they are doing and why, and the values that underpin their choices. Inevitably, a range of belief and practice was encountered, but the impression gained from the research which underpinned this book conformed to McGregor's (1970) theory Y assumptions; the managers interviewed wanted to take responsibility and to achieve, not primarily for pecuniary rewards, but because of their commitment to the work itself. As one contributor explained: 'We want to make the thing work. That's our common aim and generally we are not here for the money. We are here for other reasons. We love seeing students' work on the wall. We love seeing students do well.'

Self-reported motivators and values are of course unlikely to be self-critical, the 'He would say that, wouldn't he?' syndrome. Nevertheless, if it is accepted that nobody sets out to be an unsatisfactory manager, then all the managers whose interviews are used here are trying to be effective, and their efforts deserve serious attention. Before concluding whether management in further education is effective, and what its values may be, an important step must surely be to listen carefully to those individuals actually carrying out the task.

RESEARCHING THE WORK OF MANAGERS

The purpose and nature of research has always been subject to debate, but research in education, and educational management specifically, has recently been the focus of public discussion. Kennedy (1997, p. 10) points out that researchers 'are susceptible to the same varying waves of fads and reforms as teachers are'. The current wave of proposed reform exhorts research to be instrumental, leading in the short term to improvements in teaching and learning (Hargreaves, 1996). Tooley and Darby's (1998) contribution to the debate is a critique of educational research which claims that a sample of articles displayed partisanship, methodological weakness, lack of evidence and insufficient links with policy and practice. Implicit in the critique is the assumption that research should aspire to the positivist, quantitative paradigm, that is, be objective and value-free, attempting to find 'hard' relationships between cause and effect based on valid and reliable evidence, and, above all, providing immediate solutions to practical issues of teaching and learning (Silverman, 2000). Much of the research on further education does match this formula. As Hughes, Taylor and Tight (1996) point out, the majority of literature on the sector emanates from the government or government agencies with an emphasis on description and the identification of 'good practice'. Thus data are used to identify where colleges are achieving the required outcomes (according to government policy) and to link such success to particular actions or policies.

This approach becomes problematic when compared with the major theories of educational management. It is argued that no single perspective can adequately support an understanding of what happens in the complexity of an educational organization (Bush, 1995). Consequently, a 'conceptual pluralism' (Bolman and Deal, 1984, p. 4) is needed, i.e. multiple ways of seeing and interpreting intentions, practice and outcomes. Two of the possible 'ways of seeing' appear to demand a different research paradigm than that suggested by current exhortation as outlined above. It has been acknowledged for over two decades that schools and colleges are micropolitical organizations, where an apparently rational, logical approach to management may conceal powerful tides of values and allegiances which have at least as much effect in shaping what happens within the organization as the overt rationale (Hoyle, 1982). Hard quantitative data alone will fail to capture the power struggles and conflict which contribute to decision-making. Adopting a further alternative powerful perspective, that of Greenfield (1978), it can be argued that organizations exist essentially as the sum of the subjective experiences of the individuals involved. Attempting to reach a summary view through research which imposes a framework of order on this complexity may appear neat and satisfying, but ultimately evades responsibility for capturing the intricacy of organizations. The qualitative research reported in this book is particularly concerned to unfold the richness of individual experience and how it contributes to decisions and practice in education. Where individual experience is in question, it is neither practicable nor appropriate to attempt the sort of validity which some argue can be achieved through large quantitative samples. Rather a balance must be struck between sufficient examples to give an indication of the variety of experience and a small enough number to allow delving into the individual experience. This book attempts such a balance in collecting quantitative data from a national survey while interviewing a range of individual managers to explore their values and practice.

The research also does not aspire to the value-free approach. Rather it is based on a belief that research can be both committed and objective. In order to understand the experience of those who work in colleges, some degree of empathy is needed. In order to believe in the worth of the research, a commitment is needed to the work of the sector. The research is therefore based on what Dadds (1995) entitles her book on research, *Passionate Enquiry*. It seeks to be *for* the managers involved and not simply *about* them (Cochran-Smith and Lytle, 1998). Just as feminist research does not apologize for being 'essentially political' (Adler, Laney and Packer, 1993, p. 57), so the research undertaken for this book is about empowering the managers involved and seeking to contribute to a better understanding of the dilemmas, achievements and failures which constitute their experience of work. This is not to say that the book is an apologia. Nor is there an attempt to evade the fact that the data are self-reported and as such must be seen as merely one perspective on the totality. The underpinning value judgement is that managing in further education is an extremely difficult and complex task, and improving it must be partly based on a better understanding of the experience of those who are engaged in the endeavour.

The experience explored is linked to previous research and theoretical frameworks so that those reading can reflect on their practice in a wider context. The book aims not to offer a good-practice guide, but to stimulate reflection, to reaffirm the worth of the work and thereby ultimately to support people in their efforts. In choosing to focus on managers, the intention is not to suggest that the view of others is not equally valid or critical to the well-being of the sector and its students but, rather, within the confines of space available, to allow one perspective to be developed in some depth. It is hoped that this work can be used in synthesis with other literature which provides different viewpoints.

RESEARCH METHODOLOGY

A decision was taken to focus on colleges funded by the FEFC with the exception of sixth form colleges. The latter have a culture which is distinctive and may in some ways be closer to that of schools than other categories of college. Sixth form colleges cater largely for the 16–19 cohort and offer A-levels and General National Vocational Qualifications (GNVQs) as their main curriculum staple. Consequently, they do not meet the needs of such a diverse student profile as do general further education colleges. Therefore, the focus is on the other categories of colleges which form the majority of the sector and which serve a diverse range of students. Researching the work of colleges is problematic in a number of ways. The actual number and name of colleges change with mergers and closure. Persuading overworked and pressured staff to give time to supporting research is difficult. Speaking openly about their experience is also problematic for managers in a highly competitive environment where only the positive must be presented to the public. Research inevitably must be pragmatic in picking what is not necessarily the ideal, but the best possible option.

The population of colleges was taken from a list provided by the FEFC in February 1999, though by the time survey returns were received, the number of colleges had already changed. The questionnaire asked respondents how far they felt the sector had become more diverse, if they had restructured and why, about the tools used to bring about cultural change, their progress towards 'one staff', and their hopes and fears for the future. One hundred and sixty-four responses were received, including all categories of college other than sixth form, 50 per cent of the relevant colleges. Eighty-eight (54 per cent) respondents were principal/chief executive or acting principal. Of the remaining respondents seven were vice principals. The remainder spanned a wide array of mostly second- or third-tier posts with 37 responses giving titles that were the only example of such a designation. The range of titles perhaps reflects the variety of descriptors for such positions. Fifteen provided their personal name only, so their role could not be recorded.

The majority of respondents were from general further education colleges. The number of colleges in different categories responding expressed as a percentage of the overall number in that category was as in Table 1.1. Eight colleges did not give their category. As can be seen, Art and Design has a low response rate. The remaining categories have a reasonable rate of return.

Table 1.1   Categories of college responding to the survey by percentage of overall number in the sector

Category of college	% of colleges responding as a percentage of all colleges in the category
General Further Education	53
Tertiary	32
Agriculture and Horticulture	54
Art Design and Performing Arts	14
Specialist Designated	46

Overall, these data allow some conclusions to be drawn about the context of further education and the most significant approaches to managing cultural change.

In addition to issuing a questionnaire, a sample of managers was interviewed. Given the understandable reluctance of many colleges to release much staff time to support external research, it was felt that the most feasible way of ensuring access to staff was to limit interviews to a single manager per institution. Thus each manager speaks for their own personal view of what is happening in their own work and in their college. To ensure some degree of coverage of the geographical spread, range and level of responsibilities, managers were approached in all regions of England and in all the major areas of management responsibility. Given the difficulties of contacting and meeting very busy individuals, the people involved are an opportunity sample. Nevertheless, the spread of people gave access to a range of different perspectives. The number of colleges within which a manager was interviewed in each region is indicated in Table 1.2.

The combination of geographical convenience and willingness to be interviewed has led to differences in the percentage of colleges that were involved in each region. Overall, one in ten colleges was visited and provided an interview. The range of roles by region is indicated in Table 1.3. As argued above, the aim is not to attempt to justify generalized conclusions on the basis of a large number of interviews, but rather to explore a range of individual experiences. Finally, the gender and tier of the managers participating is indicated in Table 1.4. The lower proportion of women reflects the lower number of women in senior management posts in the sector. The range of roles and levels interviewed offers data on different aspects of management and different perspectives in terms of strategic or operational levels. In order to protect the

Table 1.2   Percentage of colleges providing an interview, by region and in total
Source: Based on figures provided by the FEFC 7 November 1999.

Region	No. of colleges, excluding sixth form colleges	Number of interviews	% of colleges providing an interview
WM	42	3	7
EM	29	8	28
ER	27	8	30
YH	32	4	13
SW	38	4	26
SE	50	2	4
GL	48	3	6
NW	39	4	10
N	18	1	6
Total	323	37	11

Table 1.3 Roles of managers interviewed, by region

Region / Role	WM	EM	ER	YH	SW	SE	GL	NW	N
Principal	1		1				2	1	
Human Resource Manager	1	1			1				
Marketing Manager				2	1				
Quality Manager		2	1		1				
Finance Manager	1	1	5	1		2		1	
Information and Communication Manager		1					1	1	
Curriculum (Students) Manager		1		1	1				1
Curriculum (Employers) Manager		2						1	

Table 1.4 Tier and gender of managers interviewed

Management tier	Women	Men	Total
1	1	4	5
2	5	15	20
3	3	7	10
4	2		2
Total	11	26	37

anonymity of individuals and colleges, each manager is referred to by a title indicating his or her role, and a number differentiating among all those interviewed who held the role in question. So, Quality Manager 4 indicates that the manager concerned had the college role to manage quality and was the fourth such person to be interviewed.

MANAGING CULTURAL CHANGE

Elliott (1996) argues that cultural change cannot be imposed from the top down, yet much of the research into further education in the 1990s indicates that the state has been successful in achieving 'massive shifts in the FE work-place and its culture' (Robson, 1998, p. 585). If a culture change has taken place, this must be at least in part as a direct or indirect result of the management of the sector. The analysis of responses to the survey and the interviews will explore how far culture has changed, or rather which cultures have changed and for whom, as each organization will be a set of different cultures. The mechanisms used to achieve cultural change will also be explored. Has leadership changed for some or for all? How have other mechanisms, such as structure, resource management, quality management, etc. contributed to culture change and in what way? The analysis is aimed at providing insight into how individual managers have understood and enacted their role, what has been achieved and what challenges or problems remain. As Quality Manager 4 expressed it: 'FE is running so hard to keep up with changes at the moment it is in great danger of falling flat on its face.'

The chapters which follow delve into how individual leaders and managers have tried to keep pace with change and keep faith with their mission, and how the management of this diverse, dynamic and vital sector is developing.

2

LEADING COLLEGES

THEORIES OF LEADERSHIP

There is no shortage of theories of leadership. The 1900s have seen a steady growth in the literature defining what leaders are, what they do and what they achieve. Farey (1993) points out that early models were dichotomous in nature, analysing leadership by positing alternative approaches; senior staff could offer leadership or management, focus on people or tasks, exhibit masculine or feminine traits. As the environment in which leaders worked became more turbulent and ambiguous, analysis of leadership based on two alternative approaches seemed simplistic, and the latter part of the century saw the dichotomies transformed into models which synthesized rather than polarized the elements. Both management and leadership were required. Style was to be androgynous. Both people and tasks were important. The resulting inconsistencies and tensions of how one might be both masculine and feminine, focus on tasks and people, offer the vision of a leader and the follow-through of a manager were neatly side-stepped by the term 'paradox'. The latter indicated that leader-managers could aim at achieving the impossible of harnessing contradictory qualities and actions. As understanding of the complexity of organizations developed (Morgan, 1986), there was less confidence that leader/managers could control events (Fullan, 1999) and certainly within the further education sector, ever-growing demands that they should do so. The nature of the relationship between the leader and those who followed took centre stage. Consequently, theories developed exploring the psychological contact between leader and led, pre-eminently transactional and transformational leadership. The former stressed a contractual approach with leaders providing good working conditions in return for workers achieving agreed contractual goals. The latter

11

stressed a deeper level of commitment where both leaders and led were focused on higher level goals to continuously improve and aim at being the best (Sergiovanni, 1990). Leaders of further education faced expectations that they would adopt both. The transformational style was endorsed as achieving an envisioned, motivated staff. The rational, transactional mode was also encouraged, exhorting managers to become ever more efficient and more sure of strategic direction and detailed tactical plans. The bureaucratic demands of the state have enforced rational, transactional modes of leadership for public service managers, while the wider picture of generic management has moved on to a greater reliance on a transformational and cultural style more suited to the complexity and ambiguity of the twenty-first century (Hesselbein, 1999).

Writers have struggled to find metaphors to capture the paradigm shift which has occurred in understanding leadership, from early rational technical approaches to an emphasis on the emergent and cultural, described for example as 'the edge of chaos' (Fullan, 1999, p. 24), 'paradox' (Pascale, 1991, p. 106). It is suggested that there is a best way, through vision, empowerment and teamwork (Drucker, 1994; West-Burnham *et al.*, 1995), and that there is no best way as all is contingent on context (Marsh, 1992). It is argued that in a chaotic environment, no single person could fulfil all the requirements of leadership. Dispersed or 'systemic' (Ogawa and Bossert, 1997, p. 9) leadership is increasingly suggested as the means of achieving appropriate guidance of the organization. The implication is that each individual undertaking a leadership role may make an individual contribution which is unique and a part of a holistic function. Consequently, different leaders in one organization may display very different behaviours and actions which in synthesis amount to leadership of the organization. Leadership may therefore be fragmented amongst individuals and assembled as a whole in the experience of all those involved with the organization. Finally, the move away from rational technical models places less emphasis on the intended outcomes of leadership/management and more on the micropolitical and cultural interpretation of the perceived outcomes. Overt and planned leadership is analysed alongside the unintended and hidden. Schein (1997) argues that cultural change is not brought about by espoused values and actions but by interpretation of signals from the leader, which may contradict publicly promoted values and assumptions. Leadership may be embodied in what people do, not what they say.

So, at the start of the new millennium, our understanding of leadership is that it may be fragmented or dispersed throughout the organization, oblique and experienced through cultural signals. It may be best achieved through empowering others, but maybe not. The experience of leaders within colleges is therefore to be interpreted though theoretical mirrors which refract the concept of leadership through different and conflicting images.

THE FURTHER EDUCATION CONTEXT

Harper (1997) argues that the term 'leader' is rarely used in further education. The managers interviewed reflected this in that the majority had not necessarily thought of themselves as leaders. The term 'manager' is even more problematic in the sector, having become associated with 'managerialism', a critique which characterizes managers as having sacrificed their educational values to a rational, resource-driven approach which does not have staff or students at its heart (Elliott and Crossley, 1997; Randle and Brady, 1997a, 1997b). The theoretical hegemony of managerialism can be challenged (Lumby and Tomlinson, 2000) but, nevertheless, the current climate where the role of manager is often not viewed positively, and leadership is rarely discussed, makes the interpretation of the role of leader/manager in the sector more difficult. Principals, senior and middle managers were asked about how they interpreted leadership. The role, gender and tier of the managers interviewed are indicated in Tables 1.3 and 1.4 in Chapter 1. The majority are men, reflecting the fact that most senior managers in further education are male. The majority are also second-tier managers. To distinguish the views and experience of first and second tier, the chapter focuses initially on the leadership of principals and then goes on to explore the leadership of other second- and third-tier managers. The chapter reflects on the managers' responses and explores whether or not their understanding of leadership appears to conform to any particular theoretical model, and if there is any connection between how it is enacted and the level or context of the management role.

PRINCIPALS LEADING

Following incorporation in 1993, 'an unprecedented number of principals' retired from their post (Cantor, Roberts and Pratley, 1995), perhaps recognizing that the job facing those who were to lead colleges into the next millennium was both more difficult and different in nature. Caldwell and Spinks (1992, p. 50) after Sergiovanni (1984), identify that self-management requires 'many facets to the leadership role: technical, human, educational, symbolic and cultural'. The principals who were interviewed described activities in each of these spheres, but were unanimous in their view that the balance among the different facets had shifted post-1993. All spent more time on the technical aspects of their work. Principal 3 described it as a dramatic increase in 'time spent on planning a business'. In the immediate post-incorporation period, much time was consumed 'bringing in systems to manage an independent free-standing college, mostly to do with financial control, accountability, personnel, estates issues which a college of this size had pre-incorporation but to nothing like the same extent' (Principal 1). Principal 2 described himself pre-incorporation as 'just being a wide boy wandering around saying yes to everybody'. Since then, 'the role has changed remarkably', now being much more driven by the Central Management Information System (CMIS) and systems. More time is spent on modelling, and controlling activities to meet targets. The principals' use of adjectives such as 'remarkable' and 'dramatic' shows just how much the leadership role has changed.

The second major adjustment was that much more attention was focused externally. Spending time on building partnerships and alliances and cultivating sponsors further reduced the time available for other facets of leadership internal to the college. This accords with theories of dispersed or systemic leadership where different facets of the role may be undertaken by a range of managers within the organization to achieve the totality of leadership. All the principals recognized the critical role to be played by the senior management team and by middle managers. The charismatic figurehead role was undertaken by some, but a team approach was much more the norm: 'I always thought that leadership was about if I was charismatic enough and wonderful enough then the world would be wonderful. Actually you are only as good as the person who is reporting to you. It is your senior management and the middle managers who are critical' (Principal 3). The sense of reliance on particularly the senior management team, but also other managers, was striking:

> My perception is that that it is not a single person's function to provide leadership. It is a Senior Management role. It goes further than that but let's just concentrate on the Senior Management role. . . . I don't consider that I have all the answers on the best way forward so I don't think it is a question of me saying this is the direction we are going in. It is much more of a tentative process of teasing out what that vision is and then moving forward collectively. . . . There are people who take a completely different view that it is the Principal's job to have the big idea and take the college from here to there following that big idea but that is not a view I have adopted or share.
>
> (Principal 4)

The practice of delegating was partly enforced, because each principal had less time owing to the demands of business planning and external activity, but also was adopted by conviction. However, the symbolic and cultural roles of leadership were undertaken as a sole responsibility on occasion. Principal 1 saw his role as most critically keeping staff focused on vision and direction: 'I think it is about taking something which is complicated and reducing it to a few simple ideas and trying to communicate those to everybody in the organization so there is an overall sense of direction and people have a handle on where the place is heading.' The entire college might participate in identifying the direction, but once decided, the responsibility for ensuring the rudder remained steady was the principal's.

The dramatic charismatic role was employed, though rarely. When Principal 2's college faced a 49 per cent reduction in funding over three years, he called staff together and literally drew a line on the floor, asking those staff who would join him in seeing through the difficult period ahead to step over the line. Some did; others left the college with as much help and support as could be offered. This 'John Wayne at the Alamo' stance, as he described it, was in response to an extreme situation. It succeeded in aligning the staff who remained to address issues of survival. However, this facet of leadership as charismatic and figurehead was the exception.

Although leadership was habitually a dispersed activity for all of the group of principals, each had a 'coherent personal "educational platform" ' which influenced their thinking (Caldwell and Spinks, 1992, p. 5) and provided boundaries within which the freedom to shape direction was shared with others. 'Sometimes I think in leadership there are certain issues which are so fundamentally how you want to see the college run, that you'll listen to other people's views, but if you're honest with them, in a few instances you'll probably be fairly steamrollerish or difficult to budge' (Principal 2). In this case there were certain qualities which Principal 2 wished the college to embody and which were not negotiable. Principal 3 worked very much through teams, but at the same time, had a clear idea of the change in emphasis she wished the college to achieve from an overemphasis on business issues to much more time and attention being given to curriculum development and creativity. Principals 1 and 4 were very concerned to create an entrepreneurial spirit, to create opportunities for students. The creation of vision and direction was therefore a dialectic between the educational platform of the principal and the process of corporate agreement with others. The principal would not arrive at a position of being forced to take action with which he or she was in fundamental disagreement, the potential result of a fully collegial process. On the other hand, the vision and direction were not fixed by the principal. They were evolved by agreement. In line with research on the ambiguous and paradoxical nature of leadership at the end of the millennium, vision and direction were shaped both by many, through team effort, and by one, the principal.

The technical and symbolic aspects of leadership were therefore in evidence. All the principals were engaged in attempting cultural transformation which is discussed in detail in Chapter 11, 'Evolving the culture'. It may be useful to distinguish educational and pedagogical leadership where the former centres on educational values and the latter on educational methodology. The principals all had educational values which were communicated as part of their leadership. None was concerned with the specifics of curriculum development and delivery. The dislocation from teaching and learning issues has been cited by the managerialist critique as a major weakness in the leadership of colleges (Elliott and Crossley, 1997). In this area the level of the manager within the hierarchy of the organization may be significant. Principals saw it as proper to delegate development of the curriculum to those who were expert in the area, the staff involved in teaching and learning. The educational values which underpinned such development were seen as the responsibility of the principal and functioned as described above in shaping the corporate agreement on vision and direction. Principal 3 did feel that the balance of activity needed to shift towards more involvement with curriculum issues, but this was in the context of facilitating the creativity of others, rather than a close personal involvement.

Despite the heavy demands of technical and external responsibilities, all the principals found time for the human aspect of their job. They all took time to move around the college, meeting as many staff as was feasible, though this process brought its own problems, which are discussed in Chapter 8, 'Managing information and communication'. Increasing motivation through contact was important. Principal 3 saw her role as providing 'inspiration to people who are feeling beleaguered, belittled and overwhelmed'. Taking note of the seemingly small, but to the individuals concerned very important, issues around the college, was a regular activity of Principal 1. Leadership by example was also in evidence. Principal 2 had recognized that a culture was evolving which expected long hours and overwork as the norm, as Principal 1 described it, the 'lunch is for wimps' approach. In response, Principal 2 had deliberately set an example to break the trend:

> I might come in early but I don't work late because I found that my working late was setting a culture so everybody was working late, so people were working until 8 o'clock and they didn't need to work until 8 o'clock. It was like a belief that you weren't on board unless you came into the car park at half past seven. I realized I wasn't happy about it, so I now come in at seven. The staff come in when they come in. I make a point of going home on most days at half five, six, though I might work at home.

He hoped that leaving regularly at half past five or six in the evening would liberate staff to feel that they too could go home and that working excessive hours would not be taken as a sign of dedication, or working reasonable hours as evidence of a lack of commitment.

The leadership of this group of principals was therefore different in nature to that pre-1993 and different in some ways to that of other managers. It was both part of a system of dispersed leadership, sharing facets of the role with others, and a unique function, providing the underpinning values. The honest assessment was that most of the available time was taken up by external contacts and the technical side of the role. Nevertheless, some time was given to human contact and symbolic activity to inspire and provide an example.

WORKING WITH GOVERNORS

Golby (1992, p. 11) identifies that educational governors have two metaphors on which they can draw to help them understand their role, 'from business life and from democratic participation'. Prior to 1993, the membership of governing bodies included democratically elected members of the local education authority (LEA) and stressed the democratic process. The post-incorporation increase in the number of business-based governors appeared to change the emphasis, and led to fears that colleges would lose the sense of democratic accountability and be run like businesses to increase funds rather than to serve the community. Ainley and Bailey (1997, pp. 38–9) reflect this fear in reporting that the impression they were given in their two case-study colleges was that governors were 'strategically distanced' and less interventionist than the more independent pre-1993 boards. They communicate a sense of two boards where the principal really decides on strategic direction and the contribution of the governors is to management, rather than leadership, i.e., technical expertise in specific aspects of management such as personnel or estates, rather than contributing to vision and strategic plans. The change of membership in governing bodies instituted in 1999 (Nash, 1999), decreasing the number of business/industry governors, may reflect similar concerns at a national level.

The evidence from the group of principals in this case does not support the picture painted by Ainley and Bailey (1997). Governors were very much involved in deciding strategic direction and, therefore, in leadership. Principal 2 explained that strategic parameters were set by governors and that these currently involved a financial loss to achieve educational aims:

> The governors have given very clear markers that they see the regionality of the college as being priority. At the present time the outcentres are not paying their way, but the governors have made provision for that, strategically, because they see the outcentres as being the next phase in development. They are underwriting them.

This is evidence of governors providing educational leadership which is strategic and value driven. Consequently the leadership role of both the principal and the governors mirror each other. There is insufficient evidence to determine whether either is dominant in resolving the fundamental values and direction of the college. As the principalship is both an individual role and a member of the corporate board such a distinction may not be possible. Principal 1 also reflected the keen involvement of governors, 'a cracking bunch', in the debate on values and strategic direction: 'They are involved strategically. I really enjoy the process of a general meeting. We have good arguments about the purpose of the place. Should we be doing this? What about the problem of HE [higher education]? Should we be doing that?' Principal 3 had experienced a similar interest in educational issues. She went so far as to believe that it was the business governors who were easier to work with:

> Generally the governors here are very good though ironically they are quite business based. The most difficult governors are often those who are not business

based. At least business governors understand the context within which you are working and they are more realistic. They understand the constraints under which you are working . . . They are genuine that they would like us to become a more community-based institution. I think they like the concept.

However, she did have doubts about the incentive to move in this direction, in that governors saw the college as successful financially and so not in urgent need of change. Nevertheless, her final judgement is that there was a genuine commitment to being responsive to the community.

Balancing this view of three boards who were involved in strategic direction and educational values, Principal 4 described the period of 1993–96 as one during which governors 'focused almost entirely on financial matters'. This was partly due to the extremely serious financial difficulties that the college had experienced. Since then the governors had come to a 'less tense view'. Just as the leadership of the principal may be contingent on circumstances, so the leadership of governors may relate strongly to the college environment.

Certainly overall, the governors as reflected in the perception of the principals did not conform to a stereotype of industrialists who did not understand educational or community issues and whose overriding concern was funding. Nor was Ainley and Bailey's (1997) impression of a non-interventionist approach borne out. Not only were governors involved in strategic direction, but they did not always support the principal. In the case of Principal 3, she felt that although they were generally supportive, they did not always agree with her approach.

At the time of writing, there is no large-scale study of the role of governors in further education. This chapter's reflection of governance through the perception of principals and other managers has shown that they can and do undertake a leadership role that incorporates the principal as a member of the board but which is also separate from that of the principal as an individual. Governors and the principal are therefore two corners of a leadership triangle which also may involve other senior and middle managers.

DISPERSED LEADERSHIP

The principals interviewed were emphatic about the importance of other managers and also just how difficult the role of senior and middle managers had become. The demands and consequent stress have risen considerably. The range of responsibilities has increased and the environment is also more problematic. The senior managers are:

the people taking all the flack, all the agro. We all have sleepless nights but they have the real sleepless nights in terms of being told, 'Well, you've got to make 20 per cent of your people redundant. You've got to close down a section. Which section do you want to close?'

(Principal 2)

Despite this certainty on the part of the principals that senior and middle managers were critical, as Harper (1997) suggests, the senior and middle managers interviewed did not necessarily consciously consider themselves to be leaders or reflect upon the leadership role. When asked if she thought of herself as a leader, Human Resource Manager 1 replied, 'No. People don't do that do they?' Additionally, the relationship between hierarchical tiers and the nature of leadership was not clear-cut. One might expect a second-tier manager who reported directly to the principal to influence strategy. In fact, Human Resource Manager 2 in this second tier position felt she did not participate in strategic discussion and that her role was largely administrative. There did appear to be two approaches to leadership, depending on the background of the manager. Where the manager came from a professional background and was appointed because of technical expertise, for example, in personnel or estates, the self-concept was much more likely to be an adviser or influencer rather than a leader. They were consciously attempting to change the culture but in oblique ways which eschewed an overt leadership role, but nevertheless were leading others into changing their perception and behaviour:

> I am the professional adviser to the organization if you like. I am the qualified personnel specialist so I have always tended to look at myself in that way rather than leading from the front so to speak. I hope that I can persuade and influence people in the way in which they manage staff.

(Human Resource Manager 1)

Just as leading from the front was not particularly related to position in the hierarchy, a conscious focus on creating vision and inspiration was not limited to senior managers. Some third- and fourth-tier managers were involved in creating a vision:

> I think it is a very difficult term 'leadership'. I see myself, I think, as having a belief in the college to start with. I think my tendency to want to lead, and therefore my job role, is based on that foundation. I have a great deal of respect for the college. I believe in what it is doing. I believe in the work that it does and the achievement of the students that are here and that go through us every year. Because I have that belief . . . I feel that it is important that other people feel the same way and my leadership, therefore, is very much based on the premise that we do make a difference. I think, therefore, my leadership is founded on a belief, and I think that's communicated to other people.

(Quality Manager 3)

This quality manager worked at the third tier, responsible to the vice-principal, but her emphasis on belief and educational values, and communicating that to others as the basis of her leadership, echoes the approach of the principals in wishing to communicate vision and to inspire. The higher level leadership function was not confined to the higher levels of the hierarchy. Many of the managers spoke of their own personal values and vision and their wish to communicate them to shape the college's development. They also reflected the paradox presented by the principals of both feeling they were providing a vision which is all their own, but which is also formed with others:

> I have worked in FE for 18 or 19 years. I am lucky enough to have a view of FE and how it should go, and a view of the way my own college should go. Basically I see my job as putting the two together, being confident enough in my view of the world and my view of where the college should go, but humble enough to understand that while that can provide a framework, I may have some of it wrong. The best way I can ensure that there is the greatest chance of making it right, is by listening and working with people, so again it's an iterative process between those two positions.
>
> (Quality Manager 1)

The leadership role of inspiring people and providing a model of relation-ships was also dispersed. Strongly held beliefs about working with people ring through the words of managers at all levels. Nobody used the word 'empowerment' but many spoke of their practice of empowering:

> The way I manage is very much seeking to work with people. As a person who is managed I believe my fundamental right at work is to be heard. I don't demand that once heard my advice is to be acted upon, but I do have a right to be heard and, likewise, the way I try to behave as a manager is to give people the right to be listened to.
>
> (Quality Manager 1)

> I have got very strong views on leadership in FE. I would see myself working in partnership with the managers I work with . . . If staff don't own the changes then they are not going to happen. Fundamentally, it's got to come from the team of staff. Fundamentally they need to acknowledge their own weaknesses and accept them. If the manager just turns around and says 'you shouldn't do this, this is not okay' staff just resent it and the change doesn't become properly embedded. It has got to come from the staff but that's completely contrary I fear to the vast majority of FE managers and it could be taken as weak management. I don't think it is.
>
> (Quality Manager 2)

Although Quality Manager 2 feared that her approach was not prevalent in the sector, the managers interviewed, at least in intention, strongly supported her view that listening to people and giving as much autonomy as possible was the right way to interpret leadership. Curriculum Manager 2 had felt unable to move away from her 'fundamental belief about enabling and empowering others', even when the degree of autonomy given to faculty heads was leading to destructive rivalries. Curriculum Manager 3 interpreted his vision of an inclusive college as meaning that staff must be included, 'trying to make sure they are included in the decision-making process, even if they didn't want to be'.

Of course these beliefs are self-reported and the enactment of them may not have matched the ideal. However, what can be concluded is that the leadership role of creating vision and inspiration, valuing and empowering staff was evident as the intention of managers interviewed at all the levels and, as such, their approach conformed to the model of transformational leadership (Bass and Avolio, 1994).

There were, therefore, similarities with the leadership of governors and principals but there were also differences. Managers acted as a bridge from the top to the bottom of the hierarchy:

> I see my role as being twofold, that I do have the corporate view but I also have very much the sort of small course-team view as well and that's where I can perhaps do the most good . . . because my role can focus. I am very fortunate in that I can leap from the sort of senior manager level right down to course-team level.
>
> (Quality Manager 3)

As a consequence, the distance between the leader and the staff was reduced. Hofstede (1980) refers to a power distance continuum, where leaders may be perceived as remote from the majority of staff and where this may be seen as desirable or otherwise in different cultures. None of the leaders interviewed wished to appear remote. All worked hard at moving around the organization and communicating with as many people as possible but, as discussed in Chapter 8, 'Managing information and communication', principals particularly, and members of the senior management team, were likely to be viewed as not seen enough. The power distance phenomenon varied amongst the managers interviewed, though not necessarily simply in ratio to the level in the hierarchy. The leap from strategic to personal was seen both as a great strength and also as a tension: 'If a particular member of staff comes in with an issue, they want an answer there and then and they want to feel that they've got something from us, but at the same time you've got your other hat on and you are trying to think more strategically' (Human Resource Manager 3). The leadership of managers other than the principals and governors, therefore, in some ways offered a greater test in being both visionary and strategic but also retaining a closer involvement with a wider range of staff.

The other possible differences were the amount of time spent in both day-to-day management or firefighting and in a close involvement with pedagogy. In both areas the principal was unlikely to have much involvement. In the case of other managers, the situation varied depending on role. Information and Communication Technology (ICT) Manager 1 reflected that despite trying to lead cultural change, his role had been largely firefighting for a long time and was likely to remain so for the foreseeable future.

THEORIZING LEADERSHIP IN FURTHER EDUCATION

The evidence certainly supports Ogawa and Bossert's (1997, p. 9) view that 'leadership flows through the organisation'. De Pree (1999) distinguishes two crucial tasks of the leader, 'Leaving a legacy – articulating and bringing to life the kind of organisational community that you want to be a part of' and setting the tone for the quality of relationships. The former distinguishes leaving a legacy from strategy which is more mechanistic. Not only creating what the community wants or needs now but also bequeathing something to the future is the most testing leadership challenge. De Pree sees this as the role of the chief executive in business and industry organizations, but the range of college managers interviewed had a passionate commitment to their own educational vision which transcended mere strategy. De Pree also singles out the role of the chief executive as setting the tone of relationships but, again, many college managers, not just the principal, had powerful beliefs about how people should relate to each other. The evidence suggests that leadership in colleges is indeed systemic. Brown, (1974) writes of the role of the vice-principal as 'assimilated', where responsibilities are shared, or 'interposed', where the vice-principal acts as a bridge between the principal and others. Times have moved on and more managers than just the vice-principal share leadership with the principals and governors, not in an assimilated or interposed model but in both.

Five possible differences in the nature of the leadership in colleges emerge. Leaders can be focused externally or internally. They can be primarily focused on creating and communicating vision or can see their role as advisory in achieving vision. They can be concerned with the creation of systems at an organization-wide level or they can be intimately caught up in day-to-day implementation, the difference between 'normative' and 'operational' activity as defined by Becher and Kogan (1980, p. 13). They can be perceived as distant from staff or as closely involved. Finally, they can see their role as one of educational leadership, in defining educational values and broad curriculum areas, or as pedagogical leadership, with a closer involvement with development and delivery of the curriculum. These differences can be presented as five possible spectra (Figure 2.1).

The nature of leadership of an individual manager could be plotted against the five spectra to indicate an individual approach in leading. It is apparent from the evidence that principals and senior managers are more likely to adopt the focus on the left-hand side of the spectra. However, there is not a consistent relationship between approach and hierarchical level. Middle managers can and do focus on creating vision and inspiration. Some principals may work in an environment where their focus is primarily internal. Taking these variations as given, nevertheless the model can be used to relate leadership approaches to hierarchical level within the organization in a theoretical sense.

EXTERNAL FOCUS ←――――――――→ INTERNAL FOCUS
(National/regional issues   (Cross-college or subunit
and partnerships)   focus)

VISION & INSPIRATION ←――――――――→ ADVICE
(Creating a vision or legacy   (Advising and supporting.
and inspiring others)   Leading from behind)

SYSTEMS CREATION ←――――――――→ DAY-TO-DAY
(Creating organization wide   MANAGEMENT
systems. Managing by   (Day-to-day
exception)   implementation.
                                      Firefighting)

DISTANT FROM ←――――――――→ CLOSE TO STAFF
STAFF   (Perceived as close to
(Power distance perceived   staff)
as great)

EDUCATIONAL ←――――――――→ PEDAGOGIC
LEADERSHIP   LEADERSHIP
(Setting educational   (Leadership of detailed
values and broad   curriculum development)
parameters for curriculum
development)

Figure 2.1   Dimensions of leadership focus

Table 2.1 shows a possible relationship between the different approaches to leadership emerging from the interviews and management level. It has already been acknowledged that individual managers do not necessarily conform to the expected profile of leadership at their level. A second facet of the fallibility of this fixed table is that leadership was seen as contingent and therefore not static: 'I think I interpret leadership continuously because it's a changing role which needs to adapt to the circumstances that you are placed within' (Curriculum Manager 4).

Building on the model for mapping leadership developed by Farey (1993, p. 120), to give a visual representation of an individual pattern, the spectra could be presented to allow the individual pattern to be seen as a distinctive shape (Figure 2.2). The components of leadership can be mapped across the spectra, and just as the shape suggests an amoeba, which is a living, changing form, so leadership of an individual might shift its shape constantly, the

Table 2.1 Relationship of management level and leadership focus

Level of management	External/ internal focus	Leading from in front or behind	Involvement in management	Distance from staff	Educational/ pedagogic leadership
Governance	Focus on local community regional and national issues	Create vision and strategy	No involvement in day-to-day management	Perceived as power distant	Focus on educational values and broad issues of curriculum definition, development and delivery
Principal/ chief executive	Focus on local community regional and national issues	Create vision and strategy	Creation of systems Management by exception	Perceived as power distant	Focus on educational values and broad issues of curriculum definition, development and delivery
Senior management	Focus on internal issues and local community issues	Create vision and strategy or advise on strategy creation	Creation and implementation of systems	Bridge between senior management and other staff	Focus on creation of systems to implement curriculum strategy
Middle management	Focus on internal issues and local community issues	Create vision and strategy or advise on strategy creation	Focus on implementation Firefighting	Bridge between senior management and other staff	Focus on implementing the curriculum

leadership map therefore appearing differently through time and reflecting the contingent nature of leadership.

True to the emphasis on paradox in the opening paragraph of this chapter, the conclusions on the nature of leadership in further education are paradoxical. There do appear to be differences in focus or approach to leadership and these have been defined using five dimensions of focus/behaviour. There does appear to be some relationship between hierarchical level and leadership, but at the same time there is strong evidence that leadership is dispersed and the left-hand side of the spectra, indicating transformational leadership, can be and is adopted from governance to middle manager levels of the organization.

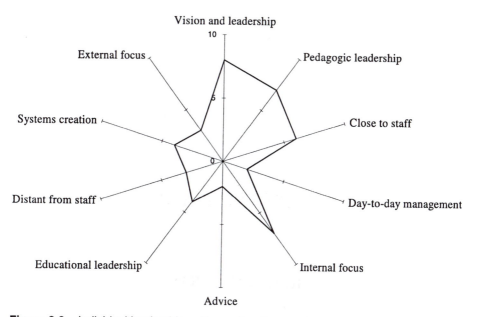

Figure 2.2 Individual leadership pattern using five spectra

A holistic view of leadership emerges, where leadership is a hologram made up of images of leaders projected from different points of the organization, the whole amounting to a function which is based on values and can inspire and create a legacy as well as enacting the vision in the day-to-day implementation of intent.

3

MANAGING PEOPLE

INTRODUCTION

People, students and staff, are the heart of further education. As a survey comment put it: 'The success of our college is the result of human resource good practice – good motivation of staff flows into all other strategic objectives.' As suggested, in any college, the motivation and skill of staff will underpin the achievement of all strategic aims, but particularly the core purpose, providing successful teaching and learning. The opportunities for students to achieve their aims will relate primarily to the staff's ability to communicate, enthuse and build meaningful relationships as the foundation of learning. Reflecting the centrality of people, the majority of each college's budget is spent on staff costs. Though colleges have striven since 1993 to reduce pay expenditure as a percentage of the overall budget, the average figure of pay as a percentage of income is not shifting significantly, as reduced pay costs are balanced by declining income. From 1994 to 1997 the figure remained approximately 70 per cent (FEFC, 1998a).

Consequently, in both an educational and financial sense, shouldering the responsibility for managing staff was one of the most significant changes facing colleges at incorporation. Prior to 1993, LEAs had managed the personnel function. Post-incorporation, colleges had to adopt the personnel brief involving a wide range of responsibilities including recruitment, appraisal, pay and employee relations (Anderson, 1994). Much of the work was shouldered by middle managers who select, appraise and direct staff with the support of a human resource specialist. Fulfilling the function was therefore a new and very challenging undertaking, particularly when institutions can be multi-sited and staffed by more than 50 per cent part-timers (FEDA, 1995).

   The sector's response to the new charge of managing people post-incorporation has been characterized by some as swiftly importing business/industry practices, such as adopting a strategic human resource perspective, moving from the previous secure tenured position of staff to using people more flexibly, viewing pay and reward as potentially fluid, the structure reflecting local need rather than national agreement and blurring previous strong demarcations between professional and 'non-teaching' staff. The adoption of such practices has been referred to as 'the hard variant of HRM [human resource management]' (Elliott and Hall 1994, p. 4), and has led to fears that FE is being run as a business, 'FE Inc.' (ibid., p. 1) rather than as an educational organization, and that this is potentially detrimental to the student experience and certainly detrimental to academic staff. The assumptions underlying such an analysis are that business practice is *de facto* inappropriate for educational organizations.

   In contrast, others have argued that a change of approach was needed as the practices prevalent in FE at the start of the1990s were inadequate and/or inappropriate to the needs of colleges and students (Gorringe, 1994a). Rather than seeing the management of people in the period immediately following incorporation as an attack on educational values, it is possible to view the changes in practice as a reinterpretation of the same values, that is doing what is best for students (Lumby and Tomlinson, 2000). Certainly the initial intention on the part of managers was not necessarily to act punitively towards staff but to break out of the straitjacket of previous conditions of service to enable colleges to use people more flexibly. Gorringe (1994a, p. 50) argues that 'the key issue here is not that staff should necessarily be working harder, but that ways of working need to be radically different'. However, the introduction of a funding system which in effect cut colleges' budgets year on year, and coercion by a government which linked funds to the introduction of new contracts, meant that colleges felt they had no option but to adopt a range of cost-cutting measures, including moving to a situation where staff are working harder, that is, more hours per week over a longer academic year (Hewitt and Crawford, 1997). Longer working hours are part of a wider European trend, leading eventually to such concerns for people's health that the European Economic Community issued the European Framework Directive on Working Hours (92/85/EEC) limiting the working week for most employees. Untangling how far the pressures on staff in the sector are solely due to FE factors and how far what is happening may be due to wider pressures in society is problematic.

   Whatever the judgement, it is clear that managers took up the human resource management role at a time when internal and external pressures made the task extremely difficult. The result was a period which has encompassed much conflict and bitterness. Although improvements for students may have been achieved, how far the cost to staff is acceptable is still under debate.

   A detailed consideration of each of the full range of management responsibilities relating to human resources could not be covered in one chapter.

Consequently, this chapter adopts a more strategic perspective, exploring the context in which colleges assumed the management of staff, the problems encountered and how far colleges have resolved inherited or subsequent issues. The perspective mainly reflects the experience of those most closely involved at strategic and policy level, the principal and the human resource/personnel specialist. It also explores how far managing people in further education may be similar or dissimilar to managing in other contexts and whether the sector has been able to reach stability and confidence in the management of people, or the contrary.

SKILLS IN HUMAN RESOURCE MANAGEMENT

At the time of incorporation there was little experience of human resource management in the sector and, according to a national survey, skills were also in short supply (Goulding, Dominey and Gray, 1998). In the view of Human Resource Manager 2, the recognition of the need of specialist skills in this area was slow to arrive. She believed that priority was given to acquiring financial management and accountancy expertise and that, being a people-based sector, there was a belief that current staff could cope with managing people without further support:

> When they (colleges) became incorporated, they realized they had to have an accounts function and that was the top priority. They didn't consider personnel to be a real issue. If they didn't have anybody in the personnel role, they either decided not to appoint at all or that what they needed was a personnel administrator. They didn't need the expertise of the professional human resource person because they knew everything there was to know . . . This phase has passed. They have recognized the need for professional input. They didn't want it in the first place. They thought they could get by without it. They've got themselves into deep water in many cases and now they know that they need to appoint a professional human resource/personnel person, as they perceived they needed an accountant in the first place.

Of course some colleges may have appointed a human resource specialist at a senior level immediately following incorporation, but the evidence of the interviews supports the view of Human Resource Manager 2 that the focus was very much on finance rather than on people. However, importing human resource management skills from outside the sector has brought its own tensions. The people who occupied such roles were potentially subject to two negative pressures. First, many within education felt that nobody who came from outside the sector could fully understand and, therefore, support education as opposed to business values and practice. They were therefore perceived as lacking the 'right' kind of experience. Second, because the personnel function, at least in the immediate post-incorporation period, was not necessarily appointed at a senior level, the post might be subject to what Human Resource Manager 2 saw as academic snobbery of the sort that historically saw all support staff as less skilled and important than academic staff. Whether such opinions were justified or not, the perceptions could make the role uncomfortable.

Such issues are partly structural. Is a human resource specialist, not necessarily from an education background, most appropriately appointed to the senior management team or is it more effective to allocate responsibility for resources, including human resources, to a member of the senior management team with an education background, appointing an HRM or personnel specialist at a lower level in the hierarchy? Whatever decision an individual college takes, the role of supporting and developing the management of people is critical and subject to severe strain, acting to support the strategic priorities of the college while simultaneously attempting to support staff at an individual level through very difficult times.

THE LEGACY OF THE LOCAL AUTHORITIES

The management of people by the local education authorities offered practice which was both excellent and poor. For example, as Gorringe (1994a) points out, the wide advertisement of posts provided a degree of equality of opportunity which is still not necessarily the case in the private sector. On the other hand, pay and rewards were low and limited largely to incremental rises in a salary scale. Flexibility in offering additional non-pay rewards was not part of the picture. This pay structure inhibited rewarding anything other than level of academic qualification and length of service. It is a legacy which still leads to incongruence between what colleges wish to achieve and to reward, and what they are able to attain:

> While managers may claim to want staff with initiative and creativity, they may actually be rewarding conformity; where they claim to stress the importance of teaching and learning skills or of experience, they are rewarding those with degrees and higher qualifications; while they aim to create teams of equals, the same teams contain staff on a multitude of grades. At a time of rapid change such as we are experiencing in further education, and with traditional patterns of rewards which were developed for previous decades, it is more than ever likely that such incongruence occurs.
>
> (Brain, 1994, p. 91)

The conditions of service encapsulated in the 'Silver Book' offered staff the protection of a nationally agreed framework, but some argue that implicit in the conditions were assumptions which were no longer tenable in the late twentieth century:

Silver Book conditions of service have implicit within them a model or set of assumptions about how colleges work. These include:

- A separation between lecturers and all other staff leading, possibly unintentionally, to higher status for the former;
- the primacy of class contact, i.e. a lecturer standing in front of a classroom group as the key pedagogic role;
- the notion that teaching is the key function of a lecturer, rather than the management of learning in a wider sense;
- the view that lecturers are 'academics' who require bursts of teaching activity followed by lengthy periods of recuperation if they are to be effective; and
- the view that traditional patterns of college terms and holidays are the only right way to deliver education and training.

(Gorringe, 1994a, p. 49)

All these assumptions are open to question. A hierarchy of academic staff supported by 'non-teaching' staff results in a hidden agenda for students, suggesting that academic 'professional' staff are in some sense more highly regarded. This is surely not the message that students ought to receive. If a college is to be inclusive and confidence-building, then the explicit and implicit avowal must be that all skills and contributions to the success of an organization, including those of the administrator and technician, are valuable. The recognition of this view has led to a determination in many colleges to try to erode such distinctions and achieve 'one staff', i.e., that the majority value equally the activities of lecturers and support staff.

The focus on teaching and class contact was under scrutiny well before incorporation, with the suggestion that learning, not teaching, ought to be central (Shackleton, 1988). The advent of new technologies which widen the range of modes of learning open to students has strengthened the trend to see class contact as a vital but not unique mode of achieving learning. Finally, the sanctity of term times, leading to college closure during weekends and holidays, and inflexible teaching hours, were in question before incorporation.

Principal 5 described how:

many staff who have been in colleges for a long time look back with longing and affection to the times when we were local authority and they taught 19 hours a week and had reduced class contact for things like course tutor duties, course management duties, looking after a laboratory or counting the spoons in the canteen. It's upset a lot of staff.

The time when there was a shorter working week and fewer teaching hours within the week are inevitably seen as halcyon days by many staff. However, the staff in question are largely academic staff. The then 'non-teaching' staff may have a less rosy view of that period when it was seen as legitimate to view them as holding inferior posts, and when there was little chance for their development into roles which could contribute more to students' experience.

Additionally, Ainley and Bailey (1997) analysing their two case study colleges, point out that there are differences of opinion amongst lecturers on how far the pre-1993 days were seen as 'better':

> All main-grade lecturers interviewed also agreed there had been some changes for the better. They might also concede under questioning that 'the good old days' were not in fact so perfect as they might nostalgically appear in retrospect. The balance between such concessions to the new ethos varied systematically amongst interviewees in the way we have suggested by age, experience (length of service) and subject specialism.
>
> (Ainley and Bailey, 1997, p. 63)

Equally, accepting Gorringe's (1994a) analysis of the inappropriate assumptions in terms of student need which underlay the 'Silver Book', change was needed. Incorporation allowed colleges the freedom to respond to the pressures already being felt to adopt more flexible and learner-centred practices. Unfortunately the freedom from LEAs was balanced by the arrival of central government action which trammelled colleges' freedom to act. One set of pressures was removed but another arrived.

THE FURTHER EDUCATION CONTEXT

Managing people in FE may be different to managing people in business or even in other sectors of education. Principal 5 felt that any changes in staffing had to be approached with some caution:

> We are always conscious that a certain cohort of students has got to a particular stage in their learning programme by being taught by a certain person. So we are always very cautious about making changes in staff. If you're manufacturing widgets, you are not going to be too concerned if the widgets are made by a different person, but here there is a direct link with student achievement if you were to break that connection without good reason. One is more cautious about it.

Action was therefore circumspect and deliberate. At the same time there was sometimes a need for a speedy response if a member of staff was not helping students to learn in a satisfactory way. The problem here was that feedback was not necessarily received instantly, but might be delayed until an end of year review, by which time the students had perhaps experienced unsatisfactory teaching for some time. Managing people was therefore subject to contradictory pressures, the need for efficient and speedy feedback systems to enable fast action but caution in making changes because 'The relationship between the staff and student is everything' (Principal 5).

All the human resource managers interviewed agreed that the emphasis on staff development and qualifications was much greater in further education than in business. Staff needed to develop to keep pace with a changing and much more diverse student profile, as outlined in Chapter 9, and with the new learning technologies. Survey responses indicated that staff development was the third most important tool, after restructuring and quality assurance systems, used to achieve cultural change (see Figure 11.2 in Chapter 11). The emphasis on staff development is very significant, perhaps reflecting that the learning and teaching in the sector in terms of age range, ability of students and the levels of study is more diverse than other educational sectors. Those interviewed saw the need for a continuing drive to develop skills, but also that this was not a universal answer and some flexibility in using existing skills would be needed for those who found it difficult to adapt:

> Many students come here because they want to learn and get qualified and that's a fairly easy teaching scenario for a member of teaching staff. Where the motivation of students is questionable, where they are disengaged because of their previous experiences within school, within their home and their lack of hope of ever gaining proper employment, that situation is much more difficult to manage, and while we have recruited staff who are equipped with those type of skills, where we haven't had it, we have tried to bring it in from outside or we have tried to develop those skills within our existing staff. I would like to think we have had some success with developing staff in order to cope with students who at times might be challenging. But there are some staff who find that area of work very difficult, and I think we have tried to use those staff where their skills and capabilities lie rather than try to fit a square peg into a round hole.
>
> (Curriculum Manager 4)

The recognition that not all staff could or would change was expressed by several interviewees. Additionally, not only was development needed for experienced staff, but also the initial training for new staff needed to be much more forward looking. Speaking of her work in managing a project developing the use of ICT in teaching and learning, Curriculum Manager 7 felt that the current initial teacher training might not be adequate in preparing staff for the present, let alone the future. She questioned the adequacy of the most common programme to train staff who enter the sector without a teaching qualification, the course commonly known as the 730:

> It is a question of getting to the people who are coming through now, getting the training right for them. When I did the 730 we didn't even dream of this (ICT-based teaching and learning) yet I've got a lecturer now who is doing all this (working on an ICT project) and doing the 730 at the same time. It is very difficult for him because they are asking, 'Show me your handouts, show me your lesson plan'. Well there isn't a lesson plan in the same way with this type of work, so that is a problem. The training has got to change much further back.

Even if development programmes, including initial training, were appropriate, staff attitudes themselves might be a barrier. Principal 3 described how staff seemed to feel very vulnerable. Praise for curriculum initiatives elsewhere in the college was interpreted as criticism of others. 'It is almost like sibling rivalry.' This vulnerability on the part of professional staff has been noted elsewhere. Argyris refers to the 'doom zoom' experienced by professional staff: 'An inappropriately high sense of despondency or even despair when people don't achieve the high levels of performance they aspire to. Such despondency is rarely psychologically devastating, but when combined with defensive reasoning, it can result in a formidable predisposition against learning' (Argyris, 1991, p. 104). Argyris suggests that such reactions are generic, but they may be particularly acute amongst educators who have both a track record of academic success and whose performance is under the constant public scrutiny of students. This may partly explain why staff do not find development unproblematic. This is the second set of contradictions in managing people in further education. Staff development is absolutely critical for success and yet staff may be predisposed to present blocks to development.

Whatever freedom colleges may have had, the challenge of managing people in such a diverse sector was quickly framed by central government by the context of significant pressures to reduce costs. The environment which resulted is one where choices are severely limited.

COERCION AND CO-OPERATION

Times of change as profound as those experienced following incorporation are inevitably deeply disturbing and unsettling. During this period, when enrolling staff to support change was of great importance, the government policy of linking funds to achieving a change in staff contracts established coercion which had a negative effect on many: 'The challenge for senior managers is to change employees' attitudes and behaviour within a co-operative psychological contract. This is where employees identify with the aims of the organisation and see those aims as being close to their own individual aspirations' (Betts, 1994, p. 9); 'In persuading managers to change, a coercive contract would be in place if there were penalties for those who did not accept the change psychologically. This is arguably not the way to encourage co-operative working, and will surely lead to a resentment of change and isolation' (Betts, 1994, pp. 8–9).

Staff did experience penalties which were often both financial, with no pay award for those refusing to accept new contracts, and psychological, with a sense of alienation from the emerging culture. Large numbers of redundancies and delayering also increased anxiety (Goulding, Dominey and Gray, 1998). Agency staff who earned less, had fewer rights and were temporary, worked alongside permanent staff. Given high levels of insecurity and rising workload, two results were predictable. First, many staff focused on their own survival rather than the organization's goals (Hewitt and Crawford, 1997). Such an outcome is suggested by Maslow's (1943) hierarchy of motivation, which asserts that primary security needs must be met before higher level self-actualization goals can come into play. Second, much evidence suggests high levels of stress and depression amongst staff (Ainley and Bailey, 1997; Stead, Fletcher and Jones, 1995). As well as anxiety about the security of any post, the nature of the posts themselves was also metamorphosing, presenting a further level of uncertainty and pressure for change. Cantor, Roberts and Pratley (1995, p. 120) detail the changing role of lecturers:

> For the individual teachers and lecturers, the demands made upon them can be divided into four main categories. Firstly, they will have to offer a wide range of teaching methodologies, from traditional teaching through seminars and tutorial work to individual counselling. Secondly, as the structure of courses becomes more complex, with more modularization and similar developments, as the need to liase with employers, validating bodies, the college's management and others becomes more pressing, so course management becomes more time-consuming and demanding. Thirdly, more and more lecturers will become involved in tutoring and acting as mentors for students and colleagues undertaking courses of teacher training. Lastly, there is an increasing need to update teaching materials and teaching methods, particularly those involving the use of information technology . . .

Lecturing staff might be concerned that their job would still be there in the future and also be anxious, that if it was there, it might be different in nature and in some sense diminished. Randle and Brady (1997a, p. 236) argue that lecturers experienced a 'degradation of work' and 'a systematic de-skilling'. There can be no definitive answer to whether the work of lecturers has been diminished or enhanced by the advent of new modes of learning and a wider range of roles employed in supporting learning. What matters ultimately is the perception of those involved. The lethal cocktail of worsening conditions, low pay, higher workloads, a more diverse and challenging student profile and a shifting lecturing role placed enormous pressures on staff and made the task of managing them full of tension. Additionally, large numbers of part-time and agency staff came into college just to teach and were unable to contribute to or be influenced by structures and meetings to achieve planning and development. Principal 5 reflected on the period from 1993 to 1999 as one where external pressures meant that the college's human resource policy was largely reactive and only in part successful:

> What I don't want to do is give you the impression that we have a human resource policy which is aimed at driving towards development where all the staff are working together as a single team and they are all committed to the development of the college and to the welfare of their students. Many, many staff are like that and I would be very, very proud if I had such a human resource policy, but I haven't. The human resource policy is really a response to other pressures and at the same time trying to go some way towards reducing the alienation of some staff. If we could find a way of enthusing staff again, to make them committed to the success of this college, committed to the success of their students, I think we'd achieve a breakthrough, but there's a lot of baggage that's got to be forgotten before we get to that.

While acknowledging the difficulties experienced and the legacy of bitterness left by pay disputes and redundancies, Principal 5 did feel that a watershed had perhaps been reached and that with the easing of financial pressures, people could start to move on. The 'residual bad taste' (Human Resource Manager 2) was lessening. Other interviewees suggested both a more positive experience of change and a sense of achievement. 'There is a real buzz when the students are here now and everyone is really focused' (Human Resource Manager 3). Principal 2 also saw the period of change as one where much could be achieved. A threat to the college's survival had really harnessed the motivation and commitment of staff. He compared the staff's attitude to that of the 'cornered animal'. His main concern subsequently was to manage the energy which had been unleashed, so that staff did not burn out, but retained a sustainable level of commitment and vigour:

> There is nothing more powerful than the cornered animal . . . You can't live on it forever because you would die, you would burn out, but we harnessed it to get us out of that corner. We were a cornered animal and the staff, instead of tearing each other apart, said, 'Come on. We are going to go for this'. It has been interesting to take the best of that, just try and damp it down now to sustainable levels.

The extreme situation increased staff commitment and teamwork. The management task is now to control the level of motivation and to make it sustainable. Human Resource Manager 1 also felt that although there had been great difficulties, people had been able to cope and to reach a point of feeling very positive. It may be that the range of situations and opinions on the success of HRM policies and practice suggests that each college faced a very individual mix of financial and other pressures and a mix of staff attitudes. Consequently, colleges have taken different paths and time spans to try to achieve a more stable and positive foothold in terms of managing people.

ACHIEVING ONE STAFF

Human Resource Manager 1 viewed teamwork as the chief method of addressing some of the polarities and conflict experienced in the immediate post-incorporation period. Achieving teamwork implied melding the historical divide between those staff whose primary duty was teaching and those whose primary duties lay elsewhere. In the survey undertaken for this book, only two colleges did not see achieving one staff as a college goal, that is 1 per cent of respondents. Twelve per cent thought they had achieved one staff and 78 per cent felt that they had made some progress towards the goal. Only 7 per cent did not feel that they had made progress.

Dismantling the divide between teaching and 'non-teaching' staff was seen by respondents as a major goal. The very terminology is problematic. 'Non-teaching' defines staff by what they do not do. 'Support' staff may refer to those who support students, but equally could imply a hierarchy where one category of staff serves another, non-teaching staff supporting lecturers. The actual descriptors in colleges were varied. As a general description, the term 'service staff' is perhaps the most neutral and will be used here.

The use of a wider range of staff to support learning has been seen by some as an attack on the professionalism of lecturers. For others, such profession-alism may be viewed as 'a piece of occupational code designed primarily to preserve demarcation' (Bright and Williamson, 1995, p. 10). The latter per-spective argues that the real concern of lecturers is not as is publicly presented, a student-centred anxiety that the growing use of service staff will erode teaching standards, but rather a lecturer-centred fear of job losses. Certainly several respondents reported an 'us and them' culture which might be particularly noticeable 'when times get tough' (Principal 4). A minority of lecturing staff were seen as 'precious' (Principal 2) and resisting the move to a situation where the contribution of all staff was equally valued: 'I regret to say that there are still some old crusty lecturers who think that support staff are a lower breed who are there to support them and to cater to their needs. Until those staff move on, things won't change' (Principal 5).

The lack of respect cut both ways. Human Resource Manager 3 spoke of service staff who perceived the lecturing staff as having an easy time as they swanned off for a lengthy summer vacation, despite the fact that this was sim-ply no longer true. She felt that service staff were influenced by society's widely held image of lecturers which depicts them as receiving unwarranted lengthy holidays and being somewhat protected. Changing such attitudes was seen as a long-term goal: 'You can't change in five years something which has been in existence for however long colleges have been around. It takes longer than that' (Human Resource Manager 1) and:

> We still have this distinction between them and us, them being academic and us being support staff. It has improved. We do try. We will never be on one condi-tions of service, totally harmonized in terms of conditions of service. I cannot envisage the day. If we ever get there it's far away.
>
> (Human Resource Manager 2)

There was general agreement among respondents that achieving one staff was an important long-term goal. The steps taken to move towards this point were varied. Harmonization of terms was one major tool. Moving to one staff through harmonization of conditions was reported by Goulding, Dominey and Gray (1998) as a goal in approximately half the colleges they surveyed, though they also pointed out that colleges were using very different defini-tions, not all of which defined harmonization as all staff being on the same conditions. The emphasis on the same treatment was evidenced in other ways. Quality Manager 2 reported that the self-assessment process, includ-ing all documentation, was identical for lecturing and service staff. The inclusion of service staff in all training and development activities was a widely used tactic. In some cases the structure was adjusted to integrate service staff and to indicate the same levels of seniority amongst lecturing and service staff:

> We have placed an emphasis on trying to integrate service staff within academic areas so that we have less of a divide. Where we had lots of central services . . . [these have] been disbanded and there are now secretarial services within the schools. We had central administrative services and we have now changed that. We now have an administrative officer for each school or shared within schools. . . . Obviously you are going to have a central finance service and a central personnel service, central student tracking service but there are now links within the schools. The people concerned actually report to the head of school. There are a lot of moves to try to eradicate the barrier of them and us.
>
> (Human Resource Manager 1)

The appointment of service staff at a senior level was seen as an indicator of the seriousness with which the message that academic staff 'are the important ones and the rest are just servants' (Principal 4) was being resisted. If the senior management team consisted of academic staff only, it may be that this is a powerful symbol of the historical hierarchy of categories of staff. Where service staff were senior appointments, the hierarchy was, if not disintegrating, at least rocking a little. The fundamental divide had not disappeared as different staff did not necessarily understand or sympathize with each other's role: 'There is always, as there is everywhere, a lack of understanding' (Human Resource Manager 1).

What the colleges were engaged with was the 'David solution', i.e., even Michelangelo started with a shapeless block of stone and achieved the final miraculous sculpture by chipping away small amounts of material that did not resemble the vision he held. So colleges are removing anything which does not look like the required result, one staff, by removing the policies and practices which reinforce the divide. In this way it is hoped that different behaviour and structure would usher in a culture change where underlying attitudes had shifted.

STRATEGIC HUMAN RESOURCE MANAGEMENT

Taking on responsibility for managing people implied adopting a strategic approach. The generic trend to a human resources approach, rather than a personnel approach (O'Neill, 1994) was felt by colleges. There was a pressure to place more emphasis on linking the management of people to the organization's strategic goals and a more dispersed responsibility for all the previous personnel functions. However, despite the theoretical base for such development, the empirical underpinning was lacking and managers had little to guide them on how to achieve a strategic approach to HRM: 'Exhortations for the personnel management function to become involved at strategic level may sound impressive; however, the reality is that theoretical and applied perspectives on how to achieve strategic integration are in their infancy' (Lundy and Cowling, 1996, p. 49).

In their survey of further education colleges, Goulding, Dominey and Gray (1998) found that over half had created links between human resources and strategic plans, but that these focused mainly on recruitment and training rather than on the full range of activities associated with managing people. The detail and ownership of plans also varied from perhaps a single paragraph written and owned by the principal to a detailed operating plan which had been developed by the human resource specialist. The report of the survey gives no indication that dispersed responsibility, i.e., the involvement of line managers in managing people, is reflected in a strategic planning process. The explanation suggested is that external pressure, and particularly financial pressure, limited the scope of strategic planning in managing people. The enforced primary aim was to cut costs, rather than a wider vision encompassing the motivation and reward of people. Principal 5 was very aware of being trammelled in this way:

> I think there are some facts in here that are very, very important. The initial phase of the dash for growth was where, upon incorporation, colleges were set targets for growth of 24 per cent over three years. That dash for growth, coupled with savings of 5–6 per cent per year over several years, was going to have a serious effect on how you were going to deliver a programme. The human resource policy, if you like, is a way of coping with those sorts of things. You can't continue to deliver a service in the way that you did because you can't afford to. You are taking students with different social backgrounds, different aspirations, different academic experience and attainment levels, and staff are going to see even less of them. So they have got to find new ways of working and the human resource policies are ways of coping with that. We don't start by saying we're putting in place this human resource policy because we want to achieve that end result, or I don't, I'm afraid. Perhaps I should but I don't. You put in place a human resource policy to help you cope with the factors that are driving your institution.

Other respondents were more sanguine on becoming strategic in their approach, with structures in place to achieve college goals. However, in all cases, it seemed that the goals were selected from the range of human resource activities rather than yet being comprehensive. The connection that eluded them, and which Goulding, Dominey and Gray (1998) also reported, was the connection between managing people and improving teaching and learning. There was a hope that such a connection did exist, but it was an act of faith rather than anything more tangible: 'I can't say to you that I can give you a definite link. I feel it [the HRM strategy] has given a better experience for the students but I couldn't say to you I know this because' (Human Resource Manager 1). Maybe it will never be more than a hope, in that connecting improvements in the core business, teaching and learning, with the impact of human resource strategies, is likely to remain problematic.

The goals expressed included achieving teamwork, placing the right person in the right job at the right price, changing the reward system to reflect more accurately what the college wished to reward and motivating staff. There was some cautious optimism that these could be achieved over time, but within continuing limitations of financial restraint and inadequate time to plan:

> I think the key objective in simple terms has got to be to enthuse staff, to enthuse them so they are committed to the development of their students and the development of the institution; so you try to hang a few action points on that. It's very difficult, but there has got to be flexibility, there has got to be acceptance of new techniques. There has probably got to be teamworking, not necessarily just with other academic staff. All these things have got to come together with the recognition that it has all got to be done to a price I'm afraid. The financial situation has eased a little but all the new money is targeted. There is no new money for the core of what we do.
>
> (Principal 5)

Lifting one's head to look forward and to look widely could still not be taken for granted by the staff interviewed, but there was a sense of greater confidence than previously and more room for manoeuvre. There was some hope of adopting a strategic approach and achieving the goals set.

CONCLUSIONS

Respondents expressed a sense of emerging from a maelstrom where staff had experienced pain and confusion to a present point where confidence could grow. The one enduring and stable factor throughout had been the commitment of staff to their students and this was a solid foundation on which to build. Human Resource Manager 2 believed that staff 'have very, very strong loyalty to our students and I think no matter what, their priority has been doing the best for students and I don't think that's changed at all.'

Staff 'professionalism which we value and treasure very much' (Curriculum Manager 4) was commented on by many:

> There really is a commitment amongst staff that they want to provide a good experience for the students, they want to improve, they want to be better. They want to be best. Those kinds of things really change the ethos of the place and get the commitment from the staff to give the students a good experience.
>
> (Human Resource Manager 3)

Despite the hammering that the sector had taken, there was still real pride in the dedication of staff and some confidence that people could be supported to make a contribution which would enhance the learning of an increasingly diverse student body.

4

MANAGING FINANCE

THE CONTEXT

There is an international search for a solution to the problem of financing the level and quality of vocational education and training required by the economy and demanded by individuals and employers. The pursuit has led to an international trend to shift the focus from the development of the curriculum *per se* to the development of a more cost-efficient means of delivering the curriculum to larger numbers of students from a wider range of backgrounds (Abrokwa, 1995; Gray and Warrender, 1993; King, 1993). This chapter focuses on the UK experience where two major mechanisms have been selected to achieve this goal: first, opening state-funded colleges to a market or quasi-market and, second, using the funding methodology as a lever to achieve lower unit costs simultaneously with higher levels of participation.

Both these tactics have been in evidence since incorporation in 1993, when colleges were given powers to:

- Employ their own staff;
- Enter into contracts on their own behalf;
- Manage assets and resources; and
- Act as a legal body undertaking activities in furtherance of their purposes as providers of education (DES, 1991, quoted in Briggs, 1992, p. 62).

The resources to carry out these responsibilities were provided by a new funding methodology devised by the FEFC which embodied 'twin objectives of more students and more achievements' (Gorringe, 1994b, p. 70). The funding was offered in a currency of units attached to three elements of each individual student's experience: entry into a learning programme, time on the

Table 4.1   Table indicating number of colleges in financial health categories A–C, 1994–98

	1994	1995	1996	1997	1998
Group A (reasonably robust)	309 (70%)	257 (57%)	206 (46%)	197 (44%)	213 (49%)
Group B (financially vulnerable)	106 (24%)	135 (30%)	148 (33%)	151 (34%)	142 (33%)
Group C (financially weak)	25 (6%)	60 (13%)	93 (21%)	96 (22%)	80 (18%)

Source: Provided by the Further Education Funding Council, July 1999.

programme and the final accredited achievement. Colleges could compete for students, and through the students, funds. The underpinning vision was perceived by Finance Manager 7 as: 'some sort of glorious insight into how marvellously efficient colleges will be in the future'. The 'efficiency' was driven by a hard edge, in that it was anticipated, and even welcomed, that in the competitive environment some colleges would thrive and others would fail: 'Colleges which are demonstrably successful will attract increasing funding. Those which are less so will be exposed, and will have choices to make about how best to secure improvements. In all of this there is a realism' (Gorringe, 1994, p. 72).

Growth in student numbers was undoubtedly achieved but at a cost. As with all policy changes, the results went beyond those anticipated and such 'realism' resulted in around one in five colleges in a weak financial position from 1996 to 1998, as indicated in Table 4.1, threatening the sufficiency and adequacy of provision.

Colleges that were struggling for survival, as well as those that were thriving, entered into the 'game' (Finance Manager 2) of the funding methodology. Mergers were largely driven by financial insecurity (Crequer, 1998), scandals of financial mismanagement, particularly in relation to franchising, hit the headlines (Leney, Lucas and Taubaum, 1998) and a new culture seemed established where financial considerations were pre-eminent. 'It got to the point where people were talking about quotas and brokering units and things like that' (Finance Manager 7), reflecting an approach where funding units were for selling on to others at a profit. A review of the methodology (Kennedy, 1997) called a halt, questioning the culture and its appropriateness for education. Government directives ordered more collaboration, less competition and a focus on providing primarily for each college's local community. Some increase in funding was made available, but targeted to particular initiatives or locations.

The legacy of this period was a financial dependency on the FEFC which colleges were anxious to lessen, primarily because of the dangers of being dependent on funds for which the rules changed frequently. Divisions were created within the sector, for example, between rural and urban, small and large colleges, each arguing a special case and seeing their treatment as inequitable compared with that of other colleges. Finally the debate went on as to how far the problems the sector was experiencing were due to the overall amount of funding available or to the methodology for its distribution (Leney, Lucas and Taubaum, 1998). Throughout this whirligig of change, uncertainty and often insecurity, managers had to make sense of the system and manipulate it to achieve the best result for their college and for students.

DEMANDS ON MANAGERS

The first impact was that, from 1993, colleges had to deal with a hugely bureaucratic system and comply with accountancy practice in a way that had never been demanded previously. In the prior culture, a good manager was one who spent at least the budget allocated and succeeded in arguing for an increase year on year. Managers were therefore prepared by experience and mentally geared for spending more, not cutting costs and achieving efficiency gains. In the new system, an ability to cut costs and to plan and to control huge amounts of data was paramount. Principal 2 described the shift from a more retrospective, casual approach to finance to a much more structured system:

> Up until '95, even after incorporation, I think there was a degree of growth which you could just achieve and it didn't have to be properly thought out, resourced and planned. Because of the drop in the average level of funding, because of the increase in auditing, now the management of growth has to be much more structured and you can't just grow and then alter the figures to fit in with what's going on.

Managers who had come up through education and training were not necessarily equipped to manage in this way. As Human Resource Manager 2 pointed out in Chapter 3, colleges were quick to recognize the need to import financial expertise. However, the twin objectives of managing a bureaucratic system designed to reduce unit costs and increase efficiency while also maintaining the quality of education immediately established a tension. The central question for resource managers was how a college could establish a system which harnessed the financial acumen and experience necessary to deal with the demands of the methodology and the year-on-year cuts in real terms, while keeping learning, rather than maximization of income, as the core purpose.

ORGANIZATIONAL APPROACH

All colleges face 'finite resources and infinite demand' (Finance Manager 1) and must therefore make choices about how to use the resources available. Underlying such choices are the values which assign priority, for example, to student learning or to survival. All of the finance managers interviewed denied that either they personally or their college were driven purely by financial considerations. However, there was a spectrum of approach to making decisions ranging from that driven primarily by learning to that driven primarily by finance. Learning was very much the primary focus for Finance Manager 9:

> I do not think the success of the college is because of a link between finance and the curriculum. The success of the college is that curriculum is the major driver. Once you start letting factors outside curriculum need influence the decisions, that is when you start getting problems. The delivery modes that we use are not a response to cuts in income or extra income or anything like that. It is because this is the most appropriate way to deliver this programme to this segment of people. . . . It is about responding to the way people need to learn in a modern technological society. That is why the place is bursting.

The need to consider finance is acknowledged, but it does not take precedence. Learning is the start point, finance follows. For other finance managers, there was a tension that was more strongly felt. Putting learning first was difficult in the face of the financial pressures. Finance Manager 1 expressed the paradox: 'There is a financial imperative which drives the decision making and it all comes back to units' and:

> As a college you have to make the decision that there are certain courses and certain provision that you have to make which are going to be profitable in the broadest sense of the word. You have to say that this is part of our social mission to provide a facility for the community which may cost us more than it generates in unit income. That is an integral part of the education world. You have to do that. It is ethically right.

'Profitable' in this case is interpreted not just as generating funds but as generating value to the students and to the community. The words 'profitable' and 'valuable' can therefore take on a double meaning, reflecting the difficult judgements facing managers about the value or profit to be given to students and the funds such activity may create or cost the college.

Some finance managers argued strongly that because of the funding methodology, rather than being in tension, creating funds and achieving learning were two sides of the same coin. Students had to be recruited and retained and had to achieve in order for the college to be paid the relevant funding units for entry, on programme and achievement. Students would not stay and would not achieve if the teaching and learning were not of a quality and appropriateness to meet their needs. Therefore educational success in recruiting more students and helping them achieve qualifications was the route to financial success. For Finance Manager 2, generating funds and supporting learning could not be decoupled: 'The way I look at things you can't decouple them. It actually comes down to the same thing at the end of the day'.

Despite this belief that finance and learning went hand in hand, and despite the certainty of all of the managers interviewed that finance was not the only consideration, it was clear that there was a tension and that sometimes very difficult decisions had to be made about what provision to offer, what students to accept and what cuts might need to be made to the resources of the college. The system to deal with such decisions established who made such decisions and how.

Just as the human resource professionals from a non-educational background were often viewed with suspicion as discussed in Chapter 3, finance managers were also subject to some distrust: 'All I know is show me a college where there is a chartered accountant in charge and I will show you a college that is failing' (Finance Manager 9). The impression is very much that educational decisions should not be left in the hands of those whose expertise is in financial management. The distrust was mutual, as some finance managers interviewed whose background was from outside education, felt that decisions had to be taken by them, as academic managers could not be trusted:

Academic managers are not very good at managing. That is possibly a very broad and insulting comment to make, but people who have come up the academic route solely tend to take a softer view of some of the decisions so ultimately some of the decisions of that nature are taken by the Director of Finance.

(Finance Manager 1)

Those in the Finance office feel academics have never been out in the real world. It's often the comment made in the Finance Department because the Finance Department staff come from outside education. Some academics go through school, university and then they come here, and they don't appreciate how things happen elsewhere. They will leave things until they get round to it and they don't appreciate that we need things recording immediately, so that we can report what is happening financially in the college. There's far more urgency than they seem to have, and we put this down to being out in the real world more.

(Finance Manager 5)

This mutual distrust is part of the 'one staff' issue discussed in Chapter 3. Clearly such division and lack of understanding of each other's perspective is a barrier in decision-making. The internal context was often then one of distrust between lecturers and finance managers, and difficulties in making choices to keep learning central in the light of continually reducing funds.

The process selected for making financial decisions reflects each college's approach to resolving the tensions. Some have selected a very precise and numerically driven system which applies a formula consistently. Principal 2 provided an example of such an approach. Asked how his practice might have changed since 1993, he described his current practice:

> You would see me much more driven by CMIS and I would be consulting the computer more and I'd be doing a lot more modelling. We have a unit allocation system which completely mirrors the FEFC's unit allocation system. So whereas before, as part of the planning, we used to go to the Section Heads and say what business are you going to do next year, and it was very unscientific, we now have ground rules and they put in bids which they then have to substantiate in terms of growth and courses . . . It's a very scientific way now, looking at models of growth. We've been doing that since '95 and therefore last year our return to the FEFC was frighteningly close to our target units. I think we were contracted to 103,149 units and we actually did 103,320.

This precise decision-making model uses numerical criteria as a basis for decisions. It is so accurate that the predicted number of units of funds which the college plans to earn is accurate to 0.1 per cent. This is the principal who in Chapter 1 described his style pre-1993 as a 'a wide boy wandering around saying yes to everybody'. The change from a relaxed approach to a very tight financial control is apparent, and this is achieved through the means of applying a formula to allocate funds. Of course, as has been pointed out (Simkins, 1998; Thomas, 1999), any apparently numerical model involves judgements on which figures to use and how, and is therefore as political as an overtly negotiated system. Power and value judgements are still contested, but in the decision about which formula to apply rather than a negotiated process of allocating funds. However, the mechanism of a formula serves to distance such judgements as once the formula is decided, then it can be applied objectively and consistently.

The quotation above also highlights another choice: how far to mirror the FEFC funding methodology internally or to adopt an independent system. The decision on whether to link the amount of income a subunit of the organization earns to how much it receives is a strong symbol of cultural intent. Is the college a whole, where areas generating more income can subsidize those which create less? Or are subunits to be allowed to thrive or die according to their own efforts and success? How much reward should subunits receive for their entrepreneurial success? Should they keep all of, for example, sponsorship funds, or only a proportion? If so, how should the proportion be decided? How can services which do not generate income be financed in a climate where other parts of the organization are under threat of survival if they fail to generate funds, without creating hostility for such services? With such questions in mind, the process of budgeting is strongly directing cultural change.

Where colleges choose to allocate funds to subunits, such as faculties or departments, in relation to what they earn, the cultural message is an emphasis on forcing the subunits to take responsibility for their future. There is no protection for those who fail to generate sufficient income. They will lose staff or courses, or close. The culture is a long way from the LEA public sector approach, where income continues to arrive no matter what. When internal budgets are linked to earnings, staff will succeed or fail by their own efforts and results, just as in the harsh world of business.

In contrast, other colleges were adopting a different approach and stressing a different culture. They were not using a formula-driven system or linking the income earned by each subunit to the funds which it received. The 'quite broad brush' (Finance Manager 1) decisions move negotiation and value judgements to the foreground, and imply a more college-wide approach where cross-subsidy can occur to protect less financially successful courses or subunits, and where decisions are driven by negotiation, rather than by numbers alone.

BUDGETING

The management of finance in colleges centres on the twin themes of establishing a system where the organization can at a minimum survive, and perhaps even thrive, but also using the powerful lever of resource to influence culture and attitudes. Budgeting provides an implicit answer to the questions posed in the paragraph above. The system elected provides an operational process but also communicates cultural messages.

Thomas (1999) points out that, historically, staff costs were controlled centrally and subunits were given a small budget for non-staff costs which was a little more or less than the previous year. The increment or decrement involved was therefore at the margin, involving small shifts in the amount devolved. There was loose coupling (Weick, 1976) between the activity and success of the subunit and the amount of funds received. That is, funds did not depend to any significant degree on the performance of the subunit. Stability reigned. Thomas (1999, p. 184) argues that the 1990s have been marked by a trend to formula approaches to budgeting with two aims: 'To change the culture of the organization to a more entrepreneurial approach by reflecting the pressures of the external environment at a departmental level: and to bring a more rational basis to the allocation of resources'. The double aim is to remove as far as possible the micropolitical element in a negotiated budget (more rational) and to force subunits to be more proactive and more responsible for their performance (more entrepreneurial). Thomas goes on to argue that a formulaic approach is more feasible in financially secure environments. If, for example, certain departments are likely to be in deficit, then a negotiated budget is more likely unless the organization is content to see parts of the institution, and therefore the curriculum, close.

In their survey of 12 colleges, Leney, Lucas and Taubaum (1998) found that the methods of resource allocation varied from those who used a formula approach mirroring the FEFC methodology to those using the methods which had been in place in the pre-incorporation period of LEA funding. The finance managers interviewed to provide data for this book evidenced the same spectrum. The reasons for adopting a particular process revealed a range of beliefs about the effect of different approaches to internal resource allocation on staff attitudes and culture.

Negotiated approaches

Internal allocation of resources based on an historical or negotiated approach was seen as appropriate for a number of reasons. The adoption of a formula approach was viewed negatively as a straitjacket which would limit decisions on how to move funds around the institution as, once decided, it would have to be followed. A negotiated approach offered managers more freedom to take decisions based on criteria other than a numerical calculation. In this way it was argued, the college could be more responsive to need, placing more or fewer funds where demand was growing or anticipated: 'It is very *ad hoc* and not scientific at all because we want to respond to things as they come up as quickly as we can' (Finance Manager 9).

As well as responding to external demand, there were internal reasons why a formula approach was rejected. One finance manager reflected that when they had adopted such an approach the result was seen as inequitable:

> Using cost weighting as a formula for allocating resources, some people were getting a disproportionate amount of resources compared to what they actually required. So we have tended to go more on historical basis and spread the resources more equally to reflect the equal numbers of students across the different curriculum areas.
>
> (Finance Manager 10)

One of the common justifications for adopting a formula approach is that it offers transparent equity, as all are subject to the same formula. The opposite is perceived as the case by this manager. Any formula will result in gainers and losers. Change the formula and a different set of winners appear. Although apparently rational and equitable, it may be, as in Finance Manager 10's perception, that decisions based on the educational judgement of managers stand as much chance of being equitable as a numerically driven system. Finance Manager 7 explained that as a small general further education college, avoiding the 'infighting' that used to happen was a major goal. The system of allocating funds tried to accommodate the winners and losers in terms of those who earned more or less income, and to encourage a corporate approach rather than cut-throat internal competition. In the view of Finance Manager 2, the dialogue of negotiation itself offered a means of taking into account the unique circumstances of each subunit, balancing educational and financial pressures:

So the starting point is a student number planning exercise, looking at the number of students we expect on individual courses and looking at how realistic that may be in the current year and the previous year, and the teaching resource that's going into it. We use that as the basis of a dialogue between the Personnel Manager, the Deputy Principal and myself with the head of each individual school, so we would look at what's required for next year, the specific staffing resource they've got at the moment and how the two match together, and identify any issues such as if the demand for a particular type of course isn't there any more, what implications that might have for members of staff that might have that specialism and no other. We might need to redeploy or look at redundancy, look at the staffing balance between permanent staff and contract staff, and go through that dialogue to see what the budget should be in each of the schools individually.

(Finance Manager 2)

In each of these examples the perceived need for maintaining motivation, equilibrium and a corporate approach underpinned resource allocation rather than a desire to engineer the delight or anxiety that result from exposure to the 'pressures of the external environment' as expressed through a formula-driven translation of what is earned into what is allocated to each subunit. However, a negotiated approach to budgeting does not necessarily eschew the use of figures. In the example of Finance Manager 2 above, the numbers of students planned is part of the decision-making process. Rather it is that numbers are not the deciding factor. Judgement tempers numerical calculation. In such an approach, the chosen cultural message is not internal competition, but the message that 'everybody shares' (Finance Manager 9).

Formula approaches

The chief explanation given for opting for a formula approach was to shift people's attitudes to a greater awareness of and responsibility for the connection between their own actions and success or failure. Internal allocation of resources which reflects the income earned by subunits has rewards and dangers for the staff in that area:

One the one hand you do more and you get more money. The downside is if you don't hit a target then the penalties hit you, but that's exactly what the FEFC are doing to us. So the whole idea of making the system respond to reflect what's happening with the FEFC nationally means that you've got to have that hard edge.

(Principal 2)

The use of a formula approach reflecting the external methodology was usually linked to a high level of devolution of responsibility and independence. In Principal 2's college, if sponsorship money was achieved, apart from a deduction for administrative costs, the unit responsible retained the funds.

Sections in trouble might be given time for a recovery plan, but there was no question of permanent cross-subsidy from more successful areas of the college. Nothing could be further from 'everybody shares'.

Various models of allocation were in evidence. In one college the costs of teacher and instructor hours, management and administrative support, accommodation, materials, etc. are calculated and deducted from the income earned. The remainder must be 40 per cent of the total and goes to central costs. Although some courses may be marginally contributing less, say 35 per cent, this lesser contribution is only possible if another course is contributing over 40 per cent within the section, so that the overall contribution of the section is 40 per cent or above. Through this mechanism, the courses which can be offered, and the resources which can be used for each course, are controlled by financial considerations. In another college, central costs were first deducted from the total college income earned. The remaining sum was divided by the number of on-programme units earned in total by the college to arrive at an internal unit value. Each subunit of the college received income calculated by the number of units they earned multiplied by the internal unit value. The system had provided a relatively unchanging allocation: 'The rate hasn't really changed much over the last few years. It's been about £10.40 and it's always based just on programme units because that gives the best weighting between areas. If you use entry and remission and things like that it distorts the allocation' (Finance Manager 3).

The net result in both of the examples above is that approximately 40 per cent of income was used for central costs and 60 per cent was devolved to academic subunits. In both the examples given, the financial outcome was very similar but the calculation to arrive at the sums involved differed. In both cases the medium is the message. How sums to be allocated are calculated is primarily a tool for cultural change emphasizing entrepreneurialism. A formula approach may on the face of it be concerned with financial issues, but is also a device to emphasise values.

The mixed model

In the case of three colleges a mixed model was in operation. There was a calculation based on costs and income but at the same time a careful eye was kept on the likely impact of following such calculation mechanistically. It was also recognized that a zero-based approach was very time-consuming and that a historical incremental approach was much easier: 'It's far easier to say you had X last year and Z plus or minus this year and of course, if they manage to struggle through last year then they can struggle through this year' (Finance Manager 1). However, it was not just that such an approach was easier but that it also seemed to provide the possibility of adjustments based on issues other than money. Asked whether the budgeting process was driven by a formula or by negotiation, Finance Manager 11 responded:

What in fact happens is that it's a bit of both. We sit down with Heads of Division, who are looking after cost centres. We look at their performance in the current year. We look at their areas of growth or contraction and we fix targets in terms of students. . . . You work largely on a historical basis. Not everything is zero-based year on year. It's a three-month process to actually finalize the budget. Overall we have 50–55 cost centres. Each of those has to be negotiated and amended.

A similar process was described by Finance Manager 4 as 'While we start with a clean sheet of paper we look back as well'.

EVALUATING APPROACHES

In each of the three approaches described above, the intention was ultimately to improve teaching and learning. In all cases, the finance available was also a management tool to achieve a cultural shift in staff attitudes. At one end of the spectrum, the use of a formula approach was seen as driving staff to be aware of their success, not only in financial terms, but also in educational terms, in that money was linked to recruiting students, retaining them and their achievement. In this way financial success was educational success and vice versa. At the other end of the spectrum might be an *ad hoc* or negotiated approach which perceived that retaining the ability to manipulate funds was in the best interests of educational balance and quality. The balance was achieved by the capacity to retain less profitable or even loss-making areas. Issues of quality were related to the belief that exposing staff to financial insecurity may result in an anxious and demotivated workforce, or one in conflict through internal competition, and that this will impact on teaching and learning. In fact the extreme ends of the spectrum were not in operation. Those using a formula approach might still set the formula aside in exceptional circumstances. Those using a negotiated approach injected a degree of numerical calculation into the allocation process. Nevertheless, the internal allocation process near to the pure formula-driven end of the spectrum is intended to encourage a culture which is closer to a commercial approach, with the advantage of arguably greater responsiveness and entrepreneurialism. At the other end, the culture is much closer to the historic public sector, with arguably the advantage of securing greater staff motivation and a corporate, less internally competitive culture. In all cases, the budgeting process was a path which hopefully led to linking resources to learning. In Chapter 11, 'Evolving the culture', the survey results presented in Figures 11.1 and 11.2 indicate that colleges acknowledge the funding methodology as the most significant factor demanding cultural change. They also point to the internal use of funds as an important tool for influencing culture.

LINKING RESOURCES TO LEARNING

Each finance manager was asked if they linked the internal allocation of resources to learning. Responses varied, though there was generally a sense that it was very difficult to achieve this:

> If you say these are the learning outcomes that we are seeking to achieve and link the resources to those, that would be wonderful and then you would have found the Holy Grail but I think it is a difficult one. I would be happy to go to the first stage of that let alone get to the end of it.
>
> (Finance Manager 1)

The 'Holy Grail' of a link between learning and resources eluded most. The term 'learning' was differently understood, with some finance managers seeing funding teaching as synonymous with funding learning, so that if resources were linked to the costs of teaching, that was perceived as linking resources and learning. Finance Manager 3 felt that, in his college, resources were linked to learning as allocated budgets were adjusted at the three census dates throughout the year, deducting funds if students had left. In this way, he argued, funding was linked to learning, because it was linked to retention. Finance Manager 6 argued that everything contributed to learning:

> I suppose it depends how you define learning. The first point would be that we take the view that every part of the college contributes to the students' experience of learning. The caretaker who opens the classrooms first thing in the morning and closes them last thing at night is contributing to the students' learning experience. The cleaners who clean the classrooms are contributing to that.

If this point of view is accepted, then funding central services is actually funding learning. To an extent the argument is therefore one of semantics, but it is clear that resources are still mostly linked to inputs, or to income, neither of which is a learning outcome. None of the finance managers were linking resources to achievement. There is an irony that the indicator used to allocate resources under the prior LEA system, the numbers of students learning, was the closest proxy any college had arrived at for the 'Holy Grail' of a link between learning and resources.

A CHANGING CULTURE

Overall, much had changed. Managers had become more aware of finance and more skilled in managing it. Staff had also increased their awareness of themselves as resource users and the need to produce value for money. The old 'LEA culture which was pretty laid back with a job for life and very cosy' (Finance Manager 8) was long gone. It had been difficult to help staff recognize and respond to the new demands:

> trying to get people to recognize that in a sense we are a business as well as an education institute and that if we don't get the money in and we don't get it right, jobs could be on the line. It's been hard to get people to think that, because they think 'it's never me'. It's always somebody else. It's not my problem if I've only got ten students and my target was 15. What can I do about it? That kind of attitude.
>
> (Finance Manager 8)

The question posed by many of the managers interviewed was how far the culture change had penetrated, and how far it was reasonable to expect lecturers to be aware of finance issues when their primary concern was rightly teaching. The issue of the extent of culture change will be explored further in Chapter 11.

There was also a strong sense of some colleges living on borrowed time. Finance Manager 7's college had survived because the LEA had been generous with capital funds for a rolling programme of replacement. That inheritance had now been spent 'several times over' and the college had no answer on how it was to fund building maintenance and equipment replacement: 'The capital programme is not just about buildings. It's also scientific equipment, engineering equipment and construction equipment. It will get to the point where we will have to withdraw the provision because safety requirements wouldn't be met. That would be the final straw.' 'Real' money was needed, described by several finance managers as money not tied to doing more, but to catch up with the backlog of inadequate buildings and equipment and poor pay. There were also fears that efficiency gains had run their course and that the methodology, which had been a successful driver to reduce unit costs, gave no guidance on where efficiency gains were no longer feasible without learning being unacceptably compromised: 'You can't go on improving efficiency year on year because effectively that would mean, just take staffing, that ultimately you would end up with no staff' (Finance Manager 11).

As well as a possible detriment to students' experience, staff had paid a price in turnover and impact on health, which was not felt to be acceptable. In contrast to the general perception that the sector had been driven very hard, Finance Manager 9 felt that solutions to finance and all else lay in the hands of the colleges themselves and that it was possible to continue to thrive if you managed well:

> I think that is another thing that some colleges have made a mistake about. They think there is a political solution, a corporate FE solution to managing their individual college affairs. Each college has got a regional accountant. I never speak to him. He tells me that others virtually ask him if they can go to the toilet now.

They do not move without checking it with the FEFC. My view is that if you are incorporated and independent, and you are given the money, bloody well get on with it.

The message is clear, that the future of the sector lies with the colleges themselves, not with government. However, this was a lone voice. The weight of evidence was very much colleges feeling that, however well they managed, funding or the lack of it might undermine their plans. In the national survey of colleges, finance was indicated as the most significant driver of cultural change, the most significant factor leading to restructuring and the most significant opportunity and threat. 'Mortgaging the future' (Finance Manager 7) cannot go on indefinitely.

5

MANAGING MARKETING

'MARKETIZATION' OF THE SECTOR

During the 1990s a rather negative view of further education pre-1993 was promulgated, suggesting that up to incorporation, the sector was myopic in relation to the needs of the community (Coleman, 1994), product driven (Hatton and Sedgemore, 1992) and unresponsive. This analysis also suggested that the government response to this perceived failure was to open colleges to a much greater degree of competition through incorporation, thereby establishing the 'marketization' of the sector. It was anticipated that this would act as a spur for colleges to achieve greater responsiveness and improved quality. A debate on the effects of opening colleges to competition has followed, examining how far the supposed intended results have been achieved, whether the curriculum and/or the student base has widened or narrowed, and the degree to which individual students and employers have greater choice to meet their needs. However, diverging from this viewpoint, a contradictory perspective has arisen suggesting that, rather than being opened to a market culture in 1993, colleges have always been markets, though highly constrained, and that they continue to be a hybrid sort of market where their capacity to act is severely limited by a number of factors, including government policy and funding (Foskett, 1996). Thus it is argued, change has been relatively limited. The degree and nature of market forces to which colleges have been subject, and the effects of such exposure are therefore contested.

The intentions of government policy in incorporating colleges and opening them to competition are also disputed. Scott (1996, p. 28) argues that the 'strategy was essentially one of centralisation not of marketisation' based primarily on 'antipathy to local authorities and the desire to increase participation while cutting costs'. In contrast, Davies (1999, p. 129) argues that the concept of 'an educational market-place where consumers exercise freedom of choice amongst competing providers' has been very influential in the UK, suggesting that colleges do indeed work within a market context. Colleges are certainly subject to a number of requirements that appear to be compelling them down a market-driven route. For example, the expectation that they will include an analysis of local needs in their strategic plans forces them to analyse market requirements. The funding system which relates funding to colleges' success in attracting and retaining students appears to give much greater encouragement to matching the expectations of customers. However, Scott (1996, p. 28) warns against being distracted by 'the "noise" of market rhetoric' from the fact that far less progress has been made towards market polices than is sometimes assumed. This chapter will try to set aside the rhetoric of marketization and explore what the data from interviews and the survey appear to indicate about how far colleges have changed their practice, and how far they appear to be implementing a marketing approach.

MARKETING

Discussion of marketing in colleges is made problematic by the myriad definitions of the term in the literature and its use by college staff to signify very different approaches and activities. As Scott (1996, p. 25) points out, even within the commercial world, ' "pure" markets have never existed outside economic text books'. If even businesses may not conform to theoretical models of markets, then educational organizations are even less likely to do so. Therefore, analysis of how far further education markets conform to theoretical models of commercial markets may not be as productive as it at first seems. If marketing is the interaction between producers and customers, then the diversity of environment and customers within the further education sector renders any monolithic interpretation of markets or marketing vulnerable to immediate challenge. College 'customers' may exist in the commercial mode, paying the full cost of their training and so be the equivalent of business customers. Or they may be indirect customers who pay nothing or very little, the costs being fully or partly borne by the state. Hence the 'hybrid' nature of colleges which have a foot in both public sector and business environments. What is clear is that education markets do not function in the same way as commercial markets and therefore demand an alternative theory. Providers are not free to offer whatever products they wish. They may be constrained by practical factors, such as available funding and an absence of an infrastructure of capital and buildings, by social factors such as the moral purpose of education and the relative autonomy of professional staff, and by political factors, where legislation limits the freedom to relate to customers. Tierney (1998, p. 125) argues that the product itself is so different as to demand a different attitude and language, recognizing the emotional and spiritual dimension of college activities:

> At its best, a college education offers something much closer to what a church is supposed to provide, than what a business is supposed to do. The Faculty and administrators help individuals grapple with difficult issues about life and death, and the meaning of life. They aid students in their quest to become productive citizens. To speak of such grand challenges in the language of customer relations runs the risk of trivializing important actions and making mundane what the philosophers have held high throughout history.

Whether one accepts that the purpose of further education goes beyond vocational training to the education and enrichment of individuals and citizens to the degree suggested by Tierney, or not, the social mission and the parameters laid down by legislation mean that FE 'is a very different kind of market from that among supermarkets or car dealers' (Scott, 1996, p. 25). The language used by individual staff and colleges indicates how far they may wish to distance themselves or move closer to the 'markets of car dealers'. Some colleges and individual staff are comfortable with using the term 'marketing' which correlates with a more commercial approach, adopting classic business techniques such as segmenting the market, analysing competitive position and maximizing income. Others use the broader term 'responsiveness' which correlates with actions to better meet the needs of actual and potential students, where social purpose predominates (Lumby, 1999a). In the survey, the term 'marketing' was employed only five times or in 0.95 per cent of the responses indicating opportunities, threats and important factors for the future. Responsiveness was more in evidence as a concept which may have significance. In fact, this semantic dichotomy may be deceptive, in that responsive organizations may benefit from adopting marketing techniques to better understand their customers. Marketing includes achieving customer care and satisfaction, and therefore relates to the social mission of aiding learners.

COLLEGE PERCEPTIONS OF MARKETING

The degree to which colleges saw activities which might be understood to be relevant to marketing as significant opportunities or threats is indicated by Table 5.1. Perceived opportunities are seen to be far more in line with a previous LEA culture, as curriculum development and partnership are of greater importance than responsiveness and competition. In fact, a number of colleges see the competitive factor as a threat, as in Table 5.2.

Colleges appear to be seeing competition not positively as a spur to greater quality or responsiveness but largely negatively as a threat. Perhaps the political insistence on competition as a lever for progress is simplistic. Colleges

Table 5.1   Factors indicated as opportunities

Factor	Number of colleges citing this factor	% of responses
Curriculum development	50	26.0
Partnership	45	24.0
Expansion	38	20.0
Widening participation	32	17.0
Responsiveness	9	4.8
Competition	9	4.8

Table 5.2   Factors indicated as threats

Factor	Number of colleges citing this factor	% of responses
Competition	50	27.0
Curriculum development	14	7.5
Responsiveness	6	3.2
Too many demands	6	3.2
Widening participation	3	1.6

may, after all, face intense competition in urban areas with many providers, or very little in a rural area or where there is no sixth form school provision. It seems likely, therefore, that any comprehensive analysis of marketing in the sector would need to focus on an understanding of marketing activity where competition is a part, but not the central driving force.

Foskett distinguishes:

> Two specific perspectives – marketing as an overall philosophy for an organisation, and marketing as a functional area of management. As a functional area marketing involves the application of strategies to effect the sale of a product or service. As an overall philosophy, however, marketing is central to the operation of an organisation and '. . . is not a specialised activity at all (but) encompasses the entire business – it is the whole business . . .' (Drucker, 1954, p 56).
>
> (Foskett, 1999, p. 34)

The functional approach to marketing focuses on products and sales and, therefore, advertising and promotion would be the primary activities with the purpose of attracting students to courses. As a philosophy, marketing would focus more on identifying needs and developing the curriculum to meet needs. The marketing managers interviewed certainly seemed aware of the difference and favoured the latter approach at a conceptual level: 'There is so much more to marketing a college than just advertising, so very much more' (Marketing Manager 3), and 'We do have more of a philosophical approach to marketing. That's not to say that that's necessarily universally held across the college, but in terms of the strategic direction, we sort of start from the premise that we are responding to customer need and/or demand' (Marketing Manager 1).

Although both of these managers are clear on their approach, the point is made by Marketing Manager 1 that not all staff may share this perspective. For some the priority may still be ' "bums on seats" and as many as possible' (Burton, 1994, p. 399). Marketing Manager 2, who was a Head of Faculty temporarily acting as the College Marketing Manager, explained that the priority for himself and his staff had to be the functional approach, recruiting as many students as possible:

> The sort of things I get involved with marketing-wise, they all stem back to enrolment. I get weekly figures on enrolment and if they are not looking good I will immediately talk to my Course Managers . . . I have a feeling that I will be largely dealing with enrolment, promoting the college, promoting courses, getting people into here and when I have got that sorted, then I might start thinking about needs analysis but it wouldn't be the first priority for me.

While there might be an awareness of a broader marketing approach, developing and adjusting products to identified needs and wants, in this college, marketing activity was still product driven, focused on selling courses to as many as possible. The explanation for this approach was that staff had insufficient time to investigate needs and therefore the urgent necessity to recruit overtook any intention to examine and respond to needs. Davies (1999, p. 139) argues that with growing experience of marketing, colleges have moved away from a concentration on selling to 'a more comprehensive vision' but acknowledges that this may be largely amongst senior staff. A recurring theme throughout this book is the degree to which culture and, therefore, practice have changed throughout the whole organization or only amongst the more senior staff. This chapter will explore how colleges are interpreting marketing by analysing how they gather information and respond to needs at a strategic top-down and at an operational bottom-up level.

GATHERING INFORMATION

Foskett (1999, p. 40) argues that colleges need to understand their markets in terms of:

- market characteristics – size, constraints, character, patterns of change and future development
- competition – the nature and behaviour of competitors
- buyer behaviour – the decision-making processes of customers.

The systems to achieve such a sophisticated analysis have developed since 1993 (Davies, 1999) but merely collecting and presenting the data are very small parts of the whole process of responding. Chapter 8, 'Managing information and communication', explores in detail the barriers which exist in helping staff to make use of data, however valid and cogently presented.

Waring (1999) argues that information gathering must be embedded in a culture of responding to information. The two halves of the equation are therefore researching need and responding to need. In relation to the former, practice varies from comprehensive, systematic and periodic research to the superficial or virtually absent. Compare the perceptions of Marketing Managers 1 and 2:

> The needs analysis is quite elaborate. We do an awful lot more than a lot of colleges which basically just reproduce the standard TEC [Training and Enterprise Council] LMI [labour market information] document and they say, well you know, there is a shortfall of people with higher level IT [information technology] skills in the area, needs analysis done. Tick. Put it against the strategic plan. We need to work on IT. We go a lot further than that. We look at a whole range of other secondary sources as well as LMI. We also do some primary research, not a huge amount, but we do a significant amount of primary research. We do quite a lot of qualitative research with our own customers, focus groups and employer clients, with full-time students and part-time students, with community groups. All of that feeds into quite an elaborate needs analysis which is quite vigorously disseminated throughout the divisions. So that underpins the planning.
>
> (Marketing Manager 1)

> One thing we don't do really, really well is market research and needs analysis and so on. Our strategic plan has a large section in it on needs analysis. The Marketing Manager next door has a whole load of stuff to help her do this but we have all struggled to do this well. The FEFC a couple of years ago brought out a very impressive guide on needs analysis. We all read it in awe really. We weren't doing half the things we should have done.
>
> (Marketing Manager 2)

The difference in the degree of confidence in the management of a needs analysis process is marked. The belief of Marketing Manager 1 that many colleges simply adapt the local labour market information from the Training and Enterprise Council raises a further issue. Government, through the FEFC, has attempted to encourage colleges to respond to the needs not just of potential individual applicants but to the needs of employers and the local economy for trained staff (FEFC, 1996). In this they are asking colleges to undertake human resource planning: 'the attempt to forecast the future demand for educated manpower' (Hough, 1994, p. 103) rather than to rely solely on a social demand approach which 'focuses on the forecasts of future student choices to determine the level of education provision' (ibid., p. 104). Hough argues that a manpower planning approach is problematic in a number of ways, including:

- difficulty of finding accurate data on the current position let alone the future
- training is undertaken in-house and by private providers so that the whole picture of training is never available

- people may transfer skills so preparing for the particular jobs which are forecast is deceptive
- occupational mobility.

Colleges are well aware of these weaknesses (Lumby, 1999b) and this may be part of the reason why the attempt to gather local labour market information is cursory in some cases. The capability may also be lacking as indicated by Marketing Manager 2 above. However, the strongest driver away from human resource planning and towards a social demand approach is the funding. Colleges are unlikely to turn away applicants from a programme which may be indicated as producing too many people trained in a particular vocational area, if turning students away means a loss of income. This is a clear example where policy is in contradiction. Various exhortations have been published encouraging colleges to plan in relation to local economic needs (FEFC, 1996, 1997). At the same time, the underlying driver for growth, the funding, encourages colleges to train all that are willing and that they can accommodate. The move to a greater emphasis on partnership implicitly acknowledges this tension and returns the sector to a regional co-ordination away from a competitive and market-driven approach, to an external co-ordination of colleges much closer to the previous LEA regime (DfEE, 1999). The social demand approach is likely to remain the strongest factor in responsiveness and marketing for the foreseeable future, but even to respond to the needs of individual potential students, information needs to be very good or it will not convince staff of the need to take note. In many colleges this position has not yet been achieved: 'I don't think the needs analysis to date has been good enough to help us or influence us in our curriculum development. I really don't' (Marketing Manager 2). Some colleges have achieved a process which is 'good enough' partly by formal data gathering systems and partly by informally listening intently:

> The managers are constantly talking to the staff, talking and listening such that we are able to hear through team review and self-assessment what is happening . . . Clearly there are other measures that have to shape it (the strategic plan) as well, like local market information, the corporation, etc. but what we want to try and do is capture genuinely all this information and make our best guesses. 'Best guesses' is an ill-considered term, but you know, get the strategic plan as right as possible for the community that we serve.
>
> (Quality Manager 1)

'Best guess' is probable an accurate description of the process of responding to information which by its nature reflects a changing situation and a partial view.

RESPONDING STRATEGICALLY

The collection and analysis of information on customer needs and wants are the first step in the marketing process. The second step is responding to what has been discovered, which implies a whole college strategic approach to making choices about which needs can be met and which cannot. Both FEFC documents and writers on marketing emphasize the importance of adopting a strategic approach to marketing (Davies, 1999; FEFC, 1998b; Foskett and Helmsley-Brown, 1999). Foskett and Helmsley-Brown (1999, p. 209–10) define strategy as: 'the process of identifying what an organisation wishes to be and to achieve (its strategic position), and how it will progress towards those aims in the context of the external environment'. This definition presents a clear agenda but meeting it is problematic for a number of reasons. First, even if colleges were free to respond as they wished, as Chadwick (1996, p. 127) points out, they lack 'a framework for categorising a diverse environment'. There are many groups in the community in competition for the resources available through the college. The evidence from college strategic plans is that the majority of plans present aims which are insufficiently defined to distinguish and mediate between the competing demands (Lumby, 1999b). For example, the aim 'to serve the community within a five-mile radius of the college' does not guide the choice of whether the limited ICT facilities are to be given to upskilling employees or to providing those returning to employment with basic skills. Although some colleges have very specific priorities, many have no agreed criteria against which to judge competing claims and so the choices are either *ad hoc*, depending on the micropolitical power of those involved in choosing, or are driven by forces other than educational values, such as finance.

Hoy and Miskel (1989) provide a model which suggests that educational organizations experience freedom to be responsive in ratio to their resource dependency. Where there is a high degree of dependency, as is the case with colleges which may depend on the FEFC for 70–80 per cent of their income, and where there is also a factor of scarcity, i.e. there are insufficient resources, then 'competition for resources among sub-groups can take the form of a zero-sum game with each sub group caring more about its share of finite resources than the overall welfare of the organisation' (ibid., p. 33). Hoy and Miskel's suggested analysis, that when resources are scarce and come from limited sources, organizational subunits start to compete against each other, rather than working for the overall good, may be relevant at several levels. It may be that course teams compete against each other, rather than working for the faculty, that faculties compete, instead of working towards college goals, and that, regionally, colleges compete instead of working for the good of the region. This being the case, achieving a strategic approach to marketing, that is, being clear on the needs which are to be targeted and met in a whole organization perspective, becomes very difficult to achieve.

As explored in Chapter 4, the finance managers interviewed reflected the range of resource dependency and scarcity with all wishing to make choices to respond to need, but many driven by the imperative of financial survival to maximize funding before all else (Lumby, 2000c). Overall, the belief was what

Chadwick (1996, p. 128) described as colleges viewing themselves 'being shaped rather than shaping the external environment'. They were done to rather than doing, subject to uncontrollable external forces. An example of the lack of college freedom, the lack of a capacity to be genuinely responsive, was given by Curriculum Manager 7 who managed a programme providing services to local small- to medium-size enterprises: 'It has already been decided that small- to medium-sized enterprises need to have ICT capability. They need to be brought up to speed on that. I don't know if they have been asked, but Europe has decided that they need it.' Businesses themselves had not been approached to identify their own needs and priorities. Europe had decided this for them and provided funding. In a resource-starved environment, the college bid for and gained the funding to implement training. This is a long way from a philosophical approach to marketing (Foskett, 1999), which would see as axiomatic a first step to know and understand the customer. This is far closer to the pre-1993 product-driven approach which appeared anathema to the government. There is a sort of bitter irony in an apparent government drive to encourage responsiveness at local level being accompanied by a range of funded initiatives which, in effect, at both national and European level, tell colleges whom they should target.

Despite the limitations of resource dependence, resource scarcity and directed funding which limits responsiveness, some colleges have struggled to listen to their local communities and to respond:

> There is a particular management style that we work to which has been much more to do with winning hearts and minds over a period of time. Throughout all of that period when we were being exhorted to be highly competitive in a free market, etc., etc., etc., I think by and large we did do that quite successfully, but at the same time, there was a lot of keeping faith with the notion that we were serving a community and in a sense it is quite well embedded.
>
> (Marketing Manager 1)

Several of the finance managers felt similarly, that their college had achieved a balance between financial and educational imperatives, and was 'keeping faith' with the community and, in some cases, using the funding to respond in ways which widened access and developed the curriculum.

BARRIERS TO ENROLLING STAFF IN MARKETING

There was a strong belief that everybody needed to be involved:

> Marketing is so extremely important for the future of a college and it is very important that everybody has an opportunity to have their views represented. There are a lot of innovative people in this college and we should give those people more of a chance to contribute. I don't think it should be the responsibility of just one person because it is such a diverse and creative role.
>
> (Marketing Manager 3)

However, the belief in the importance of involving everyone was not necessarily resulting in achievement of that aim. Two major barriers were indicated. First, the professional culture of staff may not encourage intent listening to the customer. There was still a residue of the product-driven approach which was apparent in the belief of staff that they were able to decide what courses were appropriate and how best to deliver them:

> It is actually very radical to say, you know, you don't know best. You may think you know best and there are things that you do know best about but there are people out there crying out for x, y and z. Why aren't you providing it? Why do you keep doing what you have been doing for the last 25 years?
>
> (Marketing Manager 1)

This marketing manager also found difficulty because of the same suspicion of his role to which other non-curriculum managers, such as human resources and finance managers, have borne witness in previous chapters:

> When I was appointed to my post, most people in the college thought I must come from a commercial marketing background. That was the assumption. They thought that I was going to come in and use lots of marketing jargon and be rather like one of these flash, spin doctory types that are the stereotype. In fact I don't come from that sort of background at all. So as time went on, it became clear that I actually did know about what went on in the classroom. So a lot of it was about winning people's confidence that I actually did know about teaching and about education because I had taught a number of sub-jects at a number of levels, but could still challenge people's preconceptions in terms of moving them away from a provider-led model to a consumer-led model.
>
> (Marketing Manager 1)

There is an irony in this tension. The staff appear to believe that their histor-ical approach of deciding on courses and promoting them, i.e. not listening to customers, is more educationally based and professional, and they suspect the 'flash' marketing approach. The latter actually suggests that they do listen to people in the community and value their opinions and perception of their needs. The practice seems the reverse of that implied by the lecturers' belief. In fact the so-called business approach of marketing is soundly based on the educational values of listening and responding, while the approach of simply providing what lecturers think best is much closer to a commercial scam to persuade people to buy what is on offer. The tensions and distrust of marketing professionals and a marketing approach are therefore barriers to achieving the involvement of all.

A further barrier centres on the expertise of staff and the time they have available. In the case of Marketing Manager 2, whose permanent role is Head of Faculty, neither he nor his staff were involved with the strategic marketing plan: 'It comes from the Marketing Manager, totally from the Marketing Manager. She comes up with the plan for the whole college. As a department we have no separate marketing section in our plan. As I said earlier, we hardly talk about it' (Marketing Manager 2). In the case of this manager, it was not a question of lack of knowledge or lack of commitment. He was knowledgeable about marketing and committed to a customer-driven approach. The problem was that there was no time or resource to carry out the degree of research which could underpin a real understanding of customer need. This seems to be a common situation (Chadwick, 1996; FEFC, 1998b). The difficulties of achieving a bottom-up operational involvement in marketing are therefore considerable.

RESPONDING OPERATIONALLY

Despite these barriers, Foskett (1999) makes a strong case for the importance of involving all staff in marketing. Senior staff and specialists may plan, co-ordinate and provide specialist functions but they need the support and participation of all to ensure that needs analysis and marketing plans are more than paper exercises. Participation has not been achieved at all levels in most colleges. Marketing Manager 2 gave an example of how a new course had come into being:

> It happened initially because our external verifier spoke of a college far away and said that their National Diploma in Public Services recruits very well. So we went off to the college to see what they were doing and I wrote to various people because, being an EDEXCEL course, I had to give evidence of support. So everybody round here, the army, the RAF, the police, the whole lot were very supportive, but in terms of the students wanting it, my only evidence was that other courses were able to recruit quite easily. I had no direct evidence at all that it would recruit in this area.

In this case, there was no evidence of student need. The initiation of the programme was based on success in another part of the country and the judgement of the lecturer that it would recruit locally. It was product driven rather than a response to need. Marketing Manager 2 pointed out that validation panels vary in their requirement for evidence of student need. Some 'push you quite hard for evidence'. For others there is no need and documentation can be completed in an hour. There is therefore little incentive to spend time collecting evidence which is not required. There was also little overt consideration of marketing:

> The curriculum planning starts quite soon. My department has two, three, four, however many meetings it takes to start producing our plan and the department plan is in three areas, human resource, curriculum development and physical resources. We talk about these three things but we never actually mention the work 'marketing' the whole time.

> (Marketing Manager 2)

Provision is therefore driven by proactive staff who make educated guesses about what courses will recruit. The fuller picture of the range of provision which may be in demand by local individuals and the local economy is not considered. The profile of marketing was much higher in the college of Marketing Manager 1 but, even there, the philosophy did not seem to have permeated throughout. Asked how far the response to needs analysis had spread, the answer reflected a partial success only:

> I think the honest answer is by no means far enough. It certainly gets as far as Head of Division level, and they do draw upon it but to be brutally honest, if you look at a course proposal, when they are planning a new course, they don't really engage with it as a piece of market research.

Even in this college, which has had much success in gathering information about needs and in expanding the curriculum to meet needs, the participation of all staff is still problematic.

The strategies used to change attitudes were various. In the college of Marketing Manager 1, an initial thrust had been that the Marketing Manager himself managed a fairly large team which established and provided, for example, outreach provision, to ensure that the needs identified by a sophisticated needs analysis process were met. The success was marked and the team grew to such an extent that it became equivalent to a division in size. The result was that sufficient students came though this route to begin to influence the thinking and practice of the mainstream divisions. Consequently, a restructuring reduced the team to four people and dispersed other members throughout the college. In this way, a central function had been used to inject the college with change agents in the form of non-traditional students. When the injected material had become sufficiently absorbed into the body and the change in response was permanent, the need to continue injections ceased. This suggests a neat and successful strategy, but Marketing Manager 1 was quick to dispel any impression of complete success. There are still parts of the organization which are not responding and a different strategy is needed. When one particular curriculum area failed to accommodate identified needs, the Marketing Manager set up a rival drop-in facility which has been a huge success. Internal competition with provision which is more flexible and undercuts the price of the mainstream offering is enforcing change:

> It's a sort of movement by stealth. I have no idea whether it is right, not a clue, it's totally pragmatic. It's that Drucker thing, changing behaviour before you can change people's minds. We know we won't change their minds so we have got to change their behaviour first. We have go to force them to do it.
>
> (Marketing Manager 1)

This college therefore works through slow empowerment 'winning hearts and minds over a period of time' and by forcing the pace of change through changing behaviour before hearts. The implication is that leadership and change management may be more successful if strategies are multiple and even in contradiction, both empowering and enforcing as seems required.

Attitudes may be a barrier to change, but even if this problem is overcome, there is still a need to tackle the issue of time. Staff may be reluctant to be responsive because they must survive and so control the demands made on their time: 'All our staff, without exception, teach and have one, two, three other roles either year tutors or key skills co-ordinators, managing the work-shops. There is no chance for them really' (Marketing Manager 2). Therefore despite great resources of creativity and innovation: 'Staff are keeping their heads down a bit now because if you say you've got an idea then somebody asks you to develop it' (Marketing Manager 2).

Of all the managers interviewed, only Principal 3 stressed unlocking staff's creativity as a top strategic priority by addressing issues of time management. Until such issues are solved, marketing is likely to remain imperfectly inte-grated, with lecturers maybe willing, but unable to participate:

> From a personal point of view I think we need to improve. All right, as a college we are reasonably successful but a few years ago we were establishing courses just like that and now we are struggling. We need to be innovative. When we became an independent college we went off like a rocket. The staff were so inno-vative, so proactive that we reached the top of the famous curve and are starting to look down a bit now. So the ideas are shrinking because we find it difficult to reward people. I think we've got to get needs analysis and market research straight. I just totally believe in it. I am a business-trained person and I think the reason most businesses fail is that they don't identify a strong need for their product and I think it is just the same with us. We are a business.
>
> (Marketing Manager 2)

Despite this belief, concerns about enrolment would continue to come first for the foreseeable future. Researching and responding to need would not be a priority. The will is there, and the expertise, but personal and financial sur-vival are driving much harder than any need to be responsive or to adopt a marketing approach. It is, of course, easy to posit that in theory a marketing approach would improve recruitment and might break the cycle of promoting products for which there is no proven need or demand, but in the real world of a college, an intervention to provide time is needed, and time is not avail-able. In effect, the drive for efficiency, cutting costs in real terms and forcing an emphasis on recruiting ever larger numbers of students is militating against responsiveness.

CONCLUSIONS

Assessing the degree and nature of marketing operating in colleges remains problematic. The term covers such a diverse range of approaches and practice that it is not easy to characterize how colleges understand or enact the concept. The word itself is far less prevalent in use than responsiveness, as demonstrated by the survey. Essentially, colleges are doing what they have always done, trying to develop the curriculum partly though the judgement of lecturers and partly in response to identified need with a very slight nod in the direction of the needs of the local economy. Some are competing more strongly, but this is dependent on the nature of the environment. There appears to be a greater degree of awareness and expertise in marketing techniques which are being applied largely by senior staff or specialist units. There has been a shift away from a product-driven to a customer-driven approach but this change has not permeated all levels. For many colleges, the direct and indirect pressure of funding and the need to recruit more students are more strongly felt than the need to understand and respond to the community.

6

UNDERSTANDING QUALITY

INTRODUCTION

Quality is a good thing. So far those who work in further education can agree. But as with many overarching concepts in management, while there may be universal support for a theoretical concept, in practice the debate on how to define it and to achieve it, fractures. Much of the public debate on education in the latter half of the 1990s has centred on issues of quality, though the terminology differs. Schools wish to improve and become effective. The public wishes to raise standards. Achievement rates in colleges must increase and so on. There are powerful obligations to achieve improved quality. Sallis identifies four quality imperatives:

1 The moral imperative – the link with customers.
2 The professional imperative – the link with the professional role of educators.
3 The competitive imperative – the link with competitors.
4 The accountability imperative – the link with constituent groups (adapted from Sallis, 1996, pp. 4–5).

Colleges must therefore achieve quality in order to fulfil professional obligations to provide the best possible education and training for students, to maintain their own pride as professional educators, to continue to attract students, and not least because the funding bodies say they must. So far, so good. Beyond the deafening roar of demand for quality lies a babble of disagreement as attempts are made to define exactly what quality is and how it is to be achieved.

Many writers agree that defining quality is elusive. It is an 'enigmatic concept' (Sallis, 1996, p. 1), 'slippery' (ibid., p. 12), not necessarily the same for this person as for the next (Fitz-Gibbon, 1996). Definitions of quality face Janus-like in two directions. First, many definitions face inwards and stress matching customer expectations. Quality is meeting or exceeding student expectations, students being the primary customer. At the same time, definitions may face outwards, recognizing that expectations may be low, particularly from those whose previous educational experience may have been unsuccessful, or insufficiently informed by knowledge of the vocational area in question. In this case, the professional judgement of educators may need to establish expectations. Equally, if customers are defined as those who pay for a product, then the state can be considered the chief customer and the benchmarks set by the government may be the standard against which quality is judged. Reaching a definition of what constitutes quality is difficult when the range of customers, lecturers and representative bodies of government will have different definitions and criteria for assessing quality, and fulfilling one set of expectations may compromise fulfilling another. For example, a focus on raising achievement levels as measured by the percentage of students being awarded their primary qualification aim will be argued as a measure of quality by some. Others will see such a focus as leading to an over-narrow curriculum and therefore being detrimental to quality, positing a broad and rounded education for citizenship, transferable skills and personal confidence as axiomatic to quality.

The heart of this tension is the interface between what individual students may want, the industrial model of designing and selling the product demanded by customers, and the professional imperative which assumes an obligation to provide for students' education and training which is shaped by others. Lecturers may attempt to meet needs of which the student is unaware, and may even require them to experience aspects of education which they would prefer to avoid. For example, students may be very comfortable as dependent learners. Lecturers may feel it is in the students' best interest to encourage independent learning. The state or employers' representative bodies may insist on shaping curriculum content and pathways. As a consequence, any simple definition of quality in education which is based solely on meeting customer requirements could be argued as unrealistically one dimensional. A definition of quality which reflects the reality of practice is therefore likely to be a compromise which replicates the tensions between the different sources of demand for quality and the different criteria which result. An example of this eclectic approach to understanding quality was given by Quality Manager 4. Asked how the college understood quality, his response mirrors the need to adopt a multi-layered approach:

> I think first it's that we are doing things correctly, effectively, as efficiently as possible. So we try to do as much as we can first time and do it correctly. Or that we are learning by our mistakes and ensuring that those mistakes are constantly reduced and also, once having established that base line, we are then about improving what we are doing the whole time. For me that's quality; constantly

improving, constantly asking, constantly ensuring we meet what the customer wants, the student, by and large it is usually the student who is the customer, and where possible always trying to exceed their expectations.

This definition meets the criteria of several customers, students certainly, but also the FEFC drive for efficiency and the professional pride of lecturers in striving to constantly improve learning. Sallis (1996) argues that quality is a dynamic idea and that too much definition may kill it. Equally, too much emphasis on its importance may be unwise. An emphasis on quality may have much to offer, but the concept will remain disputed and is certainly not the equivalent of a management fairy godmother, transforming all.

APPROACHES TO ACHIEVING QUALITY

Alongside the difficulty in achieving a clear definition of quality runs an equally diverse debate on the means of achieving it. Quality assurance, quality control and total quality management are defined differently by different writers, and, in the case of the latter two, used sometimes as if synonymous, sometimes as if complementary and sometimes as if in contradiction. Sallis provides a possible set of definitions:

- *Quality control* involves the detection and elimination of components or final products which are not up to standard ... It is an after-the-event process.
- *Quality assurance* is a before and during the event process. Its concern is to prevent faults occurring in the first place.
- *Total quality management* (TQM) incorporates quality assurance, and extends and develops it. TQM is about creating a quality culture where the aim of every member of staff is to delight their customers (adapted from Sallis, 1996, p. 19).

In practice colleges are likely to be involved with all of these or, alternatively, one might define the same activity in different ways. For example, student questionnaires may be designed to detect and eliminate weak teaching (quality control), to identify weaknesses in a programme and establish systems to resolve them (quality assurance) and to listen and respond to students fully (total quality management). Champions and detractors of each of these systems are likely to remain. In fact, much of quality management in education rests on evaluation, which is retrospective and therefore matches the quality control model in some respects. Improvements are made on the basis of yesterday's students not tomorrow's. As West-Burnham (1994, p. 167) argues: 'Evaluation is a classic exemplification of a reactive culture at the micro level however significant it may be at the macro level. Inspection and evaluation are in the same relationship to the daily learning experiences of the current generation of young people as the post-mortem is to preventative medicine.' The dissatisfaction with quality control evident in this quotation may partly explain the growth of interest in total quality management, where a more holistic and preventative approach is endorsed. However, the empirical base of much of the relevant literature is missing and the so-called management gurus are essentially providing normative textbooks which are not necessarily underpinned by evidence of the effectiveness of the proposed methods in business, let alone in education (Crosby, 1979; Deming, 1982; Ishikawa, 1985; Juran, 1988). Generally speaking, the approaches advocated involve either responding to qualitative evidence of customer perceptions and quantitative evidence of results, or a cultural management process of enrolling staff in seeing customer perception as pre-eminent, or both.

The issue is complicated by the imposition of an inspection system by the FEFC which scrutinizes quality indicators and uses statistical process control by measuring results against national norms. This adds a further strand of debate as to what quality is and how it can be achieved; do the systems established in colleges in response to the FEFC's requirements and inspection regime focus on proving the quality which exists or improving it, that is, giving an account or managing change? The FEFC (1998c) concluded that quality assurance continued to be the weakest aspect of cross-college provision. They do not comment on or attempt to explain the paradox of colleges which have been given excellent inspection grades for quality assurance and poor grades for learning and teaching, or vice versa. Such apparently illogical results continue to challenge theory which posits a connection between quality systems and students' experience.

UNDERSTANDING QUALITY IN COLLEGES

Hopkins (1998, p. 65) concluded that there was no correlation between inspection high grades for quality assurance and the delivery of high quality. His belief is that the system imposed by the FEFC encouraged colleges to 'see the development of excellent systems for measuring quality as an alternative to improving colleges'. Elliott (1996) concludes that the lecturers he had interviewed rejected quality assurance systems as leading to improved teaching and learning. This negative view of quality systems is partially borne out by the interviews for this book, but only partially. The Quality Managers interviewed believed that in their colleges there was a greater understanding of quality which had led to changed practice, though this was not yet complete and universal:

> Staff have a strong understanding about what is meant by the quality systems in the college. They have an understanding of the manuals that we have here. They

have an understanding of the processes of team review and self-assessment. Where the college needs to do more work is turning an understanding of systems and the processes of quality into an understanding of what that means for the students and what that means for us as a college, planning and providing for students. So it's a schizophrenic answer really. I think there is an understanding of systems in the college, but in the most important aspect of quality, that is practice, I think there is some way to go.

(Quality Manager 1)

I think with a lot of effort the staff now have a common understanding of quality systems and I think that the vast majority would say that our main methods of assessing QA [quality assurance] are through Course Boards of Study, questionnaires and self-assessment. I think that most would come up with the main aim of quality to improve, to continuously improve. I am not sure all value quality assurance and quite a number would see it as a system imposed by the FEFC.

(Quality Manager 2)

The period of time from 1993 to 1999 is relatively short in terms of establishing a different culture and it is clear that in the views expressed above there is a perception that limited progress has been made in the two colleges in reaching a shared understanding of quality and in changing practice. Quality managers are realistic in recognizing that there are still staff who do not value or may resent the system. One of the most difficult tasks was perceived to be persuading staff that quality was their responsibility:

I think people are now far more aware of the need for themselves to look at everything they do from the view point of quality. Whereas previously I think it was very much felt that it was not necessarily their responsibility but it was somebody else's responsibility, I think now there is a cultural change.

(Quality Manager 3)

Quality Manager 3 believed that understanding and commitment had come on in leaps and bounds in the previous two years. In contrast, Quality Manager 4 still struggled to persuade staff not to see quality as an irrelevant manual, but as something for which they had to take responsibility:

One of the problems we have in the college is that the staff do not all have a shared understanding of what quality is . . . People have a perception that quality equals a quality management system, in some cases more specifically, they actually think quality equals a set of procedures that are contained in a manual that sits on a shelf. If you ask people about quality, when you question them closely, they have an understanding that quality is not within their own control but quite often that quality is something that somebody else does to them, i.e. they have to fill in paper, they have tasks associated with procedures. They don't see the underpinning philosophy of it.

This manager was particularly frustrated by people interpreting quality as his job because 'I have quality in my job title'. Obviously the situation varied from college to college, with some estimating more progress than others. However, all agreed that progress had been made but there was still some way to go. Although colleges had experimented with procedures and structures, the major thrust was a cultural process of convincing all staff of the central importance of being responsive to customers and to improving continuously (Crosby, 1979).

USING INFORMATION

The FEFC has emphasized the importance of quantitative measurement of performance as an aid to improving quality. Retention and achievement rates, for example, are collected and published. League tables are used for comparison. Colleges' overall performance is measured against six major performance indicators:

PI 1 Achievement of funding target: an indicator of the degree to which a college has achieved its funding target

PI 2 Changes in student numbers; an indicator of the level of change in student enrolments at a college

PI 3 In-year retention rates; an indicator of the effectiveness of a college's teaching, and guidance and support process, as measured by the retention of students on their learning programmes

PI 4 Achievement rates; an indicator of the effectiveness of the college in enabling students to attain their learning goals

PI 5 Contribution to the national targets; an indicator of the number of students attaining one of the national targets for education and training by achieving an NVQ or equivalent at the appropriate level

(FEFC, 1998d, p. iv)

Fitz-Gibbon (1996, p. 5) defines a performance indicator as 'an item of information collected at regular intervals to track the performance of a system'. At a conceptual level, it is hard to disagree with the notion that collecting information on performance which can be compared across institutions and over time is a proper way for colleges to be called to account and for the state to ensure acceptable standards and value for money. In practice the system has problems. Perry (1999) identifies a number of factors which make the use of performance indicators to measure and compare performance problematic. His analysis includes:

- *Social factors* – differences in levels of deprivation amongst students may render comparisons across colleges questionable.
- *Creaming* – schools and colleges have found that efforts to attract the more able and to discourage those who are less able or resource hungry result in more favourable figures for league tables.
- *Measuring the wrong things* – indicators sometimes do not measure what they purport to.

- *Data quality* – inaccurate or incomplete data distort the picture.
- *Fiddling the books* – not so much fraud as creative use of figures.
- *Proxy padding* – adding additional units to a student's programme to reach the required unit target (adapted from Perry, 1999, pp. 3–6).

Chapter 8, 'Managing information and communication', explores in more detail the difficulty that colleges have in collecting data and ensuring its accuracy and completeness. Chapter 4, 'Managing finance', reflected the view of the majority of finance managers interviewed, that colleges were driven by the need to reach or exceed unit targets. The evidence presented in these chapters adds weight to Perry's analysis of the difficulties of using performance indicators in a meaningful way. Colleges do appear to be having difficulty in amassing accurate data and are manipulating them to present the best possible public face. Therefore, the two primary uses of performance indicators, to give a summative account of performance and to provide a formative location of problems, may be at worst illusory and at best an imprecise tool. Nevertheless, the quality managers interviewed clearly felt that the quantitative data being collected were of value and did indicate where improvement had succeeded or weaknesses required attention.

A further difficulty in collecting and working with data was the micropolitical aspects of the process. Yorke (1997, p. 4) paraphrases Wildavsky (1979, p. 215) who wrote that: 'evaluation consisted of one group of people making statements on the worth of activities to which another group of people were devoting their lives. Given the interests that are at stake, and the likely power differentials, evaluation cannot be other than political (small p) in character.'

Quality Manager 2 was well aware of the issues. She felt that it was most difficult to get evaluation data from those parts of the college which were the weakest and that those staff whose performance was poor or who had most at stake in maintaining a reputation for good performance, were most likely to have problems with honest self-assessment and presenting data which would expose weaknesses: 'People aren't going to be totally honest. Let's face it. They're not going to be totally honest and say my lessons are appalling, etc. You have problems with lecturers whose teaching is poor, around the 4 grade.'

As well as poor teachers, there were also problems with the most senior staff. In the view of Quality Manager 2, 'People get more defensive the higher up the organization they are'. She believed that it was difficult for the Principal to be honestly self-critical because of the imperative to present a positive picture to the governors. Equally, governors might be reluctant to expose weakness through self-assessment. FEFC inspection (FEFC, 1997) has indicated that a quarter of colleges tend to overestimate the effectiveness of their management and a third the effectiveness of their governance. Sallis (1996) takes up Deming's (1982) exhortation to remove the element of fear so that people can address difficulties openly without apprehension. Such advice is no doubt sound but very difficult to achieve in reality.

Nevertheless, some progress has been made, with self-assessment becoming more rigorous and open. Scrutiny of evidence by a validator, sometimes external to the college, was developing the process of ensuring that evidence was adequate to support the self-assessment of performance. In each college the multiplicity of sources of information provided triangulation, so that areas of weakness and strength did emerge. Above all, despite the problems with data collection and interpretation, the belief was that all students had a voice and were heard much more than previously: 'I can now measure the perceptions of students of the impact of the new car park, the new buildings, the new refectory. Though it is not perfect still by a long way, there certainly has been a shift and staff can now see students' perceptions' (Quality Manager 2).

Seeing perceptions is only the first step. The information is of no practical value if there is no response.

RESPONDING TO INFORMATION

Those actually carrying out the activity which is the subject of quality review are best placed to understand what improvements are needed and could be achieved. As Fitz-Gibbon (1996) points out, they have the closest view of the situation. Moreover it may be their actions which need to change. However, it is equally clear that the support of management may be essential, for example in providing resources or motivation. Those managing quality therefore need to work at two levels, by involving and empowering those who actually do the teaching or the assessing or the caretaking, but also setting in place structures to facilitate a response: 'You could have a very good quality assurance system which is producing the evidence which tells you where you actually need to improve, but you can have poor management which does not act to achieve the improvements' (Quality Manager 2).

All the quality managers interviewed were very aware of the need for strong commitment and support from senior managers. Quality Manager 1 strove to achieve: 'a very clear planning cycle so there is a clear relationship between team review and self-assessment and the actual management planning cycle, resources, etc. so that the two coincide and people see that the work they put into team review and self-assessment doesn't disappear into a dark hole'. Closing the loop between gathering information and taking action in response was important. Colleges wished to achieve a tight connection between self-assessment and management planning. In order to achieve this they were experimenting with structuring the organization, placing those with responsibility for co-ordinating quality where they could have most effect. The quality managers were very aware of the importance of where they were placed in the structure. Quality Manager 4 worked with both the Chief

Executive and the Deputy Principal: 'Anybody who is dealing with quality and quality systems must have access to the Chief Executive of the organization so that anything that they are reporting regarding audits, regarding non-compliance across the college, cannot be stopped by any manager in the system who is trying to achieve self-protection.'

Access to the highest level of executive authority was an insurance policy that quality issues could not be hidden or blocked. Quality Manager 4 also reported to the Deputy Principal working as a 'triumvirate' as appropriate. He did not have direct access to the Chair of the Board, but as a co-opted member of the Performance and Review Quality Sub-Committee, he had access to governors. Where there were any concerns which could not be resolved with the Chief Executive, Quality Manager 4 felt that he could ring the Chair 'but of course I place my job on the line if I do that'. Such a contingency had not arisen. Overall therefore, the Quality Manager had access to the full range of governors and management 'so that if there were unpleasant things that had to be said, I can say them'. The experience of Quality Manager 2 was different. She had no access to the governors and 'felt excluded'. She struggled to encourage a response from senior management to areas of weakness identified by the evaluation processes and felt that senior management and governors were poor role models in that they overestimated their own capability and did not validate their self-assessment. The necessity they felt to save face was a barrier to improvement. However, this college had made strides in embedding a culture of responsibility for quality across the academic/support staff divide. The same systems were in place for all and, below senior management level, a greater degree of accuracy in self-review was evident.

Quality Manager 3 had participated in a college restructure which had quality improvement at its heart. The resulting structure had addressed the historical powerlessness of cross-college roles, giving them access to a range of groupings throughout the college and the power to call other managers to meetings to consider specific issues. A complex matrix of teams and meetings ensured communication up and down and across the college. There was also an awareness of the waste of time that might result if bureaucracy burgeoned. Consequently, minutes were in a format which asked for minimum notes focusing on action. The resulting bullet point format ensured that meetings were recorded, focused on what needed to be done, but did not alienate staff by producing wordy documents which were unlikely to be used. Quality would not be improved if relevant processes constantly added to people's workload and so were resented or rejected. There was a perception that culture change would happen only if there was attention to detail and change was based on understanding and accommodating the reality of people's working lives.

All the quality managers indicated that the role of middle managers had changed, with the responsibility for quality written into their job descriptions and expected in practice. This had not been easy on either side. The first stage had been middle managers going through the motions but without any true responsibility:

> For example, they have had to go in and check the quality of programme files. About 18 months ago they just went in and audited the file, when I was tearing my hair out saying just going in to check the paper is there is not enough. They have now started to realize that auditing the file does not mean just checking the bits of paper are there. It means looking at the quality of the bits of paper, looking at the quality of the schemes of work.
>
> (Quality Manager 2)

The process towards taking responsibility had been very painful and involved a good deal of resistance, because it challenged the longstanding professional autonomy of teachers. There was no history of heads of department looking critically at the quality of learning and teaching within their area:

> It wasn't traditionally the role of a teacher to look at somebody else's quality, to go into their classes, to make negative comments, to make suggestions for improvements, to have to turn round and say I am sorry these minutes are not good enough. That's why it has been very, very difficult. Also there has been resentment of the role that I have to a certain extent, because every man is an island and teachers were the God in the classroom who could do no wrong, and now this has changed.
>
> (Quality Manager 2)

The difficulty reflected in this manager's experience goes to the heart of a tension in quality management. Much of the theory emphasizes that for quality improvement to be effective, the improvement must be owned. Teachers must review their own practice and take responsibility for introducing whatever changes they see as appropriate. Enforced change is likely to be resisted and ineffective. On the other hand, there is evidence from several years of inspection reports from the FEFC, from the views of the managers interviewed for this book and from the literature (Ainley and Bailey, 1997; Burton, 1994) that lecturers are not always accurate in their self-assessment and those who are weakest are least likely to identify and bring problems out into the open. Responsibility must therefore be shared between the staff themselves and by managers. The latter cannot escape responsibility. A mediator is needed to bridge this dual responsibility. The quality managers fulfilled this role. Quality Manager 4 saw himself as a 'champion' persuading people that quality was to help practice, not hinder it, and as 'an honest broker for many people' helping them acknowledge and move forward on issues they or others had identified. The emphasis on working with people in a supportive way was striking in all the quality managers. All of them acknowledged the difficulty of working with several hundred staff, often on different sites, but the difficulty did not deflect the basic purpose of winning people's commitment.

WINNING HEARTS AND MINDS

All the quality managers were concerned to enrol people's understanding and commitment. There was no dependence on an authority position but rather a recognition that 'we can't impose anything on people who are our equals'. The common message was that quality is about the students' experience and that success lay in the hands of individual staff. The message of Quality Manager 4 was: 'to try and put people at the heart of it and that people's endeavours are really important. They have (quality) in their own skills, attitudes, responsibilities. They are the ones that can really make a difference'. In order to achieve this, he kept 'plugging away, calmly and continuously, saying that message, repeating it, repeating it. Not getting angry with people but continuously trying to win them round'. Quality Manager 1 had a similar strategy, spending much time out of the office talking to people on the grounds that 'paper can be taken home but people can't'. This is not to say that they would allow evidence on unsatisfactory performance to pass. On the contrary, the collection of data which gave clear evidence of strengths and weakness was a high priority. Asked how she would deal with those who evaded acting on such evidence, Quality Manager 2 described how she would respond:

> I would challenge them. If staff don't own the changes then they are not going to happen. Fundamentally, it's got to come from the team of staff. Fundamentally they need to acknowledge their own weaknesses and accept them. If the manager just turns around and says, 'You shouldn't do this. This is not okay', staff just resent it and the change doesn't become properly embedded. It has got to come from the staff.

Challenging complacency was viewed as supporting the professional pride of staff in that it assumed that they would want to do the best they could for students. The repeated message was that staff must do it themselves. Some of the resistance to the quality movement has come from those who see professional autonomy as the proper means of assuring quality in education. The perception of the quality managers was that many staff did not want responsibility for improvement. They were happy to hand that over to someone with 'quality' in their title.

In leading this process of cultural change, the quality managers are challenging the hegemony that all lecturers are professional and therefore, by definition, have a primary responsibility to students which overrides self-interest. They are challenging staff to make this theoretical responsibility a reality. By demanding a self-critical attitude they are asking staff to learn about themselves and about the learning process, and thereby to provide a model of lifelong learning which is as much the curriculum which students will perceive as any formal syllabus.

COMPLETING THE LOOP

Sallis (1996) argues that concepts of quality fall into two groups: definitions which are 'procedural' or definitions which are 'transformational'. The former establishes systems to measure products against agreed standards. The latter is not centred on systems, but on transforming the culture of an organization. It is clear from the evidence reviewed in this chapter that colleges are both forced to and have embraced some procedural approaches. Despite the problems with using data, there is a general belief that the collection of both 'hard' data, such as retention and achievement statistics, and 'soft' data, such as student perceptions, can contribute to improvement. The difficulty with this approach is that it encourages single-loop learning. Argyris (1991) contrasts 'single-loop' learning, that is, learning which compares progress with the agreed indicators of success and adjusts to keep things on track, with 'double-loop learning' where the goals and routes themselves which are how success is defined, are challenged and transformed. He suggests that in single-loop learning, failure leads professionals to defensive behaviour with blame directed at other individuals and groups, or to inconsistency between what is declared and what is enacted. In encouraging staff to focus on achieving performance indicators and targets, learning may be inhibited by deflecting people from questioning the aims and targets themselves. The quality managers interviewed were aware of this and placed more emphasis on cultural transformation, on establishing a learning culture where the performance of all was open to question. They recognized the resistance of staff and saw overcoming this barrier as long-term, requiring patience and persistence. In this they were in accord with Argyris (1991) who reasons that professionals, above all, become very skilled in resisting learning. He believes that the very success of professionals in achieving their position weakens their capacity to think critically of their own performance, to deal with criticism and mistakes, and to dismantle a faulty self-image which acts as a barrier between self and accurate self-assessment:

> Even if we feel uncertain or ignorant, we learn to protect ourselves from the pain of appearing uncertain or ignorant. That very process blocks out any new understandings which might threaten us. The consequence is what Argyris calls 'skilled incompetence' – teams full of people who are incredibly proficient at keeping themselves from learning.
>
> (Senge, 1993, p. 25)

Three of the four quality managers could point to evidence from external sources which indicated progress in overcoming this resistance and encouraging staff to learn. In this they were achieving a learning organization where improvement in the quality of the students' experience was founded on the capacity of staff to learn, that is, to open themselves to self-questioning based on a range of information.

So much has been thrown at the sector demanding change that 'FE is running so hard to keep up with changes at the moment that it is in great danger of falling flat on its face' (Quality Manager 4). Nevertheless, the achievements of the sector have been acknowledged:

> Average retention rates were stable between 1995–96 and 1996–97, and achievement rates for full-time students increased slightly to 68 per cent. Achievement rates for part-time students increased by three per cent over the same period to 67 per cent. It is of some credit to the sector that colleges have shown increases in retention and achievement rates during a period when student numbers funded by the Council increased by 15 per cent against a background of demanding efficiency gains.
>
> (FEFC, 1998c, p. 2)

Such praise suggests that the sector has managed to hold in tension the different demands for quality, the different beliefs on how it may be achieved, the enforced emphasis on numerical data and the need for cultural transformation. In the survey of colleges the inspection system was indicated to be the third most important factor demanding cultural change. Only funding and market demand were more significant. In parallel, quality assurance systems were the second most important tool used by colleges to achieve cultural change. In this it was seen as more important than distribution of resources or the delivery of teaching and learning, and only fractionally exceeded in its importance to achieve change by restructuring (see Figures 11.1 and 11.2 in Chapter 11). Colleges therefore value quality management very highly as a tool to achieve cultural change. Success is not complete. 'Quality', however defined, is still seen as irrelevant or resisted by many, but there has been success. As Quality Manager 4 put it, 'It is difficult but FE has always risen to the challenge that such things inevitably bring. And FE by and large tends to achieve'.

7

CHANGING STRUCTURES AND ROLES

RESTRUCTURING

In the survey undertaken to support this book, restructuring was indicated as the most significant tool adopted to achieve cultural change for the period 1993–99. Of the 164 colleges responding, only four had not restructured. The majority had restructured more than once and 10 per cent had restructured over three times, as indicated in Figure 7.1.

The frequency of restructuring indicates pressures enforcing changed structure, or belief in the efficacy of achieving the right structure to support effective management. The survey and interview responses explored in more detail later in the chapter indicate both, with pressures driving colleges to restructure, and choices also made voluntarily to move to a different system. The chapter will explore the nature of structure, the pressures leading to structural change, including changing roles, and the current experience of colleges in establishing different forms of structure.

THE NATURE OF STRUCTURE

Definitions of structure resemble a microscope which can move its position closer to or further from the organization, or can even adopt an internal viewpoint which reflects the view of those within the organization. Assuming the latter perspective, the very concept of an organizational structure is problematic, as the organization is a theoretical concept which exists in reality only as a set of buildings and people. As the goals and experience of each individual are unique, from the subjective standpoint, an organization cannot exist

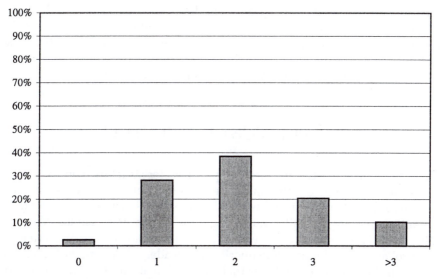

Figure 7.1   Percentage of respondents indicating number of college restructures from 1993 to 1999

as a coherent whole, but merely as the sum of the range of different perspectives and experiences. Whatever the 'structure' on paper, the reality will be a maelstrom of loosely connected beliefs and activities (Harling, 1989). Moving the microscope out, assuming that in some sense an organization can be viewed as a coherent whole, structure is the designation of roles, tasks and responsibilities recorded in organograms and job descriptions, indicating who does what and how they are related laterally and vertically (Fidler, 1997). Hanna (1997) suggests that this perspective is incomplete and we need to move the microscope out further still to incorporate the notion of the organization as an open system, where the structure is in a state of flux which responds not only to internal activity but also to the external environment.

Managers will be aware of the possibilities offered by these three different perspectives, and the limitations of each. It will be evident that the documents which describe roles, tasks and communication channels do not capture the multifarious interpretation of roles, the selectivity of role holders in undertaking designated tasks, or the actual effectiveness of communication channels throughout the organization. The richness of life escapes limited words in documents. The very plurality defeats language, so managers resort to a shorthand of documents and agreements which attempts to impose some sort of order on the diversity of activity. 'Thus all organizations have some form of structure which is more or less explicit' (Fidler, 1997, p. 53). There is, however, a sense in the new millenium that the rate of change is of such unprecedented magnitude that the previous range of structures may be inadequate. Managers therefore struggle to find metaphors which will engender new forms of structure appropriate to the very different demands colleges face in the twenty-first century. The metaphors are both a description of the relationships between groups and individuals within the organization and, sometimes, an attempt to capture the culture which the structure strives to create. Some of the metaphors currently in use will be explored later in the chapter.

THE PURPOSE OF STRUCTURE

Fidler (1997) provides two overarching purposes for structure, control and co-ordination, and points out that these are in tension, one often achieved at the expense of the other. The trend within business has been to lessen emphasis on control, moving to self-organized groups as far as possible. Wheatley (1999, p. 153) argues that we have known for more than 50 years that attempts to control are unproductive. She queries why leaders should persist in choosing a control model and concludes that such a choice derives from fear 'of one another, of a harsh competitive world, and of the natural processes of growth and change'. Certainly the external demands from funding bodies indicate a desire to control. This may be replicated internally by principals as they make their mark by restructuring, attempting to impose a new pattern on activity. Fullan (1999, p. 5) argues that some structure is required as 'too little structure creates chaos'. However, he also argues that too much 'creates gridlock'. The balance between loose and tight, accountability and creativity, control and co-ordination is difficult to achieve. Below these two overarching aims, the range of objectives to be realized by structure increases the complexity of the task of arriving at an appropriate form. A more detailed list of purposes specific to further education, provided by Field, encapsulates the tensions of matching different demands:

> In the short term colleges are having to structure their organisational arrangements to:
>
> - find the best functional arrangement to meet the current needs of their customers and staff;
> - achieve the best possible match between teaching and learning, monitoring and control systems, specialist services and the configuration of all support services;
> - ensure that their information and control systems are adequate for all the tasks which need to be performed effectively to ensure the delivery of the college's mission;
> - achieve the best trade off between teaching and social and formal organisational needs, and between the cost of co-ordination and the benefits of specialisation.
>
> In the long term colleges will have to structure their organisation:

- to be capable of adapting appropriately to changing needs and be capable of integrating new requirements into their delivery and support systems.

(Field, 1993, p. 95)

The number of objectives listed indicates the difficulty of achieving a system which can accommodate such variousness. For example, information and control systems are needed but at the same time staff needs are to be accommodated. Staff are unlikely to welcome structures to control them through the collection of data and information, as discussed in Chapter 8. The choice of structure, therefore, may motivate staff more by lessening control, or increase accountability at the cost of motivation. The implication is that any structure will be a compromise which cannot achieve all that is required. It may be necessary to identify the priority objectives the structure is to achieve from the myriad that are possible. Principal 2 was clear that the primary aim of the structural changes in his college had been 'chasing new markets'. The comments in the survey identified a range of primary objectives in restructuring, including:

- the need to balance the budget
- to improve communication
- to increase stakeholder involvement
- emphasizing teamwork.

The variety of different purposes was a response to influences and pressures inducing change. Given the range of pressures and the range of purposes, it is likely that there will be a range of structures offered as solutions to the individual situation of each college.

RATIONALE FOR STRUCTURAL CHANGE

The issues to which colleges are responding are not unique to further education. Dopson and Stewart (1993) found that in their case-study businesses most had reorganized in response to intensified competition, deregulated markets, developments in information technology, government legislation and policies. The survey indicated a similar range of factors leading to restructuring in further education. The most significant are indicated in Figure 7.2.

The factor in Figure 7.2 which appears to have been the strongest driver is funding. This fact may be interpreted in two ways: first, there is no doubt that colleges have felt driven to cut costs and, second, to increase income through a more entrepreneurial approach. Cost-cutting relates to issues of both the overall size of the organization, i.e. the number of people employed, and to the range of salaries, i.e. the number of people paid at particularly the higher salary levels. Again, in common with business, many colleges have

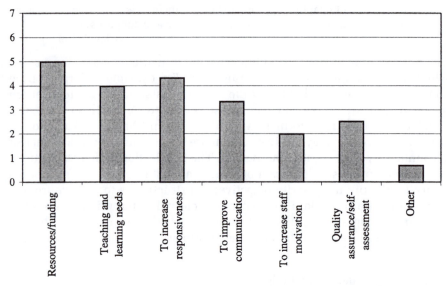

Figure 7.2   The most significant factors leading to college restructuring from 1993 to 1999

undertaken the euphemistically labelled 'downsizing', that is, employing fewer people and paying fewer high salaries (Goulding, Dominey and Gray, 1998). Merrick (1996) reported on the demise of the vice-principal post as colleges axed what they considered to be an unjustifiable luxury in the straitened resource situation. Not only vice-principals but many other management posts have been deleted, leading to flatter organizations. The overall size has also been an issue, with many colleges considering mergers in the hope that achieving a larger college would save costs, though such hopes may have been misleading (Hall, 1999). Whether reducing the size of the organization by decreasing the number of posts, or increasing the size of the organization through merger, or changing the range of posts through cutting management layers and increasing part-time and agency staff, cost-cutting is likely to be only one of the issues driving a restructure. In most cases, other issues are also involved, as indicated in Figure 7.2. Principal 2 provided an example of the cutting process, where the overall mission drives the changed structure as much as the need to cut costs:

> The governors decided that they wanted to become niche and specialist and therefore anything we were doing which was general FE we chopped. So the whole supervisory management section and all the staff went. We had a specialist schools unit which did more than just school visits. It used to do a lot of link courses for secondary schools and things like that. They considered that to be non-core activity. That went. We had a Schools and Environmental Centre which we ran in the LEA days. When the LEA ceased to fund it that went with all the staff. We took out the whole middle management structure as it was.

In this example, a range of issues are allied in driving changes in structure. In this case the number of curriculum areas of teaching are reduced in line with the new mission, but there are other issues to do with reducing layers of management to cut costs and increase responsiveness which have under-pinned structural change. Curriculum Manager 4 was clear that 'teaching has significantly changed'. The change had led to new ways of looking at how different types of staff could support students who were more challenging, because of ability and motivation levels, and who might do much of their training in the workplace, learn at an individual pace and could no longer be taught in a neat group as was previously the case. Additionally there was an increased range of administrative tasks related to tracking students and staff. The efforts to meet this new scenario had led to different staff often working in different ways. All the curriculum managers interviewed commented on the range of roles that supported teaching and learning, and though the titles adopted may have differed, staff who were not lecturers were involved in assessment, in supporting students' learning in resource centres, in guidance and counselling, tutoring and as technicians supporting both learners and lecturers. Additionally, the increasing use of the term 'core staff' (Goulding, Dominey and Gray, 1998, p. 16) to differentiate full-time employees from part-time and agency staff, indicated another layer of different structure within staffing. Staff might therefore comprise a range of roles and also be core or non-core. The result was a *de facto* difference in structure in the vary-ing types of staff. Overlaid on these changes might be a formal structure designed to support communication, co-ordination and control of the differ-ent categories.

The third most important category of factor driving restructuring indicated in the survey is responsiveness. The need to attract new markets has been paramount, initially after 1993 because of the need to increase student num-bers and thereby funds, and latterly because of the emphasis on widening participation. The 1980s saw a range of generic management texts advocating flexible, self-organizing structures to better respond to the increasing speed of change (Kanter, 1989; Peters, 1989). In the 1990s, as the information technol-ogy revolution accelerated, further texts appeared suggesting that new ways of working required new forms of structure (Handy, 1994; Semler, 1993). The suggested imperative for flexible organizational structures was adopted with-in further education. Turner (1991, p. 23) suggested that:

- The most important qualities for the members of an organisation to pur-sue are those of flexibility and innovation, not as ends in themselves but so that it can stay in touch with its changing environments, and thus sur-vive and thrive.
- Organisational structures tend to get in the way of this process. The more hierarchic, bureaucratic and sectionalised they are, the more obstructive they tend to be.

Turner advocates 'Light, flexible and flat organisations' to achieve the required degree of responsiveness. Colleges have experimented with structures to achieve such an end, though constrained by the increasing demands for accountability, which exert a contrary pressure for control.

Given the degree of turbulence, the increasing range of staff and fewer managers, the issue of communication acquires ever-increasing importance and provides a further pressure to achieve a structure which facilitates communication laterally and vertically. Both the senior management and the middle management teams are likely to consist of fewer people who therefore have a more difficult task in communicating face to face with larger numbers than previously. Additionally, a much larger proportion of staff will be in the college for a small amount of time each week or be employed on a temporary basis. The difficulties experienced are explored in Chapter 8. To complement the attempts to retain personal communication, the restructured college is likely to have a network of groups and co-ordinators whose task it is to ensure channels of communication function adequately, so that management by memo is kept within reasonable bounds. Communication also relates to motivation. If people cannot contribute to decision-making, and/or are not aware of what is happening and why, the motivation level is likely to drop. Structure needs to support communication to maintain motivation, but also embody other principles relating to motivation. McClelland (1961) suggests that people's motivation is heightened if they have some control over their goals. Put simply, an increased level of autonomy is likely to increase motivation. Self-organizing units with their high level of autonomy are likely to be able to respond to the external and internal environment more swiftly and also motivate staff more effectively.

Equity or exchange theory (Handy, 1993) suggests that people will be motivated by a sense of fair play, and that perceptions of being treated less favorably than others will demotivate. The 'one staff' issue, which has emerged in previous chapters particularly in relation to staff from a non-education background feeling subject to a degree of academic snobbery, is relevant here. If the college is structured to convey the message that all staff are equally valued, for example, by having support or services staff in very senior posts, then the motivation of this increasingly large percentage of staff is likely to rise.

The survey has therefore identified the pressures and issues leading to restructuring: resources and funding, teaching and learning, responsiveness and communication, and motivation and quality. By implication, the aims of any restructure will therefore be to achieve an improvement of performance in each of these areas. It is asking a lot of any structure to achieve all of this simultaneously. Additionally, the college itself will comprise a starting point of a series of different cultures and practice perhaps related to site or to vocational area, and so a monolithic solution will have varied success. Curriculum Manager 2 commented on her difficulties in finding solutions because of the diversity within the college: 'As soon as you go down one [route], then it just doesn't work in practice. I would love there to be clean structures and systems but there is always an exception. It is messy management and I hate it. I hate not being able to find one answer.'

It also emerged from several interviewees, that the restructuring process followed the appointment of a new principal or a merger, and did not seem to be in response to particular factors but, rather, the principal's vehicle for marking a new start, placing people in new roles where they might have a vested interest in supporting the new order. Restructuring can therefore be seen as both a process for response to the external environment and an internal political process of reshaping power. For some, structure will not be of great importance:

> When I first took over we had a real issue about barons and we had three 'pylons' converging on the VP [vice-president]. And it was a congested system so I thought we would restructure, and this is probably anarchic, but the lesson it taught me was that structure really doesn't matter. What matters is the people and if you've got people who are truly open, who are not defensive, who are prepared to take a risk, have the right interpersonal skills, you can have a traditional structure or a matrix structure and they will work in cross-teams to make things happen. If you have got people who are defensive, want to blame, don't trust, have no desire whatsoever to take responsibility for anything, then all a structure will do is expose them quicker but it doesn't actually make it work. So a structure may make things smoother and create less friction but it is not actually going to move the engine forward. All a structure will do is expose where parts of the engine aren't working.
>
> (Principal 3)

For this principal, the underlying attitudes are by far more important and are not formed primarily or even significantly by the structure. For others, structure will have great importance: 'It matters a lot. We had a restructure at the time of incorporation ... Every year since then the structure has been tweaked' (Principal 1). This principal believed that the degree of autonomy which the structure offered had nurtured entrepreneurial attitudes leading to an expanded curriculum and a better quality experience for students. Whether seen as of primary significance or not, as Fidler (1997) states, every organization makes some choices and has some sort of explicit structure. The next section examines how colleges have reshaped in order to meet the pressures identified in the survey.

RESHAPING COLLEGES

There are a number of models depicting how organizations can be structured. Cole (1996) identifies five, including structures which are based on management/production functions, (the marketing department, the design department, etc.) structures based on different products, structures related to geographical site, or a mixture. The range of organizational structure in colleges includes all these, as a college may have a structure which relates to functions of, for example, finance and curriculum, or products, being organized in vertical streams according to programme areas, or geography with specific structures on different sites. However, within educational organizations, underpinning these different variations, two basic models of structuring have been identified, the hierarchical pyramid (Turner, 1991) and the matrix (Fidler, 1997). The pyramid structure is based on the premise that everyone in the organization will be directed by one manager only, so creating lines of command which order who has charge of whom in a hierarchical sequence (see Figure 7.3). Turner argues that structure is very important and that the pyramid, based on the bureaucratic theories of Weber (1947), has advantages:

> The strength of this model is in the clear and unambiguous definition of who has responsibility and is accountable for whom and what and to whom. It makes possible a division of work into convenient specialist departments and sections. It limits the span of control any one person exercises over others. It divides the organisation into manageable units. It enables co-ordination of activities to be easily accomplished by top management. It enables control and monitoring of activities to take place at each level.
>
> (Turner, 1991, pp. 4–5)

Hall (1994) notes that the departmental, pyramid structure has dominated in colleges for 30 years and that a survey at the beginning of the 1990s showed that 70 per cent of UK further education colleges had such a structure. The disadvantages of such a structure are also noted. As early as 1981, Brannen, Holloway and Peeke commented on the negative effects of isolation, internal competition, power struggles and barriers preventing co-operation.

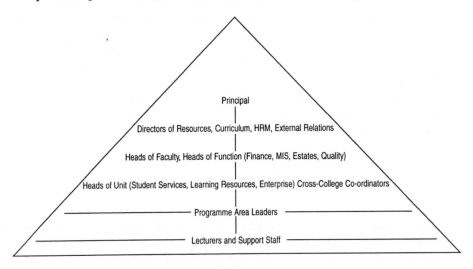

Figure 7.3   Hierarchical pyramid organization

The alternative structure of a matrix is defined by Fidler, (1997, p. 62): 'An organizational structure in which large numbers of employees are in dual authority relationships.' In such a structure, each member of staff may have two or more managers and also relate to a number of advisers. The structure is usually represented in a two-dimensional matrix in contrast to the departmental pyramid, as in Figure 7.4. Not surprisingly, a matrix structure also has advantages and disadvantages:

> A formal matrix structure offers flexibility and adaptability to change. It has open lines of communication and more diffuse managerial accountability giving greater responsibility to individual workers. However, there is evidence of conflict, lack of accountability, many meetings and paperwork particularly where the nature of the dual accountability has not been fully appreciated and allowed for.
>
> (Fidler, 1997, p. 63)

The matrix structure has been adopted particularly by smaller colleges, Hall (1994) noting that just under 60 per cent of tertiary colleges had a matrix structure at the start of the 1990s. In fact, although these two forms of structure exist as theoretical concepts, they do not exist in practice in a pure form. Departmental colleges have a range of cross-college committees and co-ordinators who exert some form of authority or control outside the line management system. Similarly, the matrix college inevitably has some degree of hierarchy, the pyramid apex ending at the principal. One approach to experimentation with structure is to harness the advantages of each of these two basic models and eliminate as many of the disadvantages as possible. Such experimentation has been fuelled in some colleges by the fashion for business process re-engineering, a radical refocusing of processes on the core business. In order to achieve the latter and escape the tyranny of the two images of pyramid or matrix, other metaphors for structure have been suggested. In some cases, the change has been merely one of softening the rather negative connotations of hierarchy, which are explicit in the pyramid. For example, Principal 1 described his structure as a 'Christmas tree' a less stark

Principal /Chief Executive					
			Head of Resources	Head of HRM	Estates Manager
Principal /Chief Executive	Director of Internal Relations	Head of Quality GNVQ Co-ordinator Key Skills Co-ordinator	Faculty 1	Faculty 2	Faculty 3
	Director of External Relations	Head of Marketing	Student Services	Enterprise Unit	

Figure 7.4   Matrix organization

image than a pyramid. Others try to suggest something more organic, less hierarchical, for example, a circle. Harper (1997) uses Mintzberg's ideas (1996) to suggest a structure of concentric circles, where senior managers are the outer circle, middle managers form an inner circle and lecturers are in the centre, as in Figure 7.5. In this way, middle managers are represented as pivotal in linking the strategic and operational levels of the college. However, it can be argued that such an image does not reflect any change in activity in that lecturers still report to middle managers who still report to senior managers. Nothing has changed. The pyramid in reality remains intact. An alternative argument is that the redrawn image does reflect a change in practice, in that it reflects the increase in power of middle managers, their centrality in the visual image reflecting their critical role in the college.

Some degree of bureaucratic hierarchy will always assert itself, but the visual image used to represent a college structure is, perhaps above all, a cultural signal of the intention to shift power or thinking to some extent. Morgan (1997) offers the image of the spider plant to suggest new ways of designing organizations (see Figure 7.6). The offshoots are supported by an umbilical cord to the parent. Both the baby plant (subunit) and the connecting cord (its relationship to the rest of the organization) may be varied by means of negotiation. The subunit baby plants have not necessarily replicated the parent by transplanting the same rules, regulations and practice. Each unit could there-

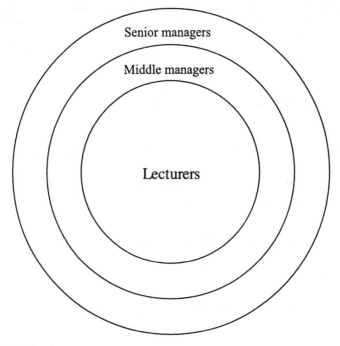

Figure 7.5   Circle diagram

fore be different in culture and practice. Bumblebees are people who go between units cross-pollinating. Again it might be argued that the pyramid is intact, but simply represented in a way which emphasizes a greater degree of autonomy allocated to subunits and a greater variety of ways of operating.

The organic emphasis is taken even further by one principal in offering the image of a flower, a dahlia to be specific:

Of Kappa college

The new principal decided that radical changes in management were necessary so that the college could immediately develop the means to ensure its own survival. She called this 'developing capability'. The old structure of 12 independent departments, which had led to duplication and overlap, was abolished and the new curriculum model, resting on three faculties – Business, Technology and Services to People – set up, providing a new management system, based on the visual metaphor of 'the dahlia' – a multi-petalled flower. The metaphor was seen as appropriate because of its organic connotations of growth and renewal and therefore its symbolic endorsement of change.

(Bennett and Hagon, 1997, p. 98)

The use of a new metaphor and visual image as a cultural signal is quite explicit. The signal is more to do with changing attitudes of renewed hope and co-operation, than a radical change in the roles and formal relationships of those who are managing.

This chapter opened by establishing that three perspectives were possible on structure: the internal subjective perspective, the whole organization perspective and the organization within its environment perspective. The first of

Figure 7.6 Spider plant with different 'cords' for different situations
Source: Morgan, 1997, p. 531.

these is particularly relevant in interpreting changed ways of representing structure. Depending on the experience of the individual, he or she will interpret a restructuring as a real change or a reshuffle, having radical significance or affecting day-to-day operations very little. Certainly the intention of those managing a restructure was to achieve important improvements in the way things are done, i.e. to have an impact on culture by adjusting both practice, and attitudes.

CURRENT PRACTICE

One common factor in the structure of colleges is that all appear to have some sort of senior management team though the title and size of the group varied. Often there is an inner group of the principal and a small number of second-tier managers. An expanded circle may incorporate other senior managers, for example, those with a cross-college role or heads of faculty. The choice of how to allocate responsibilities within the inner group was a strong signal of intent. For example, Curriculum Manager 4, who was an Assistant Principal, explained that in his senior management team, each of the Assistant Principals had responsibility for a curriculum area, the reason being that the principal saw the curriculum as the core business of the college and therefore the role of each assistant principal was to monitor curriculum performance. This was not typical. Interviewees indicated that in most colleges, roles in the senior management team were allocated according to management functions, for example for finance, marketing, human resources, etc. There might be one person with a curriculum responsibility. Curriculum Manager 2 held such a role within her senior management team (SMT). She felt that the SMT structure in her college, where other team members held responsibility for finance, marketing and human resources, had resulted in shifting the curriculum from being the centre of attention. The result was that unlike previously, the majority of SMT discussion time was given to issues other than teaching and learning. One contrary argument supporting such a division of roles within a SMT is that if senior managers are responsible for a curriculum area, they will not be able to promote a detached whole-college view, but will be the apex of internal divisions and competition (Lumby, 1996). The first choice in structure is, therefore, how to distribute responsibilities within the SMT to ensure a central focus on a whole-college approach to learning and teaching but without creating strong vertical barriers.

All colleges also seemed to have some central functions, for example, finance and estates. The position in the structure of staff who worked in central services was critical. They could be members of the SMT or largely viewed as administrative, even though third tier. There were several examples of tensions and a feeling of isolation. Such managers had the classic ambivalence of middle managers in relating to both strategic and operational staff, but often, coming from a non-educational background, with the added disadvantage of perceiving themselves as seen as outsiders bringing in a different culture. Such a position was very uncomfortable:

> Well I don't perceive myself to be a manager first and foremost. I perceive myself to be in a role where I am supporting managers and that means that I am doing my best and hoping to support managers doing some difficult things while at the same time supporting staff who are having difficult things done to them which is also a difficult role. It makes you feel like you've got a split personality. It's a very, very difficult position because whatever you do you cannot please everybody and so you don't even try. You don't try and please, because you know you can't, so you just try and support as much as you can.
>
> (Human Resource Manager 2)

This sort of third-tier advisory role fitted within neither academic staff nor senior managers and was indeed an uncomfortable perch within the structure. Although one or two of the managers interviewed had resolved this and worked effectively and happily, it was apparent that those who had a more senior position within the hierarchy had found it easier to gain acceptance, being seen as of an equivalence to the professional status of lecturer.

Beyond the SMT and some central functions, the variety of structural arrangement increased. Some degree of cross-college integration was attempted by means of project teams, committees and cross-college co-ordinators. The links between such individuals and groups and those working within the vertical divisions of the college was by means of meetings. The latter might have very carefully structured membership and agendas to ensure that the work undertaken was embedded as far as possible. The degree of centralization or integration of administrative services, resources management and student guidance varied. Principal 3 wished to give each curriculum area its own accounting and administrative officer in order to release academic middle managers to focus on teaching and learning issues. Lack of resources prevented such a move. Devolution of managerial responsibility of all kinds was seen as the way forward by many: 'You've got a choice. Either you try running everything from Moscow or you give individual managers responsibility and as much freedom as you can. The second system works better' (Principal 1). Such a high degree of autonomy did lead to issues of demarcation and rivalries but the Principal felt: 'You've got to try and manage those. They are inherent in having a devolved structure.'

The gains from the creativity and energy of people liberated to build their own part of the organization outweighed the disadvantages of the disagreements that arise as a consequence. The ultimate degree of autonomy was given in the case of some colleges to detached units, most typically those concerned with working with employers. The aim of such independent units within the structure was twofold: first, to achieve a culture and responsiveness to immediately improve performance in relation to the relevant aspect of college activity; and, second, long-term to embed changes of practice and culture throughout the structure. The first is the easier target. In the case of Marketing Manager 1, his unit had achieved spectacular success in recruiting new groups of people and had to some extent had an impact on wider practice elsewhere in the college. It was, however, after several years still in competition with other parts of the organization (and winning!). An independent unit can therefore be an effective strategy both for challenging and/or bypassing culture resistant to change. There is further discussion of the advantages and disadvantages of detached units in Chapter 10, 'Working with employers'.

There was an example of one college which was going in the opposite direction, away from devolution. In the case of this college, a greater degree of control was required to ensure that targets were understood and met and costs cut:

> The college restructured 18 months ago and moved from a very flat matrix structure. I think the matrix system had a lot of advantages but it became very difficult to manage in terms of target setting . . . We had a flatter system and we have actually moved to a hierarchy. The reason we went for a hierarchical system if I am being blatantly honest, is because of staff costs. It was a way of saving money. I don't think it was learning driven. Having said that, there are advantages in this hierarchical system. But I also think there are advantages in the matrix system in terms of ownership and those sorts of things. It was a cost-saving exercise as most restructurings are. They are not necessarily done with the learner at heart, I am afraid.
>
> (Curriculum Manager 3)

In this case the primary reason for changing the structure was to cut costs by eliminating a number of middle managers, but also to make communication easier by dividing the college into smaller groups of people.

ROLE TENSIONS

Hall (1997, p. 63) describes that 'at their simplest, roles constitute the parts people expect and are expected to play in the drama of educational life'. Staff will hold their own idea of what their role involves, but will also adjust their view and actions in the light of the expectations of their role set, that is, the people with whom they interact. Each individual will have a job description which delineates duties and responsibilities, but this is at best only a sketchy approximation of their role. The concept of role is more dynamic and exists at the interface of formal duties and responsibilities, the expectations of the role set and the status accorded to the role by the players.

There are many pressures in the sector enforcing changes in role. As discussed in this chapter, many colleges have changed their structure so that there may be fewer staff to undertake aspects of the work. The imperative to reduce costs has led to the use of different contractual arrangements, with more staff on part-time or agency contracts who may have more limited responsibilities than full-time permanent staff. The requirement for a greater degree of accountability has led to demands that staff undertake new tasks related to monitoring, quality implementation and administration. The technologies of learning and teaching have changed, leading to a wider range of modes of operation, for example, assessing off site, or supporting resource-based learning. Finally, the different forms of supporting learning are being implemented by a wider range of staff, rather than formerly, just by lecturers. Such pressures have frequently led to the extension of the range of duties and responsibilities of each role, or sometimes, as in the case of agency staff, a reduction. The changing expectations of internal and external members of the role set, students, superordinates, employers, local, regional and national government bodies, produce a melange of different priorities for the range of tasks in each role. The status accorded may also vary amongst the different stakeholders. The result is what Hall (1997, p. 62) calls 'post-modern uncertainties (in which boundaries are permeable, roles blurred and tasks constantly changing)'. Role holders will respond by a dialectic of both accepting the role given and, to some degree, shaping it themselves.

Resulting developments in role can be analysed by exploration of three areas of change:

- changes in what people do
- changes in the relationship between people
- changes in the status and power of the individual.

CHANGES IN WHAT PEOPLE DO

Changes in what people do have happened at two levels. Many lecturers *de facto* have moved to a management role:

> Without a doubt another of the changes is that we are expecting people to pick up the programme manager role, which in a way is the role which was made redundant and which is no longer called programme manager. Of course they get no extra salary or remission or whatever, so the lecturer's role has embraced the programme manager's role.
>
> (Curriculum Manager 3)

In this college, the job of programme manager was formally deleted from the structure but the task and responsibilities passed informally to lecturers, thereby enlarging their role, if not their pay. Quality Manager 2 acknowledged that although job descriptions had not changed, section managers had to take far more responsibility for quality, and that such change had been very painful and resisted. Therefore those who were already managers were given a weightier responsibility. There was much evidence in the interviews that, particularly in terms of responsibilities for quality and accountability, the management role of previously designated 'academic' staff had shifted up a gear in all parts of the hierarchy. The second level of change involved variously named 'support' or 'service' staff and technicians. The numbers of such staff had grown and their role, too, had often engaged a wider range of tasks, responsibilities and, sometimes, status. Curriculum Manager 1 described the evolving roles:

> Increasingly we are seeing the use of people who are not teachers as such working within the curriculum. For instance, we have an extensive career and personal development programme which is delivered almost entirely by our guidance staff who are actually not paid as lecturers but they do the lecturing job. Similarly, we have outreach centres which have drop-in IT facilities where the staff who are working with the students are facilitators. Similarly, our youth workers are playing an increasing role in working directly with students usually on personal development issues and things like drug taking and so on. But now they are also taking them away on things like outdoor expeditions, going camping and that sort of thing . . .

The use of a much wider range of staff in direct curriculum delivery was universal within the colleges visited.

CHANGES IN STATUS, POWER AND RELATIONSHIPS

The status accorded to roles was also changing. 'Support' staff who previously might have been viewed as of lesser status than teaching staff had an enhanced status either at senior levels, through their professional expertise in a management function such as human resource management or financial management, or lower in the hierarchy by their entry into involvement with delivering the curriculum. Lecturers had become managers who acquired greater responsibility for accountability and thereby might grow in power and status. The question which follows is, in whose eyes was status/power enhanced for any particular individual? A frequent phenomenon was individuals in interview reporting that greater status, and therefore power, had been given to a category of staff other than their own. With the occasional exception of members of senior management teams, acknowledgment of status and power enhancement was elusive, always conferred on someone other than the person in question.

There were a number of points of tension where the relationship between staff was uneasy. For example, the legitimacy of the involvement of non-teaching staff in delivering the curriculum, particularly where they were perceived to do the same job for less pay, was a critical issue. The status to be accorded to managers who might be senior but who came from outside education was another such fulcrum of uncertainty. Such debate and contention indicated role difficulties.

ROLE DIFFICULTIES

Handy (1990, p. 41) categorizes role difficulties as including: 'role conflict (two roles in conflict with each other such as the caring person and efficient supervisor, or the mother/worker clash); role ambiguity (when you don't know what is expected of you, or different people expect different things); role over-load (just too many things expected of you)'. There was a universal conviction amongst interviewees that all these role difficulties were commonly experienced. Role overload was reported as universal and serious, leading to severe stress for staff. Role ambiguity was particularly related to middle managers where the different expectations of super- and sub-ordinates caused tension. Role conflict occurred particularly in relation to boundary spanning where external organizations such as employers, funding and awarding bodies would adopt a quite different view and expectations of roles to those of, for example, students. Roles were continually evolving in response to the tensions and turbulence. On the positive side, there was room for manoeuvre and enrichment of roles. More frequently, role difficulties were sustained to a degree that led to stress and dysfunction.

ALL CHANGE, NO CHANGE

Dopson and Stewart (1993) found that in their case-study businesses, most had reorganized, most had fewer staff and a greater degree of decentralization. This trend was evidenced amongst the colleges examined for this book, but the trend was not universal. There were many variations in the form of structure and the reasons for change. It is very difficult to assess whether the changes on paper actually amount to significant change in practice, are merely semantic, or signal attitudinal shifts which will affect practice long term. Quality Manager 3 gave an example of this ambivalence: 'We have nine teaching teams which are curriculum teams, and each of those have a team leader. The team leader is what you would term the departmental head.' Is the team leader merely a different name for a departmental head? The Quality Manager argued differently, that in her view the structure was radically different. She explained this as a significant change in the role, i.e. responsibilities and range of tasks undertaken by the different categories of people in the new structure.

Little is known about the structure of colleges, partly because little research has been undertaken, and partly because each college may change its structure so frequently that there is no time to assess the impact before the organization has moved on. Much more work is needed to attempt to resolve the connections between formal structure, its communication by visual means of words or image, changes in role and changes in culture. In talking to the managers about structure there was a sense that structure was seen as highly significant by the majority but that much change had been driven by external circumstance or by a leap of faith, rather than any in-depth understanding of how structure works, particularly in terms of the impact on the psychological contract between managers and others. It may be that colleges are reaching a point of greater stability where extended research and reflection may become possible.

Whereas the degree of significance of changes in structure may be uncertain, changes in role were far more immediately felt as significant by individuals. Whether the official place within the structure of any role had changed or not, the way the role was seen by the role holder and by others continued to change, and was likely to be subject to ambiguity, conflict and overload. This has undoubtedly always been the case, but seems to have been exacerbated by the pressures within the sector post-1993. The reorganizations undertaken were at least in part an attempt to reduce ambiguity and conflict, and to provide clarity for staff in what they were expected to do and to achieve. Success seems to have been varied. Perhaps postmodern uncertainty is an abiding universal reality with which we must all live. However, before reaching that conclusion, and in recognition of the seriousness of the levels of stress in the sector, more research is needed on how far structure has the potential to contribute to alleviating role tensions and supporting the core business of teaching and learning.

8

MANAGING INFORMATION AND COMMUNICATION

COMMUNICATION AT THE CORE

The technological advances of the last decade have revolutionized the management of information and communication in many organizations. The advent of systems capable of storing millions of pieces of data has had a profound effect on the overall view of how information and communication can best be managed. The increasing emphasis on effectiveness and efficiency, underpinned by data-driven rational management regimes, has led to an emphasis on information collection and computerized systems. Approximately £36 million was invested in hardware and software in colleges, during the late 1980s and early 1990s (Parker, 1997). Since then, the information requirements of external bodies have enforced the collection of billions of pieces of information and further investment and development of systems (Harper, 1997). The strategic need is for a holistic management of information and communication, of which computerized systems are only a part. Unfortunately, the technological revolution combined with external pressure for information may have displaced a more holistic view of communication, resulting in a disproportionate concentration on management information systems (MIS). Nevertheless, the lesson has been hard learned that 'every aspect of information systems depends on people' (Alter, 1996, p. 31). One might expect lecturers skilled in communicating with students to be good communicators with each other. Andrews (1995) argues that this cannot be assumed, and that consequently there is a need to invest energy, resource and skill in establishing a system which focuses on communication within colleges as much as on information gathering. The managers interviewed recognized the imperative to communicate, particularly in times of rapid change and uncertainty. As Quality Manager 4 put it: 'The game plan is to communicate and then communicate and when you have done that to communicate some more.'

The process of communication is complex. It can be achieved by:

- words, oral and written
- pictures
- diagrams, drawings
- symbols
- colour
- sounds other than words
- facial expression
- appearance
- body language
- regalia and insignia (adapted from Savage, 1989, pp. 106–7).

Complete control and manipulation of such a complex set of interactive elements is not possible. The intended impact of any attempt at communication is always only at best a part of what is understood by the receiver. Any communication interaction may also be intended and received differently in terms of its purpose or purposes. Riches (1994, p. 247) suggests many possible objectives of communication: 'Reasons for communicating might be to inform, explain, persuade, reprimand, encourage, thank, appraise, propose, consult, apologise or praise (and one can think of many others).'

The complexity of the means of communication working in dialectic with the possible aims of the communication in the context of two or more individuals with unique histories, personalities and agendas means that, at best, communication can only be nudged along in the general direction desired, and will defy attempts to command it. While recognizing the limitations of control, college managers can still focus on their aim(s) in communicating and attempt to provide effective channels whereby the potential for misunderstanding, misinformation and ignorance of events and feelings can be minimized.

ISSUES IN COMMUNICATION

The metaphor of the machine is one that can be applied to organizations (Morgan 1986). The normative tone of some literature from government-sponsored organizations seems underpinned by such a view of how organizations function (FEU, 1993). Those texts suggest that better information and more communication will indubitably lead to better managed colleges. But organizations are not machines and communication remains a stubbornly human activity, its impact unpredictable and erratic. There is difficulty in achieving communication of any calibre. In organizations as large as colleges, there will inevitably be dependence on the written word, and increasingly the e-mail or intranet. Managers may be confident that the message sent is therefore accessible to all. Unfortunately there are two problems with this. All communication is in competition with the myriad other demands on the attention of staff. Consequently, people filter communication, choosing to respond, for example, to the telephone call or personal conversation, even when this is less high priority than the memo or e-mail (Harper, 1997). The receiver of a communication does not necessarily invest the communication with the same degree of importance as the sender. Consequently even when a member of staff 'sees' a communication they may not actually read it. In some cases even this unsatisfactory stage is not reached. MIS Manager 1 explained the complex network of communication channels in his college and then used the college newsletter as an example of how the system may fail:

> If you just take the college newspaper for instance, that's available to all the staff. Yet you can talk to staff at lecturer level and at support level who say they have never seen a newsletter. To a certain extent it is because they have never ever tried to get hold of one, but that is their perception.

Written communication is therefore uncertain. Personal communication is also problematic in a number of ways. Underlying differences in values or opinions, sometimes evident in conflict between individuals or groups within the college, touch communication with a negative magic wand, transforming apparently straightforward transactions to further fuel for resentment or anger. Where the underlying culture is one of conflict, communication is both an important means of addressing issues and a potential means of further deterioration. As Handy (1993, p. 300) asserts: 'Too often organizations react to poor communication with more communication . . . If the underlying disease is untouched, the remedy will only complicate the issue and will ultimately be discarded.'

Given the endemic conflict in further education post-1993 with widespread industrial action and redundancies, underlying conflict was the norm for most colleges for a number of years. Achieving good two-way flows of information across, down and up the organization was therefore particularly challenging.

ENCOURAGING COMMUNICATION FLOWS

Savage (1989, p. 110) characterizes the often inadequate upward flow of communication in organizations as due in part to unconscious signals given by senior managers that 'ideas, reactions and criticisms are not welcome'. Although on a conscious level managers would assert that they wished people to be open and honest in their communication, achieving such an ideal is very difficult. Even if in words a manager welcomes hearing a view contrary to his or her own, body language may leak some unease or annoyance. This leads others to filter what they say. Consequently, senior managers may be protected by a self-induced filtering process which inhibits open communication, as described by Savage, but also sometimes by a physical buffer where other senior or middle managers sanitize communication from others, presenting a version cleansed of anything which may be too disturbing. Principal 1 was aware that those who rose to a senior position did so partly because they were good at spotting signals as to what was priority and what was preferred:

> Within a big organization people who scramble up the greasy pole are quite good at interpreting what management want aren't they? You tend not to get managers towards the top of any large organization who are not good at that, good at reading the body language of what people think and which things are encouraged, and what things are flavour of the month and what things aren't. That's part of the reason they climb up the greasy pole.

Acceptance of filtering is a dangerous stance long term, as it would lead to ignorance of the true state of people's views and feelings. The managers interviewed were aware of the filtering processes and were trying to combat them. Managers can respond by attempting to build a culture where opinions which differ from those further up the hierarchy are welcomed. Quinn (1993, p. 67) goes further and suggests that 'careful executives' make sure that their network for direct communication circumvents the screens to shield them and includes 'people who look at the world very differently than do those in the enterprise's dominating culture'.

The principals and members of senior management teams interviewed were very conscious of the problem of accessing genuine opinions and feelings, particularly of lecturers and support staff. The two strategies chosen to address barriers were, first, to achieve as much individual personal contact as was feasible and, second, to set up networks of meetings. Getting to meet staff on an individual level was not always straightforward. Principal 3 had made a commitment to staff that she would get around the college and speak to them. However, she found that they were usually teaching. Staff were no longer to be found in staff rooms. She had to drop her plan to simply walk around and use a more formal arrangement to meet teams. Principal 4 both welcomed people to come and see him and tried to get to see people around the college, but it was never perceived as enough:

> I have adopted an open door policy so that the staff from anywhere across the college can ask to see me . . . I feel that I do get out and about quite a bit to various functions around the college and speak to people at the time, but nevertheless the collective view comes back that we think that the Principal is not seen enough.

His feeling was that however much time he spent around the college 'It is never going to be seen as enough' and this sentiment was echoed by others.

Being available and approachable also brought its own managerial and micropolitical perils. Principal 2 was very aware that staff might try to use individual contact as a way of short-circuiting other communication channels and avoiding speaking to the staff most directly concerned:

> The minute someone comes up to me and says 'I am really worried about x. We are not resourced for y', then I have got to show discipline by saying, 'Look fine, this it what you say, but the first person you talk to is your manager or your Head of Senior Management Team', so there is no sort of back door grassing. If any one comes to me and says 'I want to talk to you but it is completely off the record' I just say to them 'No I can't talk to you off the record because if you tell me something I want to act on, I will act on it. You've got to be prepared that, if you say something about someone else, the first person I am going to go to is that person'.

Finding the balance between open communication and usurping the role of other managers was difficult.

Two of the Principals commented on the frustration caused by those who did speak to them not always saying what they thought and then communicating a different view by another channel. It was difficult for them to come to terms with because both saw themselves as reasonable, approachable people.

> When I talk to them I forget that when I am talking, I am talking as Principal and that does muck up communication. I think well why didn't the person say something at the time? I ask them why. They respond, 'Well come on, you're Principal!' I find that quite difficult because I am quite approachable and I do talk to people and most are fairly up front. Some aren't.

The discrepancy between views expressed face to face and views communicated by less direct channels was frustrating and difficult to deal with. Despite the fact that finding staff was difficult, that however hard you worked at it, it was never enough, that staff often did not give their honest views, the process of communicating on an individual level was seen as of great importance to all the senior managers. The priorities of those to whom they spoke may be different and may seem insignificant compared with the larger college issues, but recognition of the difference in perspective was seen as important. Principal 1 explained that listening to the daily small problems was a part of showing that he really did care about the working lives of staff:

> If you walk around the place you inevitably collect a lot of points because that's what people are concerned about day to day. They are worried that their desk should be over there, it shouldn't be over here. Car parking spaces should be a lot better. Those can become issues of academic freedom can't they? They can be translated into that. So partly the exercise is collecting those as you go round and trying to follow them up, so that's the part where you show that you actually care and that the organization cares and has tried to do something to make people's working lives a bit easier.

Astutely, the exercise was both about showing genuine concern for staff and also about defusing minor issues which can grow into larger ones and provide a focus for discontent; the car parking issue which grows until it is interpreted as representing an assault on academic freedom. Encouraging upward communication by individual contact was never easy, always only partly successful, but nevertheless crucial.

Given the problematic nature of individual contact, meetings and networks were a complementary method of encouraging an upward flow. Many of the colleges had very sophisticated and elaborate structures with access to meetings and agendas formulated to ensure that people would be heard. There were cross-college meetings, open meetings and college conferences. Agendas were structured to ensure those with a cross-college role, historically one of the most difficult in terms of communication, had meeting time and access to those with whom they wished to have contact. Some meetings were held without middle or senior managers so that staff could feel free from any inhibition in expressing their views. In Quality Manager 1's college the minutes of meetings and self-assessment reports were part of an interactive process of communication where as many views and as much information as possible were used to underpin draft strategic decisions which would then be sent out for comment and development. Listening was in this case through documents as much as through actual attendance at meetings. It may be that human beings need to meet and interact individually, but that the distortion in communication caused by power differentials is less acute in paper-based communication.

The contact to establish an upward flow of information is also, of course, a means of establishing a downward route from senior to less senior staff. There appeared to be very much more information flowing down than up, with endless requests for information, and documents outlining new policies and procedures. Use of an intranet was growing as a means of circulating information and news. In one college, staff in all 108 centres had access to the intranet. A briefing note was posted on it every morning. However, as MIS Manager 3 commented: 'Just plonking a computer on somebody's desk is not going to improve communication because it won't create the ownership.'

Understanding of how the use of computerized systems is profoundly effecting communication is only just beginning to be grasped. There is and will be change. How far the change will represent an improvement in communication has yet to be researched. Tierney (1998, p. 39) points out that the advent of e-mail, the Internet and intranet have democratized communication, allowing diverse groups and individuals to interact and establish a more informal system. This should in theory particularly benefit the many staff who need to communicate across the college, rather than just the group with whom they work closely. The requirement to ensure that core skills are embedded throughout the curriculum means that those with a cross-curriculum role have a particular need to communicate with a wide range of staff. The intranet would seem to be an ideal tool. However, the use of an intranet may ensure staff see any particular communication, but will not address the micropolitical issues of persuading them to pay attention. As is discussed in Chapter 9 on managing teaching and learning, the curriculum is owned by a variety of groups, each with its own agenda. To gain a response, those communicating must make recipients feel that the communication is of sufficient importance to them and as, or more important than their own priorities. Using the intranet, with a possible consequent decline in personal contact, may actually militate against the sort of persuasiveness and interpersonal skills which can gain the attention of the recipient of communication. Therefore, despite the apparent potential advantage of the wider range of means of communication, Tierney (1998, p. 39) warns that:

> The temptation is to say that such transformations in technology have vastly improved the organisation's information system. In periods of rapid upheaval, however, rather than improve systems, individuals might first acknowledge that they have simply changed ... Yet no one should assume that any tool is a panacea. Humans still drive the response system. Humanity's foibles, assumptions, and beliefs create what the system is becoming. And we are not sure what the system should become.

Much more research is needed on how the changing medium of communication is impacting on the nature of interaction between staff. Internal evaluation of the impact of any form of communication is needed to assess the appropriateness of the amount, nature and effect of interaction.

MANAGEMENT INFORMATION SYSTEMS

In colleges of further education, a number of pressures have overlain the global trend towards a focus on the technological aspects of information and communication. The sector as a whole has grown with larger numbers of students and staff, given the ever-growing numbers of part-timers, leading to larger and more complex organizations, demanding more sophisticated record-keeping. External demands for data are huge. Leney, Lucas and Taubaum (1998) give the example of one college which submits 1.5 million pieces of data to the FEFC three times a year on six floppy disks, and has had the disks returned on one occasion with the explanation that there is an error in two records.

Prior to the 1990s, Atkinson (1989) points out that there was little history of reliance on data as a basis for management. The attitudes of the period are vividly illustrated by an incident described by MIS Manager 3. He showed the senior management team a graph, which as he saw it, illustrated important information, the large number of student withdrawals over a year. They viewed it with glazed eyes as if it was 'a piece of modern art'. They were not used to drawing on numbers to support management and had no way of relating to information presented in this form.

The increased emphasis on computerized MIS is predicated on a belief that if the right data could be collected and translated into the right information and communicated, then management decisions would be improved (FEU, 1993). However, this belief may be simplistic in the light of the complexity of communication processes as discussed in the first part of this chapter. Alter argues that the effectiveness of MIS systems is bounded:

- Usefulness depends on a combination of information, quality, accessibility and presentation.
- One person's information is another person's noise.
- Soft data may be just as important as hard data.
- Ownership of information may be difficult to maintain.
- More information may be better or worse.
- Providing the truth on some issues may be a punishable offence (adapted from Alter, 1996, p. 30).

The last point is particularly interesting in emphasizing that any communication has a micropolitical element. Clarity of information may be seen as undesirable by some in some situations. For example, exposure of drop-out rates by subunit or individual lecturers may have repercussions which potentially could improve or cause further deterioration in teaching and learning, depending on how the publication of information is received and impacts on motivation. Alter (1996) also comments that although MIS can be a powerful and valuable tool, it also has the potential for causing an enormous waste of time and resource through the collection of data which are not used or misapplied.

Much of the literature (Coles, 1989; FEU, 1993; Harper, 1997) transmits a belief that MIS can be useful if:

- it is led by user needs
- it is owned by the users
- it is reliable
- it is in a form which is accessible and comprehensible
- it takes account of the micropolitical environment.

Such 'rules' appear self-evident and yet are very hard to achieve. To take the first of these points, establishing user needs is problematic. MIS Manager 3 had tried repeatedly to involve users in identifying what they would find useful:

> Eighteen months ago I met with all the section heads and said to them all, 'Imagine you have got a blank sheet of paper. Tell me the three most important things you would want out of a new system'. I gave them six weeks to do that and I got absolutely nothing back. Then I devised a questionnaire survey based on something that FEDA [Further Education Development Agency] had done which was basically a tick box where I was trying to identify all the possible things that could come out of a management information system. This pro forma

ran to 17 pages, with 17 major sections, in each case asking how often people would want the information, and I sent a copy to SMT members and out to Heads of Section. I did get about 30 or 40 of them back. The general approach was that people ticked everything – oh yes, I'll have that, I'll have that, and I'll have that – so it was all or nothing really so neither of them worked. I got nothing in the first half of the approach, and in the second, people saying they wanted everything.

There may of course have been a need for a middle way where managers were presented with a limited set of choices from which to select but, to the manager concerned, the problem seemed more one of a deep-seated lack of interest in quantitative data about the college, and a lack of skills in interpreting and using such information. He questioned the basic numeracy skills of many lecturers. He was also genuinely puzzled why information which seemed of importance to him, such as the destination of students and the reasons for drop out, seemed of such little interest to lecturers. There are probably multiple reasons for this situation. First, lecturers are overworked, strained and having to prioritize activities. Consequently, the thing which needs doing immediately, that is, teaching students on a daily basis, is likely to take most of lecturers' attention. Second, the information may be perceived as threatening. If destination data shows that few students achieve employment, at a college level the implication may be that the course in question should be dropped or have a reduced intake as there are insufficient employment opportunities. At the level of the individual lecturer, such implications may be personally threatening in a way that would not be evident to a manager who does not teach in the area concerned. Viewed from such a perspective, lack of interest in destination data may be highly logical in terms of self-preservation.

A more subtle example of the implications of the use of hard data in decision-making was given by MIS Manager 3. During one summer period, the staff in Student Services commented on how busy they were, how the area was always crowded with students waiting to be seen and this gave rise to a degree of optimism in estimating the likely number of enrolments that autumn. In fact this optimism proved to be unfounded. There were a number of possible reasons why Student Services could have appeared so busy and yet enrolments have not been so good. The manager's view was that interviews were taking a lot longer due to growing problems amongst students, for example, concerning financial issues:

> If ten people come in to Student Services and there are only three advisers there and seven students milling around, then it looks really busy. If you come back in half an hour there are still five people milling around, it still looks busy. It might be that instead of the ten-minute interview each student would have had three years ago, it might now be a half-hour interview. So it doesn't necessarily follow that from . . . that impression that you get, you can draw conclusions . . .

The same principle of distrusting gut impressions could be applied in his view to judgements on whether classes were full, programme areas busy, etc.

Measurement was needed to support or contradict impression. From the staff's point of view, for example, in Student Services, they were happily busy and might see no need to record student interviews and subsequent enrolments more systematically.

Just as oral communication can be understood differently by the sender and receiver, so the communication of 'facts' can be interpreted differently. The knowledge that the apparently busy and effective period of time over summer was no such thing will challenge the Student Services staff's view of reality and may undermine their confidence and their belief in their ability to make judgements. The collection of data and its communication in this example would have implications which confound any simple belief that performance will be improved by basing management decisions on better information. Of course it may be useful for managers to know that interviews are taking longer and that, despite appearing busy, Student Services is not processing enquiries in any more volume than the previous equivalent period, but there also needs to be an understanding of how this information may be received by those involved, and its impact in human terms. There is also the possibility that gut feeling may turn out to be a better guide than information. MIS Manager 2 gave an example of an occasion where gut feeling had been used with great success by managers to inform a decision to set up a new programme: 'There was no real guaranteed identified market and yet they had this gut feeling and took the risk, and they have set up a successful course that no educational manager in their right mind would ever even have tried.' There is likely to remain the necessity to balance information-based decisions with gut- or intuition-led action.

Achieving user-led information is therefore difficult. The issue of achieving ownership is obviously linked. Following research in several colleges, MIS Manager 1 had reached his own conclusions on who actually owned the data:

> Who owns the data? The conclusion that I came to is that the data should be owned by the people who need the information, but I found in practice that the data was owned by the person who worried about whether it was right. That's the best definition I could come up with for ownership of data and that person may not be the person who is appointed to do that. It's the person who stays until 9 o'clock at night trying to get the figures right and who worries about it.

A picture emerged of lecturers, seeing their priority as teaching and not record-keeping, providing incomplete and inaccurate information to MIS. The data became of meaning and importance to those who tried to fill in the gaps and improve the reliability, and these could be a range of people, though generally not lecturers:

> We are talking about administrative staff, and usually that person is in an MIS department. It may not be the operational manager of that department but maybe the person whose responsibility it is. It could very well be that it is a scale 1 clerical assistant who has been shown how to do the ISR [individualized student

record] and takes a very responsible attitude to their job, so that instead of saying I've been told to type this in this particular way, they actually sit there saying, no, that can't be right and start working out why it isn't right and putting it right. You might also find it's a person in central admissions who is making sure that every bit of the data that they put in is absolutely right and if something was not right they would go and ring up the student and find out and put it right.

In the two examples quoted, the member of staff could choose to take no responsibility and input the data in the form it was given, knowing it was not right, but generally, in the experience of MIS Manager 1, they did not. Ironically, those who would not be using the data to inform their management and teaching cared about it, and would take trouble with it and therefore owned it. Those who could use it and for whose use it was intended did not care about it and did not own it. This may be partly because the design of systems was primarily driven by external demands, but given the difficulties of MIS Manager 3 in creating any interest in matching the design to internal needs, it seems that ownership by lecturers and managers is not easily achieved whatever the design of the system.

The third rule listed above was that to be useful the data must be reliable. None of the MIS managers interviewed felt that reliability was acceptable, largely due to the difficulty of wresting information from lecturers. Different approaches had been tried to overcome late or non-returns for requested information. MIS Manager 2 saw this as 'a huge problem' which was only resolved when 'there was a stick waved at everybody by the Principal'. MIS Manager 3 supported a different approach:

I think one of the things which has to be improved is communication, trying to get across to everyone why the data is required in a particular format within a particular deadline, and that does not mean do this or else. It is trying to get people on your side and helping them recognize the importance of record-keeping.

Getting people on the side of those who have responsibility for MIS is likely to remain an uphill struggle, particularly as the demands on staff have come to seem to lecturers a symbol of much that is deplored in post-1993 further education (Elliott, 1996) and provided a centre of resistance.

Translating data into accessible and comprehensible information has also proved a challenge. Staff are often clear that what they have access to is not helpful, but they are not always able and/or willing to articulate what would be better. Trying to respond to the criticisms of staff about the form of information had caused MIS Manager 3 some frustration:

I do take the view that just because I give information to somebody that doesn't necessarily get a message across. I think there is room for tremendous improvement but it is easy to be critical without putting forward suggestions as to how things can be improved. If I build a wall in the way that I know how to do it and somebody comes along and says I don't like that, it doesn't help you to build the wall differently in the future unless they tell you, I don't like it because it's at a slant, or it's leaning over that way, or you need to use Flemish Bond instead of English Bond. It's got to be something other than, 'This is useless'.

Lack of interest, lack of time, and lack of numeracy skills of lecturers and managers made such detailed communication about the form of information very difficult to achieve. The resources needed to support the compilation of information are heavy. A finance manager quoted in Lumby (2000c) comments on the irony of the need to invest tens of thousands of pounds to arrive at decisions which may only adjust budgets by a few hundred. Colleges are already concerned at the proportion of their income which is used to support activities other than teaching and learning (see Chapter 12, p. 164). Given this anxiety and the heavy investment costs in developing MIS systems, colleges need to be very sure that the information they are achieving is needed and will be used.

MOVING FORWARD

Overall, the demands on MIS managers are formidable. The external information demands, in terms of both volume and complexity, are huge. The costs appear to be out of proportion to the resources available and the importance of the outcomes. The number of people involved in running MIS had grown, in the case of one college, from two to ten people. 'The overall management of MIS and what is required is out of proportion to the size of the business we are in' (MIS Manager 1). There cannot be a pause in running the system, so the development of a new system has to be simultaneous with running the old. 'It calls for a lot of mental agility to retain in your head two or three years' worth of differences in the structure' (MIS Manager 3). Colleges cannot afford to ask commercial companies to create a bespoke system. Consequently, the systems in use are a compromise, using the products created by companies to sell to a number of colleges, all of whom will have their individual differences which could not be accommodated in a single product. Internal and external expectations of MIS systems continue to rise, and MIS managers are inevitably doomed to disappoint to a degree, despite their determination to serve their constituent staff as best as they are able. The role is:

> a bit like a juggler. You are trying to drive an attitude change through. You are trying to provide information for people. You are trying to meet the FEFC requirements. Basically, I think it has been a firefighting exercise for a long time. I think to an extent, it is still a firefighting exercise. I rather fancy that it always will be a firefighting exercise. Sometimes you get it right and you are the college hero. Another time it isn't right and you are blamed for everything which could possibly go wrong in the college. It is a very volatile position.
>
> (MIS Manager 1)

Within this difficult environment, some progress has been made. There is a belief that many decisions now benefit from the information available, and that colleges certainly have a more detailed and accurate picture of their communities. The identification of additional market sectors has led to the creation of new courses, and so a widening of the curriculum range. At the same time, the advent of the widespread use of MIS 'has tended to polarize and alienate some staff' (MIS Manager 3). Such mixed results are predictable. Alter sees the positive and negative as inextricably mixed:

- All technological progress exacts a price; while it adds something on the one hand, it subtracts something on the other.
- All technological progress raises more problems than it solves, tempts us to see the consequent problems as technical in nature, and prods us to seek technical solutions to them.
- The negative effects of technological innovation are inseparable from the positive.
- All technological innovations have unforeseeable effects (Alter, 1996, p. 26).

The mixture of positive and negative effects could equally apply to all communication undertaken in a college. Certainly the formal rational approach which sees a logical loop from collection of data, translation to information, communication of information, creation of strategy, communication of strategy followed by evaluation, is deficient. It does not accord with the complexity of what happens in colleges. Currie (1995) argues that the formal rational approach is popular because it is both 'descriptive and prescriptive'. It appeals because it lends itself to checklists and sequential steps which can be represented by nice, neat, visual frameworks. It avoids the messy, uncertain, chaotic reality of communication between human beings. Understanding the way that communication and MIS systems evolve and work in practice is important as the development of systems may constrain change. Currie (1995) sees the increased automation as creating canal banks down which information flows. Increasingly, the canal banks will provide structures which confine change and make it difficult to adjust processes without changing the automated processes:

> As information technology becomes tightly integrated into the organization's different business units, it becomes difficult to separate the business process from the technology itself . . . As business processes become automated, they become embedded in the information system, it becomes increasingly difficult to change one without the other.
>
> (Currie, 1995, pp. 52–3)

Put simply, the decision to change a process may have such implications for changing the technology that fast, responsive change becomes a problem. For example, the decision to change an enrolment process may involve such massive investment in providing new software and hardware, and training staff, that the decision is one which has to be taken with great deliberation and in relation to issues other than just the experience of students enrolling in the college. Rather than supporting management decisions, MIS could become a drag and constraint.

A HOLISTIC APPROACH

There is little research to date on how communication strategies in further education are formed and evolve, and how they are experienced in practice. Solutions to improving communication lie not primarily with technology, but with the people who work in colleges continuing to nudge forward mutual understanding and openness, recognizing that messages transmitted by whatever medium can never be confined within the bounds of intention and logic. Managers may therefore need the courage of their convictions and their training to resist the fallacy that technology will inevitably provide answers to improving communication. Lecturers have insisted that ICT can complement student learning but not replace it. It is but one arrow in a full quiver (see Chapter 9). In the same way in management activity, face-to-face interaction will remain the primary means of communication in the true sense, that is, where communication is not just sent, but also received.

9

TEACHING AND LEARNING: WORKING WITH STUDENTS

THE FURTHER EDUCATION CURRICULUM

The further education curriculum comprises the interface of students and learning. It encompasses not only learning sponsored by the national funding body, but also much other work which is supported by employers, other funding bodies, such as local authorities, and by individuals, encompassing all levels and types of qualifications. It is 'immense and wide ranging' (Kennedy, 1997, p. 29). To achieve any aggregated definition of the variety of education and training which it includes, only a very general statement is possible: 'Colleges see their role in terms of providing learning opportunities which prepare individuals for their role in society and the world of employment' (Field, 1993, p. 18).

Such a mission would apply equally to schools and universities. Perhaps the special flavour of further education is to give a very high priority to the second element, that of preparation for employment, but for many students who go through its doors, for example those who go on to higher education, the vocational emphasis would not necessarily hold true. As discussed in the opening chapter, further education is comprehensive and inclusive and these very qualities make any neat definition of its curriculum impossible. As Curriculum Manager 1 explained: 'Sometimes, I must admit, I think we are spread a little thinly in that we are acquisitive. I mean that in the best possible sense, because we always wish to do things and never like to say no.'

The desire to meet the full range of student need means that the curriculum grows organically by responding to the community. This may mean that: 'Along with the rich choices within further education, there is also a fair

115

amount of chaos and confusion' (Kennedy, 1997, p. 32). The overall dichoto-my of richness and confusion, choice and chaos is reflected in the unique curriculum of each college which will have grown to its present state by a series of choices. Thus in the college of Curriculum Manager 1, a choice had been made to particularly develop Level 1 courses offering basic education and training. In Marketing Manager 1's college, there was an emphasis on developing provision at outreach centres for adults. The college of Quality Manager 1 had extensive provision for employers through outward collabora-tive provision. To talk of the further education curriculum is therefore to mislead to a degree, in that there is no equivalent of the school's National Curriculum. Each college will reflect its environment and history in the learn-ing it attempts to facilitate and for whom. Two things did emerge consistently from the survey and interviews, that the range of students continues to increase and that there is a determination to give equal status to each aspect of the curriculum. There is a long history of higher status being accorded aca-demic study rather than vocational training (Ainley and Bailey, 1997). Managers were trying to achieve a situation where no more value or status is placed on one aspect of the curriculum than another, for example, on higher level advanced work rather than basic skills:

> . . . we do not prioritize the curriculum that we offer in terms of importance. While we offer postgraduate-level qualifications, we employ staff who are skilled in that area, but in no way is that seen as being more important than the work that we do with 14–16-year-olds or with our special educational needs groups, in fact quite the reverse.
>
> (Curriculum Manager 4)

> If you deliver something, it ought to be delivered with quality. Your commitment to delivering whatever with the highest quality should not be determined by par-ticular groups of students, whether they are higher education students, FE whatever. I think one should be aiming to deliver first-class quality to all one's students.
>
> (Quality Manager 1)

The resolve to deliver the best possible learning for all was a striking charac-teristic of the managers who spoke about the curriculum.

The increasing diversity of students was also perceived by many. Aggregated national or even regional student statistics can conceal differences in individual colleges and there is, as yet, limited data available (FEFC, 1998e). Consequently colleges were asked through the survey to identify whether they felt that their students had remained the same or become more or less diverse in terms of:

- age range
- prior educational attainment
- geographical spread
- ethnic origin.

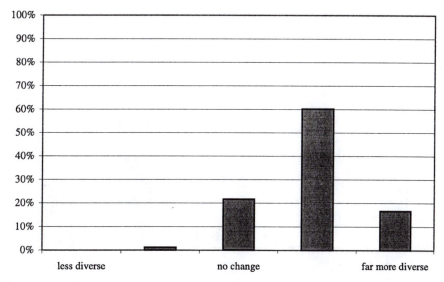

Figure 9.1   Change in diversity of age range of students from 1993 to 1999

The results show that generally, there has been an increase in diversity. Respondents were asked to indicate the extent of change on a scale of 1 to 5, where the midpoint of 3 indicated no change, 5 a far more and 1 a less diverse range. Figure 9.1 indicates the change in diversity in terms of age. Seventy-seven per cent of respondents indicate either more or far more diversity from the point of view of age. Twenty-one per cent, or one in five colleges had seen no change. Less than 2 per cent had seen their student population become less diverse.

The same pattern was repeated in terms of prior educational attainment (Figure 9.2). Fifty-four per cent of colleges believed that entrants had more diverse attainment, and 26 per cent believed their population to be far more diverse. Nineteen per cent had seen no change and less than 1 per cent felt diversity had decreased.

The change was slightly less marked in the geographical spread from which students were drawn (Figure 9.3). Here 36 per cent of colleges continued to draw students from the same geographical area. For a small number of colleges, 5 per cent, the geographical range had contracted slightly. Nevertheless, 40 per cent of colleges had seen an increase in the spread of students and 19 per cent believed their geographical spread of students to be far more diverse. Therefore, approximately 60 per cent of colleges were drawing students from a wider region than previously.

In the area of ethnicity, the majority of colleges had seen no change (60 per cent). The number of people from a range of ethnic origins in the community of many colleges is small. This would explain why the change in this aspect

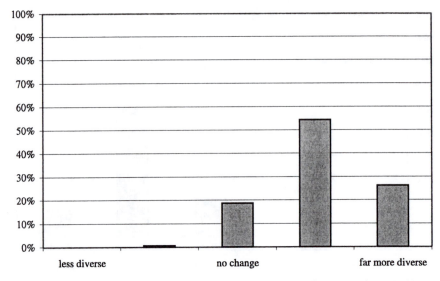

Figure 9.2   Change in diversity of educational attainment of entrants from 1993 to 1999

of the student profile is less marked. Thirty-four per cent of colleges indicated a more diverse ethnicity in their students and 5 per cent indicated students from a far more diverse range of ethnic origins (see Figure 9.4).

Taken together these results indicate that colleges are providing education and training for a population which spans a wider age range, where students come from a wider range of backgrounds and environments, and bring with them a greater spread of educational attainment. As Kennedy (1997, p. 4) believes, 'For the overwhelming majority of colleges, the driving force for excellence remains the provision of a non-discriminatory service to all sections of the community'. The evidence suggests that colleges are succeeding in the first part of the challenge, that is, in attracting an increasing range of the community. Providing learning for this more diverse population amounts to a significant challenge for colleges to help students achieve success. Responding to this challenge will build on the traditional qualities of being inclusive and comprehensive.

DIFFERENT CULTURES – DIFFERENT PATHS

To manage a curriculum for this kaleidoscope of students, some structure or form is needed to impose a shape on the diversity. Ainley and Bailey (1997) offer a categorization of activity based on pathway and level. They suggest students may follow three basic pathways:

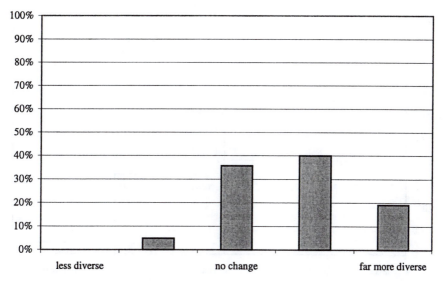

Figure 9.3 Change in diversity of geographical spread of students from 1993 to 1999

- academic (e.g. A-levels)
- general vocational (e.g. GNVQs)
- work based (e.g. NVQs [National Vocational Qualifications])

and three levels:

- foundation
- intermediate
- advanced.

They point out that although the ideal is mixing pathways to suit individual need and progressing from one level to the next, students tend to stay within one pathway and level. They also do not mix with each other much outside their learning timetable. Ainley and Bailey believe that the influence of class is still discernible. Many of the students now coming into colleges would not have received any post-compulsory training 30 years ago, and maybe in many cases even ten years ago. Students themselves are aware of this (Ainley and Bailey, 1997). Within each college may be a number of cohorts of students, each perhaps with a different culture which is an amalgam of the background of students and staff, the nature of the curriculum area within which they are working, and the college environment. For some students, going to college may be something of a negative choice; the place to go if school is unsatisfactory:

> We are very much seen as being a college you go to if you are not particularly successful at school, and we have just completed a student survey which confirms this. Now we are not sure that we think that is a great reputation to have, but it is an accurate one.

> (Curriculum Manager 1)

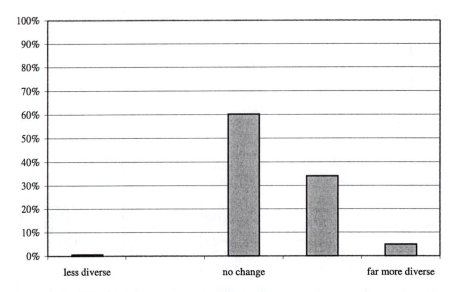

Figure 9.4 Change in diversity of ethnic origin of students from 1993 to 1999

Students come often with an unhappy experience of education and bring a variety of other difficulties, which compound the problems of providing a good educational experience.

> We have to be so much more flexible and responsive and that makes it so much more complex. I think it is much easier in HE. Perhaps it is very glib of me to say it is easier when you stream, and HE is streamed, so when you start you know the students are all of a certain ability and therefore they ought to be able, by and large, to do a lot more supported self-study. Many, many of the students who come into further education just haven't got the ability to work in their own time . . . They really haven't. A lot of them have more personal and social problems.
>
> (Curriculum Manager 2)

Students may arrive with a genuine desire to learn, or they may reflect confusion and cynicism about their future which results in an aim to use further education to fill in time, knowing they would not be able to get a job and not knowing what else to do (Ainley and Bailey, 1997). There are many students in the sector who present a great challenge to staff in finding ways to motivate them and help them to learn. There are, however, also many students who do not conform to this profile, who have been successful in their education and/or employment and are looking to further extend their skills and qualifications. The college of Principal 3 was in an economically buoyant area where jobs were plentiful. She saw the situation as one:

> where jobs are ten a penny so anybody can get a job and people move between jobs. So actually you have a very different state of affairs to where I was previously. When you don't have the prospect of getting a job, for some people

education is way of beginning to address that. When there are lots of jobs on offer, education is a way to get a better job.

If the student community were homogeneous, the issues could be addressed more easily. As it is, the diversity presents near impossible problems. Curriculum Manager 1 had tried very hard to attract and provide for students who had low levels of attainment or special learning needs. In order to provide progression routes, other sorts of provision were needed, such as access to higher education. Integrating such a range was almost unachievable:

> We are trying to encourage people who wish to go on to HE to come here on our access programmes, but at the same time I am working with local schools on the New Start Programme with groups of malcontented 15-year-olds who we strive daily to keep in some sort of line. Trying to manage all that on one campus I am beginning to think is impossible. One of our great problems in FE is the multiplicity of things that we try to do. That makes it hard to focus on what the core business or mission is, because for each of our client groups, their needs are different and I think unless you have an enormous campus where people can have distinct parts or something, or unless people are incredibly tolerant in a way I have not found before, it is not possible to do it in the same way for everybody.

One might argue that perhaps the college should choose to focus on one client group or another, to sacrifice being comprehensive in order to attain excellence for a more limited range of client groups. This was exactly what the managers were unwilling to do because to do so would involve excluding groups of people. Particularly where there were no alternatives, for example, in a rural area with only one college, managers may feel they have no choice but to try to meet diverse needs on ethical and educational grounds. Holding to this educational principle caused problems. One small example was in the reception area:

> We have had difficulties in our reception area, where our admissions are. You might have a family in there with a young child or with a 15-year-old thinking of coming to the college. At the same time, a couple of more established students come through, swearing and whatever, and the family think, 'Hang on. This is not the place we want to send our child'. That is the thing we constantly have to work with but because we believe it is important that we work with everybody and we try to satisfy everyone's needs, we are not daunted by it. We just need to find different ways of doing it.
>
> (Curriculum Manager 1)

The determination to 'find different ways of doing it' in order to remain inclusive was the theme of all of the curriculum managers, and perhaps the theme of the sector in the 1990s. The experimentation has centred on ways of addressing the increasingly diverse students within a context where resources are reducing rather than growing and where the public searchlight focuses ever more strongly on the work of the sector.

SHIFTING THE FOCUS

The requirement to accommodate the needs of a more diverse body of students is one pressure which has led to the need for a greater consideration and understanding of each student. Other pressures have also been felt. Helping students to learn how to learn has been recognized for some time as an important aim by staff working with young people and adults (Temple, 1991). As the means of studying have augmented through new technology, and as the speed of change in business and industry and society generally has increased, staff have recognized the imperative to help students respond by becoming effective autonomous learners who can use a range of resources throughout their lives to continue to increase their knowledge, understanding and skills. Finally, the need to provide education and training for more students at a reduced unit cost has enforced fewer lecturer contact hours per student (Lumby, 2000c) and, consequently, more time studying in other ways. These pragmatic and social pressures have come together simultaneously with a shift in the paradigm of education. The focus of attention has moved from the intentions of the lecturer, that is, teaching, to the experience of the student, that is, learning. Whereas previously it might have been considered appropriate and sufficient to assure the quality of teaching, there is an growing questioning of whether a connection between teaching and learning can be assumed at all:

> One of the great fallacies of late twentieth century educational policy-making at macro and micro levels, is that there is a necessary and contingent relationship between teaching and learning. Teaching can take place without any learning resulting from it and a great deal of learning is achieved without the benefit of teaching.
>
> (Davies and West-Burnham, 1997, p. 223)

Davies and West-Burnham imply that the centre of attention and development must be the learner and learning itself. This suggestion is not new. The aim to become 'learner-centred' has been evident in further education since at least the 1980s (Shackleton, 1989). However, the urgency to achieve this shift has increased and intensified the debate on just what constitutes being learner-centred. At one level, the implied shift seems to involve a transfer of power, from the teacher to the learner. No longer will students be taught as one of an undifferentiated group following a syllabus devised and controlled by the lecturer. The learner will take control of his or her learning. There are, however, problems with this definition. Thomas points out that it is to a degree misleading to suggest that the learner has or should have more power and control than is actually feasible or desirable:

> The danger of putting the learner at the centre, from whichever perspective we view the model, is that other things are seen as off-centre. This is not to say that we think that the teacher or the technology, for instance, should themselves be

at the centre. It would be a brave heretic who dared to say that programmes should be designed around what the technology could currently do or the teacher felt like teaching. A model similarly skewed in favour of the learner does not attract anything like the same opprobrium but it may be equally unrealistic, because at many levels at which the purposes of learning are determined the learner is not even present. If 'learner-centredness' is still emblazoned on the banner, though, somebody must represent the interests of the learner.

(Thomas, 1995, p. 6)

As Thomas argues, in many ways students cannot make decisions about their learning. It would not be possible to have an entirely individual qualification for every student. The content and assessment of particular programmes may be agreed at regional or national level. Industry standards must be upheld. Some common skills are needed. Students may have insufficient knowledge to make informed choices about what is appropriate preparation for a particular vocation or role. A more realistic aim may be one of shared control where the learner can influence the nature and course of his or her learning more than previously, but there is still a need for a partnership where the interests of the student are partly represented by the individual and partly by the staff who support their learning. While it is no longer acceptable for students not to be given a choice or power of negotiation, neither is a rhetoric of giving students total choice and control plausible. The real definition of 'learner-centred' appears to reside in a balance of input into designing a learning programme from both learner and teacher. This places very great demands on the skills of the lecturer:

- an ability to see the learning process in context, whether within the confines of an undergraduate class, in a company, in a region or industrial sector, or in the economic and social needs of an institution's international market
- within that context, an ability to identify the learners' needs
- an ability and willingness to respond to the learners' capabilities, expectations and uncertainties
- skill in taking into account a number of learning variables such as available technology, sources of expertise, and, yes, available funding, in the design of a learning solution which meets the purpose
- the ability to keep on doing it (Thomas, 1995, p. 1).

As Thomas points out, the above skills relate as much as anything to an attitude on the part of the lecturer and the learner. As staff are aware, such an approach is far more demanding and time-consuming (Ainley and Bailey, 1997). The reduction in funding, and therefore contact hours, militates against developing this approach. Two of the Curriculum Managers were concerned that with more students and fewer contact hours, lecturers were struggling to achieve the standards they wished in supporting learning. Not only had formal contact reduced, but the informal social contact through which relationships were built had also contracted:

There is less out of taught time interaction, so I don't observe staff going and sitting with students in the refectory in the way they would have done before
incorporation or sitting on a hot day out on the grass with their students. There
is less social activity then there used to be.

(Curriculum Manager 2)

This manager worked in a large general further education college. Another
manager who worked in an art and design college believed that the roots
of successful learning did indeed lie in the attitude and actions of each
lecturer, but working within the environment they did provided an
advantage:

I do actually talk to students a lot because of the nature of the disciplines we are
in. I could wander round the studios and talk to students and it is quite nice. I
don't think you can wander round a general further education college quite so
easily and talk to students. Students want to show you their work. There is
something physical. They have done something practical. They have done something they are proud of. They want to talk about it. It is quite difficult to get a
student on a business studies programme to talk in the same way. It is not quite
the same somehow.

(Curriculum Manager 3)

The interaction with individual students was very strong because the medium of the students' work, a physical product, provided the vehicle for
frequent individual communication. The situation varied from college to college, but the need for individual attention was a constant: 'It's this thing about
'big is beautiful', sometimes. I don't necessarily agree with that. I think every
individual needs to be known and to belong and to feel part of . . . I think
whatever their age they need to be nurtured and cared for, more so in a big
college' (Curriculum Manager 2). In this case, the manager felt that the reduction in course hours meant that students did not always get the nurturing they
needed and used to get. Satisfaction with the current situation varied, and
colleges were experimenting with ways to achieve the same care but perhaps
in different ways, for example, through tutoring systems. In the face of imper-
meable resistance, Curriculum Manager 2 gave the only directive she had ever
issued, rather than negotiating a way forward, that there should be a
timetabled one-hour tutorial each week for all full-time students. This
instruction was accompanied by a great deal of staff development on counselling and tutorial skills. The process of introducing considerable tutor time
in GNVQ courses at Loughborough College, approximately 40 per cent of
available hours, also met resistance (Middlewood, Coleman and Lumby,
1999). The move was eventually accepted because of evidence of the
improvement in students' performance. Staff are often reluctant to transfer
time from vocational education to tutorials. Helping staff find the time and
commitment to focus on the individual as a learner and as a person emerged
as a priority for colleges. The solutions may vary but the need for 'nurturing'
remained invariable.

FLEXIBLE LEARNING

Colleges need to find ways of meeting the dual aim of helping students become autonomous learners and reducing costs. The issue is not just one of coping with reduced funding. New ways of learning and assessing demand increased resource levels. As Curriculum Manager 4 explained, there is a large resource difference between bringing 16 students into a college and having a lecturer teach them as a group for an hour and sending a lecturer out to support and assess for NVQs in 16 different work placements. Colleges therefore suffer the double whammy of greater resource needs and lower funding. The use of more flexible learning has seemed to offer hope of meeting both educational and financial needs. Flexible learning has displaced open learning as the term indicating the range of teaching and learning technologies open to colleges:

> Open learning came to imply any situation in which all those features and characteristics of learning programmes and systems which reduce opportunities and access, are identified and modified to avoid closure . . .
>
> The more recent term 'flexible learning' appears to be a way of recognizing the myriad possibilities open to educators, as new ideas, new procedures and new media appear.
>
> (Gillham, 1995, p. 54)

Temple (1991) argues that the name given to vehicles for learning is not necessarily indicative of the nature of activity, 'class teaching' being possibly very interactive and negotiated while 'independent study' might be a grind through worksheets with little interaction or learner control. The important element in defining the nature of the work is the degree of involvement of the learner in deciding what is learned and how, and the degree of support offered for that process. This is not to suggest complete control by the learner. As argued above, 'learner-centred' means a partnership between learner and teacher, not the disappearance of the latter. The curriculum managers were also very clear that the degree of autonomy, the amount of face-to-face contact and support and the appropriateness of ICT, all varied according to the nature of the student and his or her programme. In the case of one college, a general policy was not to reduce face-to-face teaching. Curriculum Manager 1 explained that his college had not taken that route and had 'quite deliberately developed a curriculum model which is not based on reducing the number of taught hours'. This was related to the nature of students in the college, many of whom were studying at Level 1 and needed much personal support. Curriculum Manager 7 had similar doubts about the appropriateness of computer-based learning for certain people. He had doubts about the government's apparent intention to use ICT as a learning vehicle for University for Industry (UfI) students:

Within the UfI they are looking hard at widening participation for the 'hard to get to' people who have failed in the educational system, and yet they seem to think they are going to get progress which won't require so much face-to-face. These students are going to be the ones that need more face-to-face interaction so even in learning centres under UfI we are looking at having permanent members of staff to give face-to-face interaction.

The assumption that computers can replace lecturers is not viable. At the same time, it is clear that many managers do see the advent of ICT technologies as having huge potential and importance for learning in their college:

> It may well be that over the next three or four years with the new software packages that are coming out that colleges like this disappear. There might be no need for them. Everybody will be able to do it over the Internet. The only time you meet your fellow students and staff is at graduation.
>
> (Principal 5)

When pressed on whether this was a serious belief, the principal reiterated his belief that 'within a surprisingly short time' some programme areas would be run by electronic means. However, in contrast to this view, generally there was caution in admitting too great a change in the amount of face-to-face teaching available for the most challenging students, but overall a movement to less teacher contact and more use of a range of learning technologies was acknowledged. Encouraging autonomous learning did not mean abrogating responsibility. Curriculum Manager 3 was working very hard to improve the quality of what he termed 'non-human support', that is, paper- and computer-based resources. Curriculum Managers 2 and 4 were particularly concerned to use the full range of staff, instructors, assessors and technicians in a way which enriched learning rather than compromised quality. In one college lecturers feared their role was becoming redundant as the whole curriculum went on the intranet. Curriculum Manager 7 was anxious they be encouraged and supported to identify what they could offer the learner which was unique and valuable and which needed to be retained. The question for most was one of balance:

> Information communication technology is very, very, important to our future, as is resource-based learning, as is flexible learning, as is accreditation of prior learning, as is the use of assignments and projects and vocational education and training and formal lectures and discussions. I think what I am saying is that our approach is one of a variety of approaches which gives us a balanced curriculum offer and a balance in terms of delivery styles.
>
> (Curriculum Manager 4)

This manager made the point that if you walked through the college you would see a very wide range of activities, each offering different benefits to the student. He also pointed out that if the college did not exploit the use of ICT and offer it to students, then other, possibly private, providers would.

VOCATIONALIZING THE CURRICULUM

A concern that emerged from the managers interviewed was the vocationalizing of the curriculum. Armitage *et al.* (1999, pp. 25–6) state the case:

> Mainstream education is dominated by the vocational themes of a work-related, often competence-based curriculum, the introduction of pre-vocational or personal and social development under the guise of 'employability', and above all by the supposed need to adapt to a life in a new 'communication' or 'technological' age. Education as a whole has become vocationalized in the sense that the connection between the world of work and education is seen as necessary rather than contingent.

Further evidence is provided by Ainley and Bailey (1997) of lecturers' concern that the need to focus on providing what the employer or potential employer required militated against a focus on the needs of the individual student. The view that emerged from the curriculum managers was partly supportive of this and partly different. Some agreed that students' curriculum might be diminished by an overemphasis on vocational aspects. However, one expressed the view that the emphasis on vocational aspects was to the benefit of disaffected students. In an area of high unemployment and low educational attainment, schoolchildren came to the college for vocational education. The fact that both they and their parents could see the relevance engaged both. The result was an improvement in attendance and performance not only in vocational training in the college but also in their broader education in their schools. However, this was a sole example. Other managers were concerned by the narrowing curriculum. Curriculum Manager 2 had as a primary aim: 'to integrate the whole notion of vocational skills, academic skills and other skills into one experience. I am still a great believer in the entitlement curriculum. It saddens me when staff start to emphasize pure vocational education without looking at the wider educational picture for that person'. The implication here is that lecturers themselves are complicit in displacing broader education. This may be entirely understandable. They are held to account for results and therefore may be constrained by the industry-led standards and awarding body requirements. However, this did not appear to be the whole story. There were two other issues that emerged. One was the adequacy of training received by lecturers and the other was commitment to their own craft:

> There are lots and lots and lots of lecturers whose experience of being taught was by a craftsman. Many of them left school at 16 or even younger. Their experience was being trained by a craftsman or another trainer often in a very formal and disciplined way, so they know their industries very well but trying to get them to understand the whole thing about broader education and entitlement is very hard.
>
> (Curriculum Manager 2)

Seventeen per cent of lecturers, nearly one in five, enter further education with no teaching qualifications at all (Rudden, 1999). Additionally, they may have a commitment to the standards to which they were trained. Many were trained in a very disciplined way by craftspeople and are proud of their own vocational skills. They want to pass them on. Examples were catering, where some staff were still very committed to teaching silver service, and construction, where staff wished to pass on traditional building techniques. Younger staff fresh from industry felt the world had moved on and that such skills were not in response to student or industry need but a replication of the lecturer's own training for a previous and different situation. Scott (1989) suggests that educational organizations have four types of accountability:

- to the public/government
- to the market
- professional – to students
- to culture.

The last-named accountability may be very important in further education, as lecturers feel an obligation to pass on skills. The concern of some of the curriculum managers is that this was in contention with accountability to students, i.e. that the lecturers' desire to pass on skills might override a more individual assessment of student need. Such tension takes us back to the issue of balance within 'learner-centred'. Where is the appropriate balance between lecturers controlling the curriculum from their greater knowledge and experience, and students controlling the learning in response to their individual need?

WORKING TOGETHER

Gillham (1995, p. 56) notes that as long ago as 1976 the consequences of innovation were known:

- an increase in *workload*
- a period of *acute anxiety*
- feelings of *confusion and disorientation*

Certainly in the area of changes in curriculum delivery and teaching methodology, this analysis remains valid, except that increasingly, innovators have had to deal with a fifth consequence:

- the manifestation of disbelief and cynicism about the innovations and the motives of those concerned with it.

All of these effects are well documented in the literature (Elliott, 1996; Ainley and Bailey, 1997; Randle and Brady, 1997a). The cynicism mentioned perhaps relates to the fact that the curriculum does not exist in isolation. It is owned and fought over by groups of people who accrue or lose power in relation to whether their curriculum orientation is adopted, their programme area grows or contracts. Proctor and Wright (1995) describe how over a number of years staff in their organization had tried to isolate and attribute low status to the innovation of using workshops for English. There was competition for ownership of and credit for innovation. The struggle to introduce workshops was sustained and bitter. The curriculum is a field of battle. This comes as no surprise. Change provokes resistance (Lumby, 1998). Resistance is sometimes enacted through criticism of individuals or groups who are accused of not acting in the best interests of students. One of the characteristics of the public debate on the innovation of the post-compulsory curriculum has been the tendency for blame to be attributed to single groups. Managers of the sector are blamed for eroding quality and betraying educational values (Elliott and Crossley, 1997; Randle and Brady, 1997a, 1997b; Hartley, 1997). Lecturers are blamed for clinging rigidly to outdated methods (Ellis, 1989). Students are seen as unsatisfactory in their attitude by some lecturers (Ainley and Bailey, 1997). As Thomas (1995, p. 2) asserts, the responsibility lies with all: 'I think it would be misplaced to lay the blame for slow progress on the, variously, unimaginative management, a teaching profession resistant to change, or the conservative expectations of students, though they all have some responsibility.'

The need is for all parties to be self-critical in their assessment of their contribution to supporting learning. Lecturers have legitimate concerns about upholding standards, the deskilling of their profession and maintaining quality. Managers must find ways of improving education within resource constraints. However, both are not immune to arguing a case using 'student benefit' as a way of legitimizing an argument for action which is for their own benefit. The result is mutual suspicion, with lecturers and managers distrusting the motives of each other:

> Health and Social Care will argue to the nth degree that a 16-hour course is not appropriate. 'It needs to be much, much longer and so on' . . . Now that could be about perpetuating their jobs because they are so down in student numbers . . . So there is an example of having to work through what it is really about and I think that's probably true in a lot of other areas in the college.
> (Curriculum Manager 2)

This suspicion is met with equal distrust on the part of lecturers who may believe that curriculum innovation is purely about cost-cutting, not educational need, and there are indeed examples in this volume of actions which have been taken purely to cut costs. The restructuring described by Curriculum Manager 3 in Chapter 7, 'Changing structures and roles', was undertaken to cut costs by removing management posts, not to benefit students.

Finding the answer to such problems is not easy or short term. Managing curriculum change is a cultural process which may take years. Principal 3 believed that one way of changing behaviour to build trust was to provide a role model of behaviour throughout the organization. If the principal acted in a way which was self-seeking or bullying, that behaviour was likely to be replicated by others. If the contrary were offered, openness and corporateness, then those qualities might be seeded to grow in the organization. Leadership, particularly of the principals and senior managers, provided a model of ethics and relationships which had tremendous influence. The issue of 'one staff' was also important in trying to move away from affiliations and power struggles:

> One of the things that I have been keen to do is to blur the distinction of what we tend to think of as teaching and support staff. Increasingly we are seeing the use of people who are not teachers as such working within the curriculum. It is my dream to get away from this distinction entirely, that what we are all in the business of doing is supporting the learners and we all do it slightly differently, and some will spend more time with learners than others but basically the core business is supporting learning.
>
> (Curriculum Manager 1)

Of course, lecturers will want to deter the erosion of salaries caused by lecturing being done by those who are not paid as lecturers. Managers will continue to feel the responsibility to achieve learning for the largest number of students at the lowest cost, even at times to the detriment of lecturers' conditions. Tensions will remain, but the vision of a mutual recognition of contribution, of equal value placed on the work of lecturers, guidance counsellors, youth workers, IT facilitators, assessors, etc. is one which may contribute to a gradual achievement of greater co-operation and trust. A range of factors, including leadership, the gradual move to one staff and the determination to find different ways of doing things to meet student needs, have the potential to lessen the micropolitical tensions and allow all staff genuinely to work to become learner-centred.

10

WORKING WITH EMPLOYERS

THE ECONOMIC CONTEXT

Long-term projections of the skills needed to develop the economy have for some time predicted an increasing demand for higher level skills. For example, over a decade ago Handy (1989) quotes a study estimating that 70 per cent of all jobs in Europe in 2000 would require cerebral skills. The debate on rising skill demands and the disenfranchisement of those who do not have such skills is so well rehearsed that it has lost its impact of immediacy. Yet the implications for colleges remain profound, as they are the organizations with the national responsibility for upskilling particularly those in danger of being left behind, those whom compulsory schooling has failed, those who are in low-skill jobs or unemployed. They also share with universities the responsibility of developing the higher-level skills that will be so critical to the economy.

As well as an increase in the level of skills required, other macro changes have implications for the types of skill needed. The traditional craft and manufacturing base of the economy has been severely eroded, undermining one of the historical foundations of the sector's mission. In its place has arrived the 'knowledge economy', centring on service industries, which emphasizes the importance of education as key to competitiveness (James and Clark, 1997). Both employers and colleges are well aware of this change. A DfEE (1998) skills needs survey showed that 68 per cent of employers thought the skill level required in a typical employee was rising and that 15 per cent felt there was a significant shortfall in the level of skills of their current employees. The cry that entrants to employment have not been adequately prepared by their education and training has become a repeated refrain echoing down the decades of the 1980s and 1990s. Colleges have been left in no doubt of the level of dissatisfaction by government surveys and reports which communicate the concerns of business and industry and glumly present tables comparing the qualification and skills levels in the UK with those in other countries in Europe and elsewhere (DfEE, 1998). It is in intermediate-level vocational qualifications that there is the greatest shortfall, precisely the area where further education is the main arena.

The government for its part has responded with 'a complex amalgam of ideas, policies, legal and regulatory structures and practical endeavours' (Skilbeck *et al.*, 1994, p. vii). It attempts to introduce coherence while at the same time, on its own admission, contributing to the confusion. For example, the DfEE (1998) acknowledges that the complexity of the funding system is not understood and may be distorting provision away from the needs of the labour market. The government can, however, be relied on for regular exhortations to the sector to become more responsive and flexible (ibid.). It is very keen that colleges should gain more funds from business and industry thereby lessening the demand on the public purse. Consequently, it is equally regular in its exhortations to industry to invest in human resource development.

EMPLOYERS' ATTITUDES

Most employers of over 25 people provide off-the-job training for their employees, though the majority of this may be in areas such as health and safety and induction (Employment Department Group, 1999). Companies which employ fewer than 20 people, (and 96 per cent of businesses employ fewer than 20 [Hughes, 1996]), are notoriously reluctant to provide training. Overall, employers have concerns about the cost of training, and the perceived negative impact of staff leaving when trained or of acquiring unrealistic expectations (DfEE, 1998). There is also an absence of 'robust evidence on the benefits of training to employers' (Employment Department Group, 1999, p. 35). The interviews provided confirmation of the unwillingness of employers to pay for training in the north-east, the north-west and the 'supposedly affluent south-east' (Finance Manager 6) partly because of the cost itself and partly because colleges were in competition with free or lower-cost training provided by other government agencies. In one South East region college, rather than expecting to pay for training, employers expected the college to pay them for loss of productivity in releasing their employee for a day (Finance Manager 6). It seems reasonable to assume that such problems span all regions, given that the three identified above include both economically disadvantaged and buoyant areas. However, despite employers' reluctance, the training provided by colleges to employers is a multimillion pound business targeted by colleges as one of the main market segments for which they wish to cater (Davies, 1999).

Colleges have to work hard to earn such funds. Employers are becoming ever more demanding in where and how they train:

> More and more we are coming across firms who do not want to send people to college to train. They want them to train at their desktop and they want the materials there, and they want interaction with mentors rather than teachers. We are spending a lot of time and effort on trying to develop these systems. I think that is the single biggest threat to the college's sustainability. If we do not have a full quiver of arrows of different methodologies of responding to learning needs we will lose students to this type of learning method. People can pass their Legal Executive exams at their desk now, having an hour's study over their lunch time, and then get back to work. This means people in the firm feel they have control. There is no worry that staff are bunking off. We are finding more and more that organizations are looking for the means of training without having to release people.
>
> (Finance Manager 9)

Where employers are prepared to release employees to go off site for training, the demand is for training which is ever more tightly shaped to specific individual and company needs, and therefore likely to be for smaller groups of individuals, raising issues of scale and, consequently, economic viability:

> One of the problems we have in our area is that the vast majority of companies are very, very small and therefore cannot afford to buy bespoke training for a number which would make it economically viable for the college to operate. So we put on a lot of open courses where employers can send one or two people perhaps.
>
> (Curriculum Manager 5)

Clearly there is a range of important strategic and curriculum issues implied in the two interview extracts above, including the planning process, staff development, investment in ICT infrastructure, materials development, and structure and roles to embed and sustain development.

COLLEGES' INTERFACE WITH EMPLOYERS

Colleges' involvement with employers is significant. The sector is the largest single provider of skills updating (Hughes and Kypri, 1998), though the scale of activity varies widely amongst colleges. A survey of the number of employers with which each college had contact found that the number of contacts per college annually ranged from seven to 3,720 (James and Clark, 1997). The income achieved is equally wide-ranging, with 40 per cent of colleges generating over £250,000 per annum from cost-recovery courses for employers, with a further 10 per cent generating over £1 million. However, for the majority of colleges this revenue amounts to less than 20 per cent of their total income (Davies, 1999). Being responsive, that is, being an institution which 'assesses and attempts to meet the needs of students, employers and the community' (FEFC, 1996, p. 3) is of importance to colleges. In the survey undertaken for this book, 14 per cent of colleges mentioned responsiveness as an opportunity for the future, but this was not a high priority being rated sixth in importance. Similarly, only 6 per cent of colleges saw a failure to be responsive as a threat to their future. This confirms previous evidence that, whatever the rhetoric, many colleges consider responding to employers as marginal (Hughes, 1996) and a low priority for development (FEFC, 1996). The assessment of marginal importance is reciprocated by employers who equally do not accord great importance to the contribution of colleges. In many regions, the FE college is one of the top five largest employers (James and Clark, 1997) but is not accorded the status of other similar size employers by the business community. Colleges are seen as 'second order players' (Hughes and Kypri, 1998, p. 8) and regional strategic discussion on training infrastructure or regeneration is 'the economic development party to which FE was not invited' (James and Clark, 1997, p. 15). Colleges have a poor image which may be just that, an image which is in contradiction to a successful track record, or may indeed reflect reality, being justified by a history of inflexibility and intransigence. It is hard to unravel the source of this mutual cycle of lack of status and attention. What appears to be the case, despite mission statements to the contrary, is that colleges may not have a sufficient focus on employers, and employers may not sufficiently recognize and value what colleges can offer.

As with all negative relationships, there is disadvantage to both parties. Thorne (1995) argues that learning in the workplace and away from the workplace are equally necessary in the process of vocational education. Experience of doing a job without reflection may not result in learning. Equally learning in the college without experience of applying what is learned in the work environment means that students will miss the knowledge being 'transformed by the process of being used' (ibid., p. 78). There is a symbiosis which is necessary for the full potential of learning to be reached. The perspectives of each party may differ. Employers may be concerned with immediately applicable skills. Colleges may wish to take more of a career-long view. Some mutual accommodation has to be reached. Employers are more likely to be engaged if they are convinced of the relevance of the training. They are usually consulted on curriculum design, but the typical advisory body may work as a rubber-stamping process, rather than being truly dynamic. Employers are often not involved in evaluation of programmes FEFC, (1996). This picture was confirmed by Curriculum Manager 7:

> A lot of colleges have advisory boards but they are asking them to rubber stamp what they are doing instead of really saying to them, 'If this was a clean slate, what would you really want to do? How could we make this better for you?' We all do evaluations of programmes but we are not really getting employers in at

the early stages . . . I think the key message is really to bring them on board and talk to them.

The mutual lack of involvement undermines the relationship, with colleges giving scant weight to the importance of learning on the job and employers unimpressed by the training colleges can offer.

Colleges may adopt a very reactive approach to employers. Curriculum Manager 7 distinguished between responding to immediate market gaps and income-generating opportunities rather than working proactively, getting to know the business, analysing needs and linking training to a business plan. The latter was her preferred way of working but it was not typical in the college. However, there was also a perception amongst the interviewees that where colleges got it right, quality would attract and retain employers: 'Although some employers may have left us for a year, some even more, we've found that by and large they always come back to the quality that I think they can rely on to get from further education' (Curriculum Manager 4).

Further education has the skills and facilities to work successfully with many businesses and industry, but there is a range of ways in which the relationship between colleges and employers is often unsatisfactory. Breaking the cycle will involve moving the response to employers away from the margins, and therefore managing issues of planning and structure is particularly critical.

PLANNING

The basis of good planning is good information. As discussed in detail in Chapter 5 on marketing and Chapter 8 on information and communication, such information is lacking and its internal communication is problematic. For information to be of use in responding to employers' current and potential needs, it must be detailed and combine local, regional, national and industry sector data. While colleges may have access to the range of data, most do not have the skills and resources to transform it into the sort of synthesized information required. Consequently, planning takes place, if not quite in a vacuum, in something rather like it. An insight into the planning process was provided by interviewees. Three of the Curriculum Managers interviewed had specific responsibility for managing the curriculum in relation to employers. Two worked in specialist units and one managed a project to develop work with employers. They explained how the planning for their work was undertaken within a whole-college perspective. In the case of Curriculum Manager 6, his role was: 'not a stated role, but it is a role to provide a series of activities that can be a catalyst for change. It sounds as though it is almost *ad hoc* but it's worse. It's pretty chaotic at times'. This is not to say that the unit was not achieving excellent things, but the day-to-day experience was, in his words, worse than *ad hoc*. Curriculum Manager 5 was concerned at what he saw as the college view of this area of work, as 'about short-term income'. He considered that there was an underlying absence of understanding of the wider and longer-term benefits of working with employers:

> The benefits of doing work of this sort are obviously far wider. I think the people that get involved in the teaching can actually learn as much as they impart by talking to people, seeing what is going on in modern business and seeing how they are operating, what problems there are. Hopefully that sort of information can be fed back into the academic provision. I also think that getting people in to do short, sharp training can be a shop window for the rest of the college. If we can get people in, deliver a very good course and get them interested in further learning, then that should have a knock-on effect back into mainstream involvement. So I think there are a whole lot of other benefits that could come from this sort of work rather than just pure income. One of my most pressing concerns for the future is that we take a rather narrow view of what the unit's about and we need perhaps to take a wider view.

This narrow view translated into a marginalization of planning the work of the unit at a strategic level:

> My view of the planning process is that it tends to be very much concerned with FEFC income and, although we have general statements about increasing the amount of business in the full cost arena, I don't think it does much more than get added on to the general income targets. I don't think we plan on an annual basis to say, 'Well, if we are going to have this amount of business, how on earth are we going to resource it?' It tends to be a wish at the start of the year, or when we go through the planning process, and if that wish does become a reality, then it's 'God, how are we going to cope with it?'

This manager makes the important point of the necessity to plan resources of staff and facilities to do the work as it comes in. Unfortunately, in his experience work comes in erratically, either very little or far too much simultaneously. Consequently, staffing and accommodation were problematic. He had dedicated space, but leaving high-quality rooms empty when there were no courses on was not acceptable, so other classes moved in at such times. When work arrived, they had to move out, 'so while we were meeting the needs of one lot of people we were actually not doing a great job for another'. There is no easy answer to this issue, but this college had resolved it in part by making sure that high-quality dedicated space was available at need.

Planning staffing was also critical. Curriculum Manager 5 negotiated the use of staff on an *ad hoc* basis. These were part-time, either in the sense of either being people who worked in the college for a limited number of hours each week, or lecturers whose major commitment was elsewhere, but who were released to give designated hours to working with employers. He argued that long term this would not be enough to build a sustainable business. 'To substantially grow a business in my view you do need some dedicated staff to carry that forward.' Curriculum Manager 6 had a strong dedicated team and a similar system of staff released from their major commitment by use of college funds made available for this purpose. Curriculum Manager 7 used project funding to acquire additional staff, some of whom were new staff and some of whom were released from their full-time college roles. In all cases, staffing was therefore a mix of full-time and part-time, the latter being either new staff brought in or permanent staff released for part of their time. The issue of how to staff such work is critical and raises structural questions.

STRUCTURES

Hughes and Kypri (1998) make the point that having a specialist unit which does excellent work with employers does not necessarily improve the image of the college as a whole. The real challenge is to embed changed attitudes and practice throughout the organization. The issue of embedding curriculum innovation is, of course, far wider than working with employers, and confronts managers attempting to improve the curriculum in whatever area. It is perhaps more stark in working with employers because success requires changing to accommodate a business and industry culture which is quite different to that of education. In terms of achieving such a change, there is a choice of whether to use specialist staff in a dedicated part of the structure, or to use staff throughout the college in an integrated way, or a combination of both. Such work will not be appropriate to all staff (Hughes, 1996), nor is there much incentive for many:

> Mainstream staff don't want to know. They have no energy left to think about running a Saturday course for example, because they know how long it takes to prepare. It might not recruit. It takes a lot of time and effort and the system here doesn't allow them to get a direct reward as they don't get any of the income. There is no incentive for them to do it.
>
> (Curriculum Manager 2)

Even were a financial incentive made available, as is the case in some colleges as described in Chapter 4 on managing finance, staff are tired and, balancing the possibility of additional students and income if the course recruits, against the certainty of more work whether it recruits or not, may willingly relinquish such gambles. It seems the case that a focal point of energy and commitment is needed to galvanize others. Interviewees provided examples of different ways this issue had been resolved. In the case of the project manager, she had been given funds to carry forward work with employers but, as a new member of staff outside the mainstream structure, felt isolated: 'It has been very difficult. I have often felt like I am on the Isle of Wight and everybody else is on mainland England' (Curriculum Manager 7). The issue of linking with the rest of the college quickly became very important. It seemed that using permanent staff for this innovative work may have been a better structure. However, this was not necessarily the case. A permanent member of staff was recruited but immediately she changed role, her status changed: 'I can already see that she is beginning to get cast aside and starting to come to the Isle of Wight. She has taken the ferry I am afraid. I am just hoping she has got a return ticket.'

The metaphor of an island to which people sail when removed from their usual role is a powerful one. Linking island to mainland remains problematic. The existence of an offshore piece of land raises micropolitical currents. Mainstream lecturers fear that the island people are trying to take over their jobs. There are attempts at conquest. Curriculum Manager 7 described the power struggle that took place as people tried to annex the island:

> Sometimes you get this power thing with people feeling that 'It is part of the business sector so it should be under me', or 'It is international so it should be under me'. So I have had this dog and bone situation where I have been torn in two directions . . . If you've got something that is good, if you've got something that is wonderful, and this is a star, you've got lots of people wanting it, trying to get involved in it and trying to gatecrash your party.

She also found people withholding information, trying to go round the project by contacting employers independently and setting up provision in competition. The project has achieved a great deal, but the experience has been uncomfortable. Despite strenuous efforts to involve staff through advisory groups and secondment of individuals, communication and ownership remain partial:

> I will continue to go to Programme Leader meetings and they are fine, but I noticed that is where the bottleneck is. The information goes down as far as Programme Leaders but there it stops and it doesn't get down any further . . . It is also difficult when you have lots of part-time members of staff who will have stuff imposed on them because they just haven't got time to get involved with the development quite often. I haven't got a magic wand. It's a culture change.
> (Curriculum Manager 7)

The knowledge of what is going on remains at the upper reaches of the hierarchy. The majority of staff hear little and, in any case, have little time or inclination to be involved.

If the specialist unit is the island, then maybe the solution is to keep all activities on the mainland, i.e. within the main structures of the college, but this raises problems of its own. First, the fact that staff are permanent and within mainstream structures does not protect them from isolation. They can be viewed as 'an innovative élite' (Curriculum Manager 7) and bring with them a history which in itself may be a barrier. Such staff were described by Curriculum Manager 7: 'They have been there (in the faculty) for years and years and years but they have more difficulty than I do because they've got baggage that goes back. They were Programme Leaders and they may or may not have got on with people in the past.' Even if such staff have very positive relationships and do an excellent job, tensions are set up as other managers 'see this as losing their best people or their best people have been stolen'. There is also a cost to students:

> I have to say that I am constantly reminded by middle managers and Heads of School that taking their best staff away from the students does have a cost. I think that's a cost that we sometimes fail to quantify. Taking a first-class practitioner out of the classroom and giving them development work to do, which then results in someone who is less capable taking their role, does have an impact upon the students' performance and achievement.
>
> (Curriculum Manager 4)

Despite possible resentments and educational concerns about the continuity for students, Curriculum Manager 4 was convinced that it was vital to use mainstream staff in any development work:

> I think if you separate it entirely from the curriculum that is creating a problem because the curriculum staff have not been involved in it and therefore might feel reluctant to incorporate whatever the project produces or recommends. I think staff involvement in these things is really, really important. Although they all complain about lack of time, they appreciate being involved in projects like this which are obviously tapping into their expertise. I think it is part of the general strategy to get staff involved.

A combined approach of using specialist staff to provide focus and direction, but working largely through mainstream staff may provide a compromise. Curriculum Manager 5, himself the manager of a specialist unit, had tried to build such a partnership:

> If for example, an employer contact comes in from me but involves a technical area, I would actually pull the appropriate person out and we would go and make a joint visit. The same would apply if someone else gets an initial contact then they normally take me out on the visit as well. Partnership is a very good way of seeing it.

Achieving such an integrated approach can be based on *ad hoc* personal relationships when the scale of the work remains small. If it grows, then more formal arrangements may be necessary, such as an account manager for each company to ensure a co-ordinated response. Additionally, strong support will be needed from senior managers to embed growth in the strategic plan together with resources to support it. Whatever the publicity states, if the reality is that working with employers remains at the margin of planning and structure, the attitude is likely to be reciprocated by employers who will see what the college has to offer as of marginal significance.

INNOVATING TEACHING AND LEARNING

If Finance Manager 9's experience is common in finding companies are more reluctant to release staff to train off site and that they require ICT-based solutions, then there is a need for a high level of innovation in teaching and learning in responding to employers. Senge (1993, p. 6) distinguishes between invention, when something new is created, and innovation 'when it can be replicated reliably on a meaningful scale at practical costs'. The most forward-looking work on ICT in the curriculum in FE is currently at the stage of invention rather than innovation, owing to the problems of embedding new work relating to the structural issues discussed in the previous section. Innovation then is something which 'creates a new dimension of performance' (Hesslebein, 1999, p. 13) consistently throughout the organization. Colleges may have a limited capacity to achieve innovation. Senge (1993) believes that business is the centre of innovation because it has greater freedom than the public sector and, by using the quantitative measure of profit, is more easily able to evaluate the impact of innovation. Certainly it is true that the further education sector is constrained by limited resources and by legislated rules of action. Additionally, the squeeze on resources has drained capacity:

> There has been a reduction in the capacity of organizations to respond. You've only got to look into the FE sector and see that about 30 per cent of colleges have made large-scale redundancies, cost-saving initiatives, employ people at lower levels than they would have done in days gone by, a leak of IT staff from the sector into the private sector, lack of ability to pay for true business support activity, a whole range of issues.
>
> (Curriculum Manager 6)

Building capacity in such circumstances is very difficult.

Another barrier may be the structure of colleges. Morgan (1986) suggests that segmentation and a mechanistic approach are fundamental barriers to innovation. Colleges are certainly segmented in structure, by faculty, by site, by programme area. They are forced to be mechanistic in their approach by government requirements. For example, Curriculum Manager 6 believed his college was 'increasingly bureaucratized with self-assessment reports. We have had nine quality reviews in the college over the last six months'. The focus of staff on issues other than curriculum development, particularly finance, and its detrimental effect on curriculum development, is widely reported (Lucas, 1998; Lumby, 1996, 2000c). Further evidence of the distraction emerged from the interviews:

> It feels more difficult. I think people in this college always do remember the students, and that's one of the strengths of the college, but their energy is deflected on to things to do with – 'I am designing this course on how many units it is going to bring in' – so that there is a distortion and a deflection of energy because of the pressures that incorporation brought. People are so conscious now of units

and finance and being good managers in a more holistic sense, that the energy for curriculum design and development is not always there.

(Curriculum Manager 2)

Time and energy are therefore in short supply. There may be barriers to curriculum innovation at a deeper level also. Senge (1993) quotes Drucker's argument that innovation is often preceded by abandonment, letting go of what is no longer relevant or no longer works. Abandonment is a word redolent of emotion, and is relevant to innovation in the FE curriculum because the move from, for example, face-to-face class teaching to ICT-supported study feels like abandonment of traditional practice and values. The latter may define the basic identity of the member of staff and when such values are challenged:

> The fear of loss which this entails thus often generates a reaction that may be out of all proportion to the importance of the issue when viewed from a more detached point of view. This unconscious dynamic may help explain why some organizations have been unable to cope with the changing demands of their environment, and why there is often so much unconscious resistance to change in organizations.

(Morgan, 1986, p. 221)

Innovation is therefore an emotional process as well as a technical one. The range of factors inhibiting staff from developing the full range of teaching technologies has been discussed in the section on flexible learning in the previous chapter. The result is very circumscribed success in some areas, with limited take-up of new ways of learning (Hughes, 1996). It may also be, as suggested in the previous chapter, that although government and employers may believe that ICT is the answer to more flexible learning, it may be less widely appropriate than they imagine. Certainly staff need to develop the full range of possibilities to meet different needs, achieving a balanced curriculum offering which harnesses the advantages of different delivery modes.

Attempts to encourage innovation have focused largely on providing resources to release staff and give them time. There have been additional efforts, for example, to release the creativity of staff:

> We are actually going to go away and look at the teams and how we manage and try to bring innovation back into how they work. They will then take that back to their teams. I started it recently with my own Senior Management Team where we had a problem to solve. I gave them a completely bizarre project and asked them to try to think of ways in which they might solve it, which they were very suspicious of. I was trying to explain to them that you don't always have to cut the cake in the same way. You can actually try something entirely different and end up with the same answers.

(Principal 3)

For this principal, the return to the development of teaching and learning was the highest priority, and as part of that, unlocking the creativity and innovation within staff.

LOOKING TO THE FUTURE

Curriculum Manager 7 believed her college was fairly typical in not having shifted practice very much:

> I think the college as a whole is very similar to other colleges. The staff aren't always looking at customer service. They are still being product led, but we are trying to change things with the use of ICT to make it a more flexible system. From that point of view, we are making the system and the accessibility more flexible to meet the needs of SMEs (small to medium-sized enterprises) but I can't honestly say that that is in response to SMEs. That is in response to the environment in which we work. This is what government says we will do or Europe says we will do.

For this manager, some progress had been made in achieving greater flexibility and accessibility, but this development was overlaid on basically unchanged attitudes. Rather than being market led, colleges were developing programmes when UK or European funding allowed. This area of college management is a good example of where practice has changed to a degree but culture change has not followed. The underlying values and attitudes are largely untouched. Colleges will need to reconsider their perspective on employers, and view them as so much more than just another source of income.

11

EVOLVING THE CULTURE

DEFINING CULTURE

Culture may be recognized by managers as a critical element of how organizations function, but they have difficulty capturing just what it is. Schein (1997) recounts his realization that, when discussing culture with managers, they ascribe completely different meanings to the term, or may even deny any involvement with it, but cannot say what the 'it' is. Researchers have tried to overcome the semantic confusion either by providing very simple definitions 'the way we do things around here' (Deal and Kennedy, 1982) or by more complex characterisations:

> A pattern of shared basic assumptions that the group learned as it solved its problems of external adaptation and internal integration, that has worked well enough to be considered valid, and, therefore, to be taught to new members as the correct way to perceive, think and feel in relation to those problems.
>
> (Schein, 1997, p. 12)

If the 'shared basic assumptions' were known to all, then discovering the culture of an organization would be relatively simple. In fact, the issue of understanding culture seems to bear comparison with complexity theory. This branch of science is founded on the hypothesis that apparently complex or even random systems are actually the result of simple rules, if only they can be uncovered, 'Surface complexity arising out of deep simplicity' (Lewin, 1997, p. 14). Similarly, culture may be embedded in the complexity of myriad actions and artefacts within any one organization, but is the expression of an underlying simplicity, a 'set of core beliefs and assumptions' (Johnson, 1993, p. 61). Understanding culture in any college is therefore a question of decoding the signals to arrive at the central beliefs of the organization.

This apparently satisfactory statement is, however, undermined by the fact that organizations have not one culture but many cultures, 'multiple realities' (Morgan, 1986, p. 133). Within colleges, different sites or different curriculum areas may constitute distinct cultures, resulting in a kaleidoscope of cultural signals relating to the culture of different groupings of people. The organizational culture may also sit within external cultures such as the national culture. Hofstede's (1997) work on characterizing behaviour in different countries in relationship to leadership, defines four different spectra against which national norms can be measured. What becomes clear is that there are expectations which mean that the sort of leadership and followership which might be the assumed norm in North America would not necessarily be so in Hong Kong, and vice versa. Reading the cultural runes therefore becomes highly problematic, trying to relate myriad embodiments of culture to the many different groups of people and different levels. However, Johnson believes that, despite this, a single core set of beliefs does exist in each organization and can be discerned:

> Whilst individual managers may hold quite varying sets of beliefs about many different aspects of that organizational world, there is likely to exist at some level a core set of beliefs and assumptions held relatively commonly by the managers. This has variously been called ideational culture, myths (Hedberg and Jonsson, 1977), interpretative schemes (Bartunek, 1984) or the term used here, paradigms.
>
> (Johnson, 1993, p. 61)

One of the hypotheses of this chapter is that there is indeed a dominant paradigm in further education and that this paradigm is different to that which prevailed prior to incorporation.

Wallace (1999) warns that a single perspective on culture may be too limited and explores the possibility of dual or multiple perspectives. Certainly, drawing on the analysis in previous chapters, the changes explored often seem to involve conflict. Consequently, the micropolitical perspective, with its emphasis on power and conflict, may be relevant. With the aim of detecting the underlying core set of beliefs, the 'deep simplicity' (ibid.), a second hypothesis can be posited: that at its most fundamental level, cultural change is a shift in power, and that in further education from 1993, there has been essentially a shift of power away from lecturers and towards students and managers. The shift in power is both created and communicated by the many different expressions of culture.

LEADERSHIP AND CULTURE

There is a growing conviction that managing culture is one of the most important tasks of leadership. At the same time there is no agreement that culture is amenable to being managed: 'Many authorities do not accept that something as powerful as culture can be much affected by the puny efforts of top managers' (Turner, 1990, p. 11). Turner compares confidence that managers can influence culture with a belief in witchdoctors. Morgan (1986) is equally sceptical, though he concedes that managers can perhaps influence rather than control culture. As well as positive attempts to shape the development of culture, it is also suggested that one of the decisive actions of leadership may be the deliberate destruction of existing culture, even though what emerges to take its place cannot be controlled. In contradiction to the school of thought that culture arises from the environment and cannot be manipulated to any significant degree, some suggest that managing culture is the single most important task of leadership:

> One could argue that the only thing of real importance the leaders do is to create and manage culture and that the unique talent of leaders is their ability to understand and work with culture. If one wishes to distinguish leadership from management or administration, one can argue that leaders create and change cultures, while managers and administrators live within them.
>
> (Schein 1997, p. 5)

Culture will continue to evolve and leaders may abrogate responsibility, believing they have no power to change it, or they can manage it, attempting to influence the direction and nature of its evolution. Certainly many of the managers interviewed for this book believed they were deliberately changing culture: 'At the time of incorporation and for two or three years after that, we made considerable efforts to change the culture in a number of ways' (Principal 1). Principals 2, 4 and 5 had also tried to change the culture of their college. Principal 3, in her own view, had not. She was happy with the culture she inherited from her predecessor, but though she may not have consciously made the decision to change the culture, she was involved in such a process: 'I haven't deliberately tried to change the culture. In fact I would like to make further development of culture which is about people actively wanting to take responsibility for themselves and actually take responsibility for their learning because we are all learning, every day.'

Both Principals 1 and 2 use the term we rather than I. The change in culture is achieved by many, not one. All the managers interviewed, whether they were conscious of a deliberate decision to change the culture or not, were in fact engaged in a process of shifting staff's perspective on what was important and what was the appropriate way to think, act and feel. They were evolving culture. This is not to suggest that in all of the colleges all efforts were necessarily aligned. Schein (1997, p. 230) makes the point that the culture which emerges in an organization: 'will reflect not only the leader's assumptions but the complex internal accommodations created by subordinates to run the organization in spite of or around the leader'. A metaphor which may summarize the situation is that of sailing a ship in stormy seas. The direction and speed of the ship will be affected by the wind, currents, tide and waves whatever those on board do. The captain at the helm manipulating the rudder and the other crew members adjusting each of the sails will also affect the ship's progress. It may be that despite the crew's efforts the ship goes in a different direction to that desired, or even founders, because the crew did not work in harmony, or the forces of nature were too strong, but it may be that if the efforts of all create sufficient synergy, and the rudder is held steady, the ship moves as required.

This chapter assumes that college managers can and do influence culture, and explores how and to what end this is happening, based on the two hypotheses outlined above. The first hypothesis suggests that there is a discernible dominant culture, a core of beliefs in further education and that though this dominant paradigm is of course not static, it is stable enough for analysis. The second hypothesis posits the idea that as the culture developed to this point, it may most fundamentally rest on a shift in the locus of power.

PRESSURE FOR CHANGE

Colleges were asked what were the most significant factors demanding a change of culture. Figure 11.1 indicates the responses. The strongest pressure is that of the funding system. Chapter 4 explores the compulsion many colleges felt post-1993 to grow and to retain students in order to remain financially viable. The pressure exerted through the funding system resulted in a need to focus more strongly on students and their progress. The pressure of competition also indicated in Figure 11.1 will have compounded the need to exert greater efforts to enrol students. The changing market demand and changing student profile necessitate internal change in adjusting the curriculum and teaching methods. Finally, the inspection system opens the college to scrutiny and imposes a particular approach to quality as discussed in Chapter 6. Overall, there are considerable pressures which have emphasized a stronger focus on students. The change in the funding system, the most significant pressure, placed many colleges in financial jeopardy, leaving them little choice but to put their major efforts into raising their income through recruiting more students and by other means (Lumby, 2000c). The urgency of this imperative may have undermined attempts at culture change, which need to take place over time:

> There are instances when the organization is in crisis or confronts situations in which there is simply not sufficient time to develop shared premises about how to respond. For this very reason, the military services rely not only on techniques that build loyalty and esprit de corps . . . but also on a hierarchical chain of command and a tradition of obeying orders.
>
> (Pfeffer, 1993, pp. 202–3)

Pfeffer implies that where there is a strong shared culture, people will work towards the same end and there is less need for hierarchy and instructions.

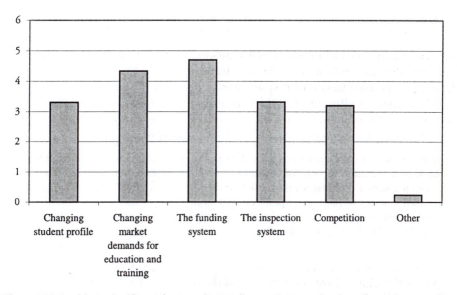

Figure 11.1   Most significant factors demanding a change of culture for college staff

The need to act quickly to survive post-1993 may have resulted in senior managers feeling impelled to issue orders rather than build shared understandings. This may be part of the explanation of the gulf which developed between managers and lecturers as discussed in Chapter 2, 'Leading colleges'. The size of colleges, both in terms of the size of buildings or number of sites and the number of staff, the fragmentation caused by multiple sites and many part-time or temporary staff, and the urgency for change made building a shared culture a near impossible task for further education managers in the period immediately following incorporation. For some, as the financial situation eased, the possibilities for achieving a truly shared new paradigm may have increased.

THE AIMS OF CULTURE CHANGE

Questioning interviewees about what culture change was intended, a degree of consistency emerged. Many managers characterized pre-incorporation further education as rather complacent, rather sleepy and going through the ritual of class teaching rather than any dynamic process which incorporated the whole student experience from recruitment to exit. Principal 1 did some work near St Petersburg in Russia and discovered 'a completely hidebound system':

> If you look at the set-up for Russian vocational schools, you have a lecturer who just sits there and waits to see how many students are sent each year. If only five come it doesn't make any difference, you've still got 15 staff. Nobody's worried

about the experience from the student point of view. Nobody's saying well can
we go out and get some more students or what about adult students?

He compared this to LEA-managed colleges. Principals 2 and 3, though not
painting the situation in such extreme terms, also saw the previous system as
lacking responsiveness and responsibility. The aim of these three principals
was to achieve a situation in which lecturers were more aware of the consequences of their actions or lack of action, more aware of the students'
experience and more enthusiastic about improving it:

> It is encouraging a business ethos. The difference is, pre-incorporation I'm a
> head of department or a head of section and I'm allocated a number of staff and
> given a number of classrooms and the students enroll. I might have control over
> a small amount of money to spend on part-time staff, but that's it really and you
> go through the year and you finish it. The cultural change is to something which
> says I'm going to do some planning for next year.
>
> (Principal 1)

> It sounds a bit mercenary to use the word 'entrepreneurial' but to me it encom-
> passes the whole of whatever the role of the college is. The staff have a role in
> ensuring that the college survives, not just by doing the specific tasks that they
> have but by their behaviour generally, by how they talk to people and relate to
> people outside the institution.
>
> (Principal 4)

Principal 3 wanted to move staff from a fatalistic view that they could not deal
with change to something more confident and proactive:

> As the workload has become greater and the managers themselves feel belea-
> guered, their expectation is that staff can't cope. Instead of saying, 'well let's look
> at it, let's discuss this and I think it is something we can cope with . . .' there is
> a sort of expectation culture here of we can't cope . . . One of the things I want
> to do is to shift that expectation.

Managers other than principals echoed the same intentions. The arrival of
a new principal triggered a culture change in the college of Quality
Manager 3:

> The cultural change I think began then; it put everybody on a different footing.
> It virtually said to this college, look, in many respects you have to pull your
> socks up, both from the financial point of view and from a performance point of
> view, and you have to take the responsibility for doing this.

There are common threads in the aims expressed in the quotations above. The
foundation change is to move staff from habitual patterns which reflect a lack
of interest in the connection of their actions to the fortunes of the college,
both educationally and financially, to a belief that their activities are central
to success, not just in teaching, but in their whole attitude and in their planning and management. The impression of the attempt to generate more energy
emerged repeatedly in the words of interviewees: 'There is a real buzz when

the students are here now and everyone is really focused. It is a completely different set of expectations amongst staff' (Human Resource Manager 3); and 'It is more fun. You've got more control over your own destiny and it's better for students' (Principal 1).

The underlying assumptions were changing to:

- Students are central.
- All of us can have an impact on the whole student experience, not just on teaching.
- A focus on planning and finance is an appropriate and necessary part of providing the best service.

The language used to describe this change often involved the term 'business' or 'entrepreneurialism'. The former correlates with negatives for some in education. The latter appears more neutral. Interestingly, for some of the managers, business was not seen as holding different values to education, but embodying educational values in a way that public service culture did not:

> There is this notion that there is a business culture and an education culture and they are different. I think the more I do what I do, I am sure the cultures are different, there is no doubt about that, but the central notion of responding to the client, if you want to call them that, the customer, the student, whoever, that notion actually needs to be central whatever you are doing, whether it is a public service or the proverbial selling baked beans.
>
> (Marketing Manager 1)

For this manager, though business and education may be distinguished in many ways, the overriding assumption to achieve success in both must be that the customer/student is central. Quality Manager 3 held a similar view:

> When I first came here I was sitting in a meeting at one point and I happened to say, quite innocently, that it simply wouldn't happen in an industrial environment. And I remember somebody saying to me 'But we are not in industry, this is education' as if it was something entirely different ... That was education. It couldn't ever be compared with industry and how business operated. Of course, we are proving that not to be the case. I think there is a cultural change and what we are trying to do now is to generate a feeling of enthusiasm for what we can do, which was not apparent and certainly I don't think it was particularly apparent in the sector. It certainly wasn't apparent here.

Much of the literature since 1993 has argued that previously quality of teaching was paramount and that students have suffered since incorporation because their learning has been sacrificed through an espousal of business values which place money at the forefront. The second part of this argument is that lecturers were the guardians of learning quality and have been displaced and disempowered in this role (Elliott, 1996; Randle and Brady, 1997a). This is in contradiction to a second body of literature which depicts a pre-incorporation lack of responsiveness and lack of focus on students in the sector (Hatton and Sedgemore, 1992; Smith, Scott and Lynch, 1995). The perception of the interviewees was very much more in line with the latter interpretation. For them, the focus prior to 1993 appeared to be on teaching and lecturers, not students and learning, and there was a sort of domestication (Carlson, 1975) of lecturers as they had no need to worry about the impact of their actions or about quality, because the LEA would keep stumping up funds no matter what.

Turner (1990, p. 5) argues that culture is often an expression of myths which amongst other purposes 'maintain and conceal political interests and value systems'. The myths are ways of legitimizing values and interests which, if openly declared, would not be acceptable. It may be that prior to 1993, there was a myth that lecturers always put the interests of students first despite evidence suggesting the contrary to be true, that colleges and the curriculum were organized at least partly for the convenience and stability of lecturers (Gray, 1991). This is not to suggest that individual lecturers did not do their utmost to provide good teaching, but the system as a whole was not organized to put students' needs at the centre. The culture change since 1993 has attempted to make a reality of the myth, genuinely to put students at the centre, to empower them, and as with any power shift, there has been resistance (Lumby, 1998).

THE EMBODIMENT OF CULTURE

There are a number of suggested frameworks for understanding how culture is embodied and enacted in organizations. Beare, Caldwell and Millikan, (1989, p. 176) define three modes:

- concepts and language
- behaviour
- visual images.

Language may be verbal or written. Behaviour involves rituals and ceremonies and the interaction between people. Images encompass the symbols or physical artefacts and settings. However, such a framework is rather all-encompassing. It is difficult to see what human activity or physical aspect of the organization would lie outside this definition. It is as much as to say that culture is expressed in everything. Though this may be true, it is not helpful to the manager trying to understand how culture may be influenced. Consequently, a less universal framework may be of more use. Deal and Kennedy (1982) suggest the framework of:

- shared values and beliefs
- heroes and heroines
- ritual
- ceremony

- stories
- informal network of cultural players.

This section will examine each of these facets, with the exception of shared values and beliefs which has already been discussed in the previous section, drawing on evidence from the interviews and survey.

Heroes and heroines

Those who were held up as heroes and heroines tended to be those who were focused on the student or who were entrepreneurial. For example there was repeated praise for lecturers who continued to work hard to offer excellent teaching and learning in the face of increasing workloads, as outlined in the concluding section of Chapter 3 on managing people. Such lecturers were spoken of as exceptional and to be emulated. Their achievements were seen as heroic. Equally, those who went out and built new opportunities for students were singled out as forging new paths ahead and creating an example to be followed: 'The Head of Section went out and got six-figure sponsorship from two companies . . . So suddenly she set up two programmes which we could not have funded . . . So by actually going and getting the money herself, she could actually fund something that she thought was high priority' (Principal 2).

Enterprise and student-centredness were the two qualities most evident in those who were held up as a hero or heroine. This is in line with the underlying values of assuming more responsibility, being more proactive and working for students.

Rituals

Turner (1990, p. 5) defines ritual as: 'A relatively rigid pattern of acts specific to a situation, which constructs a framework of meaning over and beyond the specific situational meaning'. He suggests that the pattern of acts is designed to bind individuals together through building shared values and to gain acceptance of organizational aspects which they might otherwise challenge. Inspection and later self-assessment may be one such ritual. During inspection the college gathers together documents in a special room which takes on additional significance as being the base of those with considerable power, the inspectors. From this central point, inspectors emerge to enact a series of meetings and observations which are conducted in an agreed format. The inspection report which results is a public tribute or humiliation. The dance of inspection embodies messages about expectations and power. First, it implies that neither managers nor lecturers hold the final judgement on the quality of teaching and learning. The inspectors do in their role as representatives of the public. They personify external forces. In consulting students and student evaluations they lend power to this previously relatively powerless group. The most emphatic message is that colleges are not closed organizations but accountable. This assumption was accepted. Principal 2 referred explicitly to 'the rules' of this ritual whereby the FEFC:

> keep their distance and do not interfere with what you do in your college, until you do well, whereupon you get the gold star and the grade A college rating. But then if you do badly, they send the audit team in and rip it apart. I think that's perfectly sound myself. That's the rules.

The ritual aspect of the process is evident. For example, all parties know that inspectors cannot possibly read all the material which is collected in the inspection base, and yet all sides expect that the full range is collected and placed in the room. Similarly, the fact that the time given to inspection may be out of proportion to the impact on teaching and learning is acknowledged: 'You take the time and effort from the job you are here to do, which is to deliver, in order to prepare for the inspection' (Human Resource Manager 2).

The real significance of the exercise is cultural, using a ritual to gain acceptance of actions which might otherwise be challenged, that is, that external individuals and groups have the right to judge the success of teaching and learning. It may be that as this premise became more accepted there was less need for the ritual, hence the move from inspection to self-assessment which has less involvement from external individuals.

Ceremonies

Deal and Kennedy (1982, p. 205) suggest that effective companies have regular ceremonies, the purpose of which is to 'dramatize and reinforce core values and beliefs'. The annual talk by the chief executive to employees is an example which takes place in many colleges. The annual strategic awayday of the college board or of other departments is another example. The group of people concerned absent themselves from the college for a day or two to plan for the future. The value of entrepreneurialism is therefore reinforced. The fact that such days often take place in hotels which are much more luxurious settings than the college dramatizes the connection between planning, being proactive and material reward.

Symbols

Schein (1997, p. 10) defines symbols as the 'material artefacts' of a group which embody the ideas, feelings and images with which the group strives to characterize itself. Finance Manager 10 contrasted a local college which had continued to use the same payroll system after incorporation with his own college, which took on paying staff itself, and therefore achieved the potent symbol of a new payslip. In the other college: 'All the staff continued to get the same payslips that they had got in March 1993. On their bank statements their pay came from exactly the same source as previously. This leaves a message in your mind that nothing has changed.'

The message of independence and responsibility was communicated through the symbol of the payslip. A similar role is played by management information in the form of statistical documents. It is clear from the analysis in Chapter 8 on managing information and communication that the actual content of such statistics does not hold much significance for the majority of staff. Such documents are, however, powerful symbols of a new order, where concern for how many students come into the college, how many stay and how many achieve, and consequently how much money the college has, is a heroic activity. Morgan (1986) compares statistical documents to the entrails read in earlier times to discern the future. One could debate whether the documents produced by MIS are a more accurate predictor of the future than animal entrails, but they certainly have the same ritual and symbolic significance.

Stories

The interviews were full of stories which encapsulated either how things were prior to 1993 or how things were after. The story recounted in Chapter 2 on leadership which graphically describes the principal drawing a line for staff to step over to join the fight to save the college is one such story. Another which encapsulates how things were before was told by Principal 5. He was seeking to persuade staff to sign up to the new contract. All the managers did, but only about half of the lecturers:

> I had a core of about 100 dissident staff. The nadir of that if you like was that during our first inspection when the inspectors arrived, that core were walking around with placards suggesting that the inspectors didn't know their parents. But we got a Grade 1 for governance and management in spite of that.

The point of this story is that the college heroically overcame the obstruction of the lecturers, even when the latter publicly abused those as powerful as inspectors.

The stories in the interviews fell into two types. They either, as above, reflected the values and behaviours pre- and post-incorporation, the former being unresponsive and complacent, the latter more responsible and proactive, or they lionized those who achieved increased opportunities or better learning for students. The shared assumptions and beliefs were consistent with those discussed in this chapter in the section on the aims of culture change. Ainley and Bailey (1997) provide a number of stories from the counter-culture of lecturers, some of which portray the new system as negative in a number of dimensions. However, they conclude that the post-incorporation culture had been adopted throughout their case-study colleges at least to middle manager level and that there was ambiguity amongst lecturers, the most negative views being held disproportionately by older staff. Students appeared to share a similar perspective to managers.

Network of players

The network of players who acted as priests and storytellers, as in Deal and Kennedy's typology, were the managers themselves. There will of course be a network of players promoting a counter-culture, for example, suggesting that a focus on finance is inappropriate and villainous rather than heroic, that those who raised the placards in protest at the first visit of inspectors were the heroes. This book reflects the perspective of managers and as such it is a single perspective. Nevertheless, the belief of the managers was that though counter-cultures existed, the culture they were promoting was becoming dominant. One story was told to illustrate this:

> We had a meeting between managers and governors last week, and I was frightened because one of the governors asked the managers, 'Do you understand the decisions made by the Senior Management Team?' And there was much debate on it. Yes they did. The next question he asked was 'Is the funding sufficiently transparent? Do you understand where your money comes from and how it is affected by external factors?' And, after some debate, they all said yes, 100 per cent, they did. The third question he asked them was 'Do you agree with the decisions made by the Senior Management Team?' Well I could have shot him, and it was very funny, because they sort of debated for a while and then he asked that they summarize the answer and one of them said, 'Most of the time'. I thought that was actually the best result you could have got . . . So there's the difference. That actually demonstrates we have achieved a slightly different culture.
>
> (Principal 2)

The point of this story is that when the governor publicly asked those gathered if they were in agreement with senior management, a heaven-sent opportunity for them to air their grievances had any existed, all of the managers seemed aligned and not in aggressive opposition to the senior management team. It is also an example of openness, in a governor asking for feedback on the SMT's performance from other staff. Overall, the conviction it represents is that the culture is aligned for many staff.

THE ROLE OF THE PRINCIPAL

Deal and Kennedy's framework provides one way of approaching an analysis of culture. The examples above for each of the categories give a broad picture of how the underlying paradigm has changed and by what means. Bridge (1994) believes that the principal and senior management team have a particularly critical role in such change. This was the belief of many of the managers interviewed: 'I think quality has contributed to the change in culture but I think still the biggest change in culture is how the Principal dictates his policy and he acts upon that policy and the Senior Management Team and the Middle Management Team act under the guidance of the Principal' (Quality Manager 4).

Schein (1997) provides a model for identifying the behaviour of leaders designed to influence culture (see Table 11.1). The model suggests that the cultural message is transmitted by what the principal and other members of the senior management team say, do and decide, and that these words, actions and decisions are interpreted by others as cultural signals. There is insufficient space in a single chapter to communicate the many examples in the interviews of senior managers' awareness that their actions would influence culture. They were aware that one of the strongest cultural indicators was what they gave their attention to most consistently. This focus was interpreted by others as signalling what was of most importance in the college. They were also aware that how they allocated funds, as discussed in Chapter 4, was a strong cultural indicator. The process was less one of unconscious influencing than a deliberate campaign. This deliberation was reflected in the responses to the survey which asked which tools had been used to bring about cultural change. Figure 11.2 shows the relative importance attributed to the systems colleges had used.

Table 11.1 Culture-embedding mechanisms

Primary embedding mechanisms	Secondary articulation and reinforcement mechanisms
What leaders pay attention to, measure, and control on a regular basis	Organization design and structure
How leaders react to critical incidents and organizational crises	Organizational systems and procedures
Observed criteria by which leaders allocate scarce resources	Organizational rites and rituals
Deliberate role modeling, teaching and coaching	Design of physical space, façades and buildings
Observed criteria by which leaders allocate rewards and status	Stories, legends and myths about people and events
Observed criteria by which leaders recruit, select, promote, retire and excommunicate organizational members	Formal statements of organizational philosophy, values and creed

Source: Schein, 1997, p. 231.

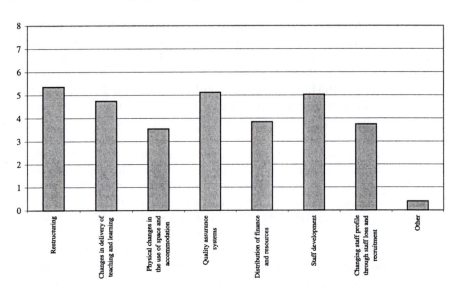

Figure 11.2   Primary tools used by senior management to manage cultural change

The responses shown in Figure 11.2 and the comments which were added in each questionnaire indicated the wide range of means being used to bring about cultural change. Each of these elements have been discussed in preceding chapters. Taken as a whole, they indicate that managers use a variety of structural and developmental tools as a transmitter of cultural codes. The clear intention rings though the words of managers again and again: 'Through team development, greatly enhanced communication systems, greater openness and involvement in business decision making and role development, the management team set out to change the culture of the institution' (Survey comment); and 'The most important factor has been effective communication, motivation of staff (mainly through the way they are treated) and focusing on the improvement of the learning experience for the student (which everyone subscribes to)' (Survey comment). The underlying value of focusing on the student is explicit in the second comment. The greater proactivity and business approach is explicit in the first. The deliberation of managers in their determination to change culture and the consistency of the values which the change was aimed at achieving were both very marked.

THE EXTENT OF CULTURE CHANGE

In the view of the managers interviewed, the answer to whether culture had changed in each college was a unanimous 'yes'. However, there were two variations in the answer. For many the change was still partial, with some staff outside the dominant paradigm:

I do think there is a shift and I do think that a lot of people have got more street-wise, more savvy but there are a lot of people still who are not and who do not like the way things are going and look to the good old days which will never return.

(Finance Manager 1)

There is the ethos in some people's minds that we are more of a business than we used to be. Certainly people are becoming more aware of the financial results of their decisions. We have had a lot of staff restructuring and we have winnowed out a lot of people who either couldn't or wouldn't change their views. There has been a lot of change in some places, a little change in others and in a very few places, little change at all.

(Finance Manager 5)

The culture change is still making its way through the organization. It is clear that changing staff, as some who hold to the previous culture leave and are replaced, is an essential part of the process. As well as the belief that the culture change may not yet have reached all, there was a harder edge for particularly the finance managers, where the third of the assumptions outlined in the section on the aims of cultural change – a focus on planning and finance is an appropriate and necessary part of providing the best service – took precedence over the other two of making students central and the belief that all can impact on the whole student experience. For other managers, a focus on students, 'that the student is the most important thing' (Quality Manager 4), not in rhetoric or mythology but in reality, was the major cultural assumption that had changed for most.

Principal 5 was 'sure we've all made terrible mistakes moving from the culture that we had to the culture that we've got now'. There has been bitterness, resistance and pain, but change has been achieved: 'It has taken some years and it is only now you can sit back and look at how it was. There really is quite a culture shift. People's expectations are somewhat different now' (Human Resource Manager 3).

Though it may not be possible to impose culture, the evidence collected points to a deliberate and successful process of influencing culture. The government used levers such as the funding mechanism to exert pressure for cultural change and this pressure then rippled outwards into colleges. This chapter has had space enough only to offer a few examples of how things have changed and why, but sufficient to tentatively conclude that the hypotheses posited at the opening of the chapter are true. There is an underlying paradigm within further education which rests on a small number of assumptions:

- that students are the most important priority
- that staff have a responsibility to ensure that they receive the best experience in all contact with the college, and
- that adopting a business-like approach to planning and resources is part of achieving the best experience for students.

The change to the point where these assumptions prevail has involved a power shift whereby students have accrued a little more power by means of the first two assumptions and managers have accrued more power by means of the third. The public service ethos, which is taken by some to be the guardian of professional values, that is, putting the clients' interests first, may have been the opposite, and the business culture, characterized by some as fixated on money to the exclusion of all else, may be promoting the interests of students, and so establishing a culture based on educational values. The irony is inescapable.

12

LOOKING TO THE FUTURE: LEARNING ENTERPRISE

SEA CHANGE

The world in which colleges function and the way they are managed have changed in many ways. The previous chapters have explored the pressures on colleges to develop their practice and their culture. Resources have been reduced, competition has increased for many and the curriculum has developed so that the means to deliver teaching and learning are more diverse. This amounts to the 'sea change' in teaching and learning referred to in Chapter 9, which has meant that previous approaches to vocational education have metamorphosed into a new order:

> They used to pay us to produce Rolls Royces. They are now paying us to produce Minis or middle-range Rovers at the best. You can't produce a Rolls Royce with no engine, because that's worthless, or a Rolls Royce with only three wheels because it doesn't go. If you are going to produce Minis you have to design it and say, okay we want something that's going to cost less than £10,000. This is it. When it is finished, okay the boot doesn't fit perfectly, the engine sounds a bit noisy, you haven't got acres of room, but it's got to go and you've got to be able to drive it. It's got to be safe. It's got to go from A to B. So that's the pragmatism which I think you've actually got to have . . . If your objective is to produce a perfect educational system, there is nowhere in the world to go now.
>
> (Principal 2)

In the interpretation of this principal, the determination to offer vocational education to larger numbers of people without a proportional rise in the resources available to do so has meant that training and education now lay the foundations, rather than build the entire house. If people face the need to continue learning and developing all their lives, perhaps this is no bad thing. Foundations can be built on and colleges can continue to offer lifelong learning to the community. The point is that many more people have been hooked into the system and are likely to keep returning. An alternative interpretation would assert that standards in teaching and learning had declined. There is little evidence for the latter. The Chief Inspector's report for 1997–98 (FEFC, 1998c) concluded that average achievement rates increased from 1995 to 1997. It would seem that colleges have adapted and continue to offer quality teaching and learning despite resource cuts.

Colleges are also more proactive and more responsible for their own fortunes. The previous cosy days when issues such as retention and achievement were not to the forefront have long gone. As Principal 5 put it, 'the world has moved on a bit since then'.

The title of this book 'learning enterprise' implies a double question. Are colleges still institutions with learning at the heart? Have they adopted a new approach to providing learning by being enterprising and entrepreneurial in their attitudes and management? That is, have they learned enterprise? This final chapter will attempt to find an answer to these questions. However, though general changes to the context and practice of colleges can be discerned, it is equally true that each college is unique. In the final part of the survey, where colleges were asked about their perspective on the future, the range and variety of perceptions was marked. So, true to the spirit of paradox which was noted in Chapter 2 as one of the features of leadership in the twenty-first century, the conclusions of this book will suggest that there are general trends in the management of colleges and also that the individual situation and approach of each college may be unique, that is, there are patterns and no patterns. To highlight the threads of pattern, this chapter will review how colleges see their mission, what they see as threats and opportunities for the future, and how they will manage in both senses of the word.

COLLEGES' MISSION

The survey response from one college to the question on how it perceived opportunities for the future was one terse word, 'survival'. A minority of colleges feel so insecure in their prospects that mission is displaced by the need to secure their continued existence. However, the survey responses in total indicated that the majority of colleges were much more positive and deliberate in how they wished to develop. Chapter 1 discussed the comprehensive nature of the curriculum offered by colleges. This appears to remain the case. One college described how it saw its future as: 'The development of the culture of lifelong learning which should support the college's view of itself as a comprehensive provider of post-16 education, including work with adults and local industry'.

The agenda for college development was truly comprehensive in two senses. First, the emphasis of many survey responses was on lifelong learning, that is, comprehensive in time span. Second, many emphasized widening participation, that is, comprehensive in including the whole local community. Many comments indicated that colleges were encouraged by the direction of government policy in highlighting such issues and interpreted this as an affirmation of the mission which further education had always held: 'The inclusive learning and widening participation agendas are close to the college's philosophy. We have a good track record so current political thinking helps us.'

One college felt that only the further education sector could actually achieve what was required, but the optimism at having its mission moved to centre stage politically was tinged with doubt as to whether government policy would remain consistent and whether politicians truly understood the extent and difficulties of the task. Overall in the survey, 17 per cent of colleges mentioned widening participation as an opportunity for the future and seven per cent lifelong learning. Thirteen per cent commented positively on government policy and the opportunities which it would create (see Figure 12.2 in the following section).

As well as a reaffirmation of a comprehensive approach to providing lifelong learning to the community, many comments added a second dimension on being business-like in approach. The intention to offer teaching and learning to the community existed pre-1993, though perhaps without the same emphasis on widening participation and lifelong learning. What has changed is that colleges understand that the mission to offer a comprehensive service is predicated on an ability to manage competently:

> I have a very strong sense in FE of serving a community and engaging with people who don't have any money to spend on a course or a programme or whatever. At the same time, particularly now in the '90s post-incorporation, I am a manager of a business that can go broke.
>
> (Quality Manager 1)

This dualism also emerged from many survey comments. The three selected here give examples of how, in describing their future, colleges were linking sound financial management to offering the best experience to students: 'Embracing raising standards agenda whilst maintaining financial position'; 'The college is cautiously optimistic about its future. A lot of work is being done to secure our future by teamwork, sound finances and a responsive curriculum offer which optimizes the quality of every student's experience'; and 'Concentrate on a portfolio of courses which are financially viable and represent significant added value to students'.

The thinking exemplified in these comments considers learning and finance as dialectic, that is, the two were not separate elements which were

chained together but rather worked in synergy. There is no point in considering student experience without considering the resources to achieve it. At the
same time there is no point in considering finance divorced from student
experience because the whole point of the finance is to achieve the best experience for students. This may seem self-evident but is a long way from the
pre-1993 assumptions where finance and management were relatively minor
considerations. It reflects a development in mission, a new way of defining
the task. Learning is still at the heart, but embedded in enterprise. Learning
enterprise is an accurate description of the mission of further education
colleges.

THREATS AND OPPORTUNITIES

Threats

Colleges were asked to identify what they saw as the significant threats and
opportunities for their future. An overview of the survey responses identifying threats is given in Figure 12.1.

The factor mentioned most frequently was funding. One college expressed
threats for the future in one word 'Money!' The threat was seen in a number
of ways. The differential funding with schools was mentioned. Rural colleges
felt they were disadvantaged by the funding methodology. The most frequent
anxiety was, however, simply that the government kept changing the rules
and therefore made financial planning very difficult: 'Strategic planning within the sector is a joke when such substantial changes are continually being
implemented from afar' (Survey comment).

The jeopardy posed by inadequate or uncertain funding was linked to several of the other factors identified as threats. Staff pay, mentioned by nine per
cent, was obviously related to the level of funding which colleges received.
This issue, and its effect on recruitment and motivation, cropped up frequently in interview and survey comments: 'The continuing downward
pressure on salaries is demotivating staff and making the most able leave.
Recruiting good staff is increasingly difficult. We compete with schools for
students but not for staff' (Survey comment). There was no easy answer to
this issue except the highly unlikely scenario of government making substantial additional funds available which were not ring-fenced for specific
initiatives. Three colleges highlighted a connection between poor staff pay
and reduced quality in teaching and learning.

Competition with schools and with private providers was identified as a
threat factor and was also linked to funding issues. Some feared that other
providers could select the most able or most homogeneous sectors of the community and take government funds to provide for these groups as being the

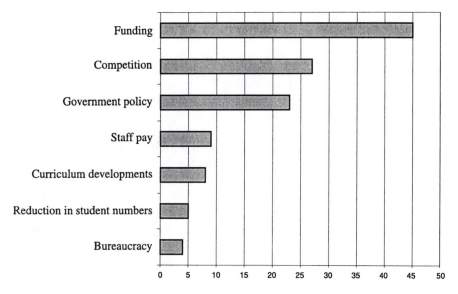

Figure 12.1 Percentage of colleges identifying factors as a threat

most lucrative, leaving colleges to fight to retain an inclusive curriculum when 'easy' income had been creamed. Planned legislation was predicted to exacerbate the situation. Although government policy was seen as encouraging by some, as discussed in the previous section, it was perceived as a threat by a substantial number of colleges, nearly one in four:

> The recent White Paper on post-16 funding threatens the whole structure of FE. Now seen primarily as one set of providers among many, rather than as a major employer and community resource, we stand to lose franchised work as collaborators are funded directly, and to lose high value work as commercial monotechnics 'cherry-pick'.
>
> (Survey comment)

The fear expressed is that private providers, perhaps offering only a single area of training, will consume funds which would otherwise have gone to colleges as part of a total budget to maintain a broad and balanced curriculum.

As well as the threat created by specific policy decisions, continuous change was seen as a threat in itself. The instability induced by frequent new legislation and government action was vividly painted in one survey comment:

> It is really difficult for anyone to see the future. The really destabilizing changes of the past ten years have been policy induced – incorporation, White Papers, Public Sector Expenditure squeeze, new exam systems, new funding systems, waxing or waning enthusiasm for college mergers, new contracts, new sixth forms, European employment legislation, arrival and departure of FEFC and TECs, etc. What makes the future of colleges uncertain is not the Tom Peters style societal and technical change as much as policy hysteria, and this is more

inherently unpredictable. I can find out the number of 16–19-year-olds in five years time; I can't even guess as to what will be the obsessions of the Minister of Education.

The 'policy hysteria' was a strongly felt frustration indicated by many. There were also real fears that the combination of changing policy and funding rules, and competition leading to a reduction in student numbers would force closure of valuable provision: 'The college overall is stable. However, parts of the college are vulnerable owing to consistent changes in the Funding Methodology. Important provision which we value as a service in the community might become too costly for us to support' (Survey comment).

Bureaucracy was the final threat identified by a significant percentage of colleges. The bureaucracy was frustrating but the real threat was again linked to funds, in that bureaucratic demands ate up resources. The threat identified in one survey response was:

> The imposition of further layers of bureaucracy and data demands. The college currently disperses over 40 per cent of its income on 'non-teaching and learning' activity, e.g. MIS, insurance, legal and audit fees, etc.
>
> If the emergence of the national Learning and Skills Council results in a greater burden of administration in this college, it is likely to be funded by removing programmes with marginal numbers.

Colleges distinguished being business-like or entrepreneurial from bureaucracy, that is, external demands for information and paper records. Being business-like focused on the needs of students. Bureaucracy focused on the demands of funding bodies. It is anticipated that further requirements in bureaucracy, unnecessarily absorbing resources, would result in a narrowed curriculum.

Opportunities

On a more positive note, colleges indicated a wide range of opportunities and much optimism. An overview of the factors identified is indicated in Figure 12.2. Just as funding is the factor identified most often by colleges as a threat, so it is also the most frequently cited opportunity. Thirty per cent of colleges saw possibilities for increasing their funding in the future and/or making best use of what was available through sound management. There was real satisfaction at what had been achieved in many survey comments: 'College in financial health category A and able to deliver year-on-year growth'; and 'A secure financial position predicated on good management and growth'. There was much confidence that reliance on government funding could be lessened: 'Increased opportunities for securing work from sources other than FEFC. The college currently secures 48 per cent of its income from non-FEFC work'; and 'Diversification into non-FEFC training is increasingly vital'.

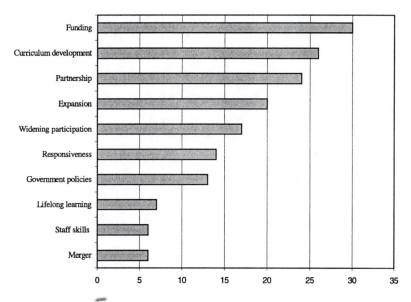

Figure 12.2 Percentage of colleges indicating areas of opportunity for the future

There was also acknowledgement that the government had made more funds available and the situation had consequently eased. The survey comments often linked financial issues with learning issues. Twenty-six per cent of colleges saw potential for developing the curriculum in a variety of ways, whether by improving the quality or developing a particular mode of delivery. Opportunities identified included:

- major innovations in the delivery of teaching and learning
- quality of teaching and learning is at the centre of management planning resulting in a growing student population
- continuous quality improvement in learning, teaching and continuous professional development
- more learning, less teaching
- ICT-based learning.

Partnership was acknowledged as a powerful aid to achieving the teaching and learning in question. The specific elements of widening participation and lifelong learning have been discussed in the opening section of this chapter which concluded that they were considered core elements of the mission of further education.

Many survey comments harnessed several elements as inextricably linked. Quality teaching and learning would lead to more students, would lead to expansion and more funds. Quality could be achieved only where the college was responsive to local needs. For a significant number of colleges, 13 per cent, government polices were welcomed as creating opportunities to be responsive and to improve learning. Staff skills were mentioned as an essential ingredient in realizing opportunities, but only by a small number of colleges. It may be that the funding situation and its impact on pay, as discussed in the previous section, has made managers less sanguine about how far staff skills can be further developed. However, for some colleges it was very important. Opportunities stated included:

- motivating and energizing staff/releasing creativity
- a committed staff body who are aware of the college's aims
- staff flexible/positive.

Clearly, staff are valued and seen as key.

WEIGHING THREATS AND OPPORTUNITIES

Respondents were asked to judge whether the senior management team viewed the future of the college as secure or uncertain. The majority, 119 colleges (73 per cent), were positive. Thirty-eight colleges (23 per cent) believed the SMT saw the future of their college as uncertain. Some of this uncertainty may be accounted for by anticipated mergers, whereby the college would no longer exist. However, in Figure 12.2, only 6 per cent of respondents identified merger as an opportunity. Therefore, the majority of respondents sensing an uncertain future may fear retrenchment or even closure. Consequently the environment in which many managers must work may well be stressful and demotivating. Respondents were also asked to give the senior management team's view on how the college staff as a whole felt about the future of their college. This response was slightly more positive. Eighty-seven per cent of responses indicated that staff had a positive view. Thirteen per cent saw the majority view as disheartened.

Staff may be disheartened for a number of reasons including pay or possible job losses, for example, through merger or because their college is in a vulnerable position in relation to local competitors or because of its history. In order to triangulate this result and to confirm that the majority of staff are positive and to identify the factors which may be disheartening staff, a much wider survey would be needed of a large number of further education staff. For the moment, it can only be concluded that it is the belief of senior managers that the majority of staff look forward positively to their college's future.

MANAGING COLLEGES INTO THE FUTURE

The range of survey comments on how colleges were managing for the future was very wide but there was generally a sense of confidence. 'Competent management – nothing else matters!' In reply to the question of how his or her college was managing, one respondent replied, 'Expertly!' Perhaps the sector has gone through so much that those who have weathered the storm have a renewed strength. The sense of the value of the sector's task was very strong. In the interviews, particularly the commitment of those who worked in colleges was affirmed again and again:

> Like most colleges we came through a fairly difficult period with contracts and so on and I think that those who were least likely to change were enabled to go. . . . The people who have stayed did so because they are local people by and large. If I look around me, most of the people are here because they feel some sense of ownership.
>
> (Marketing Manager 1)

The college is a vital resource for the community and staff who work there feel a commitment both to the community and to the college. A belief in the dedication of staff was a constant for the managers interviewed: 'There really is a commitment amongst staff that they want to provide a good experience for the students, they want to improve, they want to be better, they want to be best' (Human Resource Manager 3).

Harnessing the commitment, energy and skill of staff was seen as the key task by many of the managers. Curriculum Manager 4 described the challenge:

> I think that it is really important to make sure staff feel valued for the work that they are doing, that you celebrate success, that you make staff feel that they are doing a good job. You address issues as and when they arise in terms of under-performance, but you concentrate on the positive while still taking stock of the negative and dealing with it. Harnessing their full potential and making them feel that they are valued in an invaluable task is one of the most important tasks I have to do day to day.

As well as this central message, much else has been learned during the period of intense change. The concept of flexibility was central, as the diversity and inclusive approach of the sector ruled out monolithic solutions:

> When you think you have got the answer, there isn't one. There never, ever is. I think that is the most important thing that I have had to learn. People say 'Well, we can't do this because of this', and you say 'OK. Try it this way', and the moment you say that, they say 'Well that won't work either because of this', so you are constantly trying to find new ways. There isn't one answer. It's being flexible and having to live with that.
>
> (Curriculum Manager 2)

Working with people, taking account of their views, being creative and allowing oneself to be content with what is possible, are all themes emerging from this manager's words. As a survey comment put it, the need is 'to remain responsive, flexible and ever changing'. Complementing this willingness to be flexible is an understanding of the need to act incrementally. Despite the fact that very large and immediate changes had often been imposed on the sector, managers seemed determined wherever possible to mediate the effects internally and to achieve development in a way which took account of people's need for time to absorb and rework innovation. A survey comment stated that future management would be 'by incremental developments; the "big bang" theory is OK for astrophysics but has no place in education'. If such are the attitudes of management, then turbulence can be endured and even enjoyed:

> All of a sudden the wind has changed dramatically and the outreach centres are being frowned upon by the FEFC, and the same officers who were imploring you to compete are now suggesting you refocus. Now that causes immense difficulties really. Then there is the White Paper. Challenging, interesting all those sorts of things, but how long will the consensus last? . . . It is difficult if you allow it to be difficult but one of the reasons I enjoy FE is because of that very turbulence, but you can end up tearing your hair out.
>
> (Quality Manager 1)

The dramatic changes in policy and the sector's fortunes are rather like a roller-coaster, terrifying and exhilarating. The picture of management which emerged from the interviews conforms quite closely to the view that emergent strategies may be the most appropriate method of steering an organization in times of turbulence (Mintzberg and Waters, 1985). Such an approach accepts the need to plan but also recognizes that whatever the intended target, the actual goal reached is likely to be different and the result of the interplay of planned actions and unpredictable circumstances and responses from others. There is a disavowal of reliance on 'awesome rationality' alone (Quinn, 1993, p. 83). Detailed plans, quantitative measurements and stern logic all have a place, but intuition, flexibility and creativity in working with people are equally critical. So managers would plan, monitor and evaluate, but this was in the context of a need to keep adjusting the goal. Rather than single-loop learning, that is, monitoring and adjusting to reach the planned targets, these managers were involved in double-loop learning, that is, monitoring progress and evaluating and adjusting the targets themselves as events unfolded (Senge, 1993). The trick (and the paradox) was summarized long ago in Wildavsky's (1973, p. 146) words 'be flexible but do not alter your course'. The managers adhered to their basic mission to offer inclusive education and training opportunities to their communities, but in doing so they weave with and through the changing circumstances and other staff's views: 'Inching forward on a knee-jerking process, seizing opportunities as they arise but not all fronts and not at the same speed. Where are we going? I don't know. Where are we heading? I ain't certain. All I know is we are on our way . . . just' (Survey comment).

LEARNING ENTERPRISE

The management of further education colleges has always been about managing learning. In the period since 1993, managers have adjusted to a plethora of new demands and have accepted the charge of continuing and expanding the tradition of inclusive learning while also taking wider responsibilities for their self-management. They have survived and learned to 'duck and dive with the best!' (Survey comment). Learning has increased in quality and quantity. More students have entered the system from more diverse backgrounds and achievement standards have continued to rise. Colleges have therefore risen to the challenge presented by the state to provide better learning for more people at a lower cost. They have continued, by and large, to hold true to an educational mission to provide in an inclusive way for their local community and beyond. They have continued experimentation with improving the quality of learning by developing the range of their curriculum offering, both in terms of the content and the modes of delivery. They have put in place self-assessment systems which listen systematically to students and to staff. They have achieved all this while enduring cuts in real terms year on year, unremitting government policy and funding changes, and a continued lack of interest from the public compared with that offered to schools and higher education. There have been unacceptable costs for this achievement in terms of the levels of workload and stress experienced by staff. There is, of course, still much to do to improve retention, achievement and responsiveness. The detail in previous chapters has shown that managers have achieved much but still foresee significant hurdles to be overcome. However, as an overview, it would seem that colleges are indeed learning organizations, that is, they have moved to a culture where one of the underlying fundamentals is the need to focus strongly on the needs of learners.

There has been high-profile publicity surrounding the colleges where things have gone badly wrong, but the situation of this handful of organizations has perhaps skewed the view of the sector. Though some colleges are still in jeopardy because of their financial situation, many have grown stronger. Self-management has been a spur to consider the meaning of concepts like business-like and entrepreneurial and how they should properly be enacted in an education environment. Although there is inevitably a range of interpretation, and at one end of the spectrum some colleges may have moved too far towards a commercial culture, the majority seem to have arrived at a positive and education-focused view. Behaving in a business-like way is interpreted to mean that the college must put meeting the needs of customers/students at the heart, and must plan in deliberate fashion to use all their resources and skills to this end. The spirit is one of enterprise, that is, discovering needs which demand a response and using management skills creatively to access and distribute resources to this end. It is a long way from the previous 1980s public sector culture in which it was possible to wait for students to arrive and not be too concerned with the quality of what they received, or if they left before time. 'The fact that you were losing students and had poor retention was no bother really' (Burton, 1994, p. 399). It would be easy to overstate the positives and negatives. There was good management and quality teaching and learning prior to incorporation. There has been poor management and poor teaching and learning since. However, overall, the evidence presented in previous chapters has shown a sea change in the sector. Further education colleges have become more self-aware and more deliberate in implementing a culture which links learning and enterprise, learning and good management. As they move forward to face new challenges as the learning and skills sector of the twenty-first century, they have challenged the old dichotomy which saw public sector workers as immune to 'business' concerns about, for example, investigating demand and managing finance. This success is a tribute to all the staff who work in the sector and to the managers who have steered though tempestuous times. Colleges make an enormously important contribution to education. They have done so and will continue to do so because they have grasped the opportunity to embrace a spirit of learning themselves. What they have learned is to go out and create opportunities, to harness a range of resources and to shape their own future. 'Learning enterprise' in both senses is an epithet well earned by the sector.

REFERENCES

Abrokwa, C. (1995) Vocational education in the Third World: revisiting the debate, *The Vocational Aspect of Education*, Vol. 47, no. 2, pp. 129–40.

Adler, S., Laney, J. and Packer, M. (1993) *Managing Women: Feminism and Power in Educational Management*, Buckingham, Open University Press.

Ainley, P. and Bailey, B. (1997) *The Business of Learning*, London, Cassell.

Alter, S. (1996) *Information Systems*, 2nd edn, Menlo Park, Benjamin/Cummings.

Anderson, J. (1994) Human resource strategies in the new FE, in C. Flint and M. Austin (eds) *Going Further*, Blagdon, The Staff College in association with the Association for Colleges.

Andrews, J. (1995) Effective communication, in D. Warner and E. Crosthwaite (eds) *Human Resource Management in Higher and Further Education*, Buckingham, SRHE and Open University Press.

Argyris, C. (1991) Teaching smart people how to learn, *Harvard Business Review*, May–June, pp. 99–109.

Armitage, A., Bryant, B., Dunhill, R., Hammersley, M., Hayes, D., Hudson, A. and Lawes, S. (1999) *Teaching and Training in Post-Compulsory Education*, Buckingham, Open University Press.

Atkinson, D. (1989) MIS: an introduction strategy in management information systems, *Coombe Lodge Report*, Vol. 21, no. 4, pp. 253–61.

Bartunek, J. (1984) Changing interpretive schemes and organisational restructuring: the example of a religious order, *Administrative Science Quarterley*, Vol. 29, pp. 355–72.

Bass, B. M. and Avolio, B. J. (1994) *Improving Organizational Effectiveness Through Tranformationary Leadership*, London, Sage.

Beare, H., Caldwell, B. and Millikan, R. (1989) *Creating an Excellent School: Some New Management Techniques*, London, Routledge.

Becher, T. and Kogan, M. (1980) *Process and Structure in Higher Education*, London, Heinemann.

Bennett, N. and Hagon, L. (1997) Managing for learning after incorporation, in R. Levacic and R. Glatter (eds) Managing change in further education, *FEDA Report*, Vol. 1, no. 7, pp. 85–111.

Betts, A. (1994) A focus for human resource management, *Mendip Paper 069*, Blagdon, The Staff College.

Bolman, L. and Deal, T. (1984) *Modern Approaches to Understanding and Managing Organizations*, San Francisco, Jossey-Bass.

Brain, G. (1994) Reward systems and management culture, in G. Brain (ed.) *Managing and Developing People*, Blagdon, The Staff College.

Brannen, R., Holloway, D. and Peeke, G. (1981) Departmental organisational structures in further education, *Journal of Further and Higher Education*, Vol. 5, no. 1, Spring, pp. 22–32.

Bridge, W. (1994) Change where contrasting cultures meet, in The Staff College (ed.) Changing the culture of a college, *Coombe Lodge Report*, Vol. 24, no. 1, pp. 183–277.

Briggs, P. (1992) Finance, in A. Limb, J. Avery, P. Briggs, M. Jack, C. Monk, J. Skitt, P. Sokoloff and J. Wilson *The Road to Incorporation*, Blagdon, The Staff College and the Association of Colleges for Further and Higher Education.

Bright, D. and Williamson, B. (1995) Managing and rewarding performance, in D. Warner and E. Crosthwaite (eds) *Human Resource Management in Higher and Further Education*, Buckingham, SRHE and Open University Press.

Brown, D. (1974) The role of the vice principal, *The Technical Journal*.

Burton, S. (1994) Factors affecting quality in the new FE – principals' views, *Coombe Lodge Report*, Vol. 24, no. 5, pp. 349–439.

Bush, T. (1995) *Theories of Educational Management*, 2nd edn, London, Paul Chapman.

Caldwell, B. and Spinks, J. (1992) *Leading the Self-Managing School*, London, Falmer.

Cantor, L., Roberts, I. and Pratley, B. (1995) *A Guide to Further Education in England and Wales*, London, Cassell.

Carlson, R. (1975) Environmental constraints and organisational consequences: the public school and its clients, in J. Baldridge and T. Deal (eds) *Managing Change in Educational Organisations*, Berkeley, CA, McCutchan.

Chadwick, S. (1996) Resource dependence, competition and environmental assessment in further education, in N. Foskett, (ed.) *Markets in Education: Policy, Process and Practice*, Proceedings of an International Symposium organized by the Centre for Research in Education Marketing, University of Southampton, Chilworth Manor Conference Centre, University of Southampton, 4–5 July 1996.

Cochran-Smith, M. and Lytle, S. (1998) Teacher research: the question that persists, *International Journal of Leadership in Education: Theory and Practice*, Vol. 1, no. 1, pp. 19–36.

Cole, G. (1996) *Management Theory and Practice*, 5th edn, London, DP Publications.

Coleman, M. (1994) Marketing in education, Leicester, Leicester University, materials produced for the MBA in Educational Management.

Coles, C. (1989) What use the user requirement?, in Management information systems, *Coombe Lodge Report*, Vol. 21, no. 4, pp. 229–35.

Crequer, N. (1998) Fearful principals sought mergers, *Times Educational Supplement*, 16 October.

Crosby, W. (1979) *Quality is Free*, London, McGraw-Hill.

Currie, W. (1995) *Management Strategy for IT*, London, Pitman.

Dadds, M. (1995) *Passionate Enquiry and School Development*, London, Falmer.

Davies, B. and West-Burnham, J. (1997) Mapping the future, in B. Davies and J. West-Burnham (eds) *Reengineering and Total Quality in Schools*, London, Pitman.

Davies, P. (1999) Colleges and customers, in J. Lumby and N. Foskett (eds) *Managing External Relations in Schools and Colleges*, London, Paul Chapman.

De Pree, M. (1999) The leader's legacy, in F. Hesslebein and P. Cohen (eds) *Leader to Leader*, San Francisco, Jossey-Bass.

Deal, T. and Kennedy, A. (1982) *Corporate Rituals: The Rites and Rituals of Corporate Life*, Reading, MA, Addison Wesley.

Deming, W. E. (1982) *Out of the Crisis: Quality Productivity and Competitive Position*, Cambridge, MA, Cambridge University Press.

DES (Department of Education and Science) (1991) *Education and Training for the 21st Century*, London, HMSO.

DfEE (Department for Education and Employment) (1998) *Towards a National Skills Agenda*, London, DfEE.

DfEE (Department for Education and Employment) (1999) *Learning to Succeed: A New Framework for Post-16 Learning*, London, HMSO.

Dopson, S. and Stewart, R. (1993) What *is* happening to middle management, in C. Mabey and B. Mayon-White (eds) *Managing Change*, 2nd edn, London, Paul Chapman.

Drucker, P. (1954) *The Practice of Management*, New York, Harper and Row.

Drucker, P. (1994) *Managing the Non-Profit Organization*, Oxford, Butterworth-Heinemann.

Edwards, R. (1993) Multi-skilling the flexible workforce in post-compulsory education and training, *Journal of Further and Higher Education*, Vol. 17, no. 1, Spring, pp. 44–51.

Elliott, G. (1996) *Crisis and Change in Further Education*, London, Jessica Kingsley.

Elliott, G. and Crossley, M. (1997) Contested values in further education: findings from a case study of the management of change, *Educational Management and Administration*, Vol. 25, no. 1, pp. 79–92.

Elliott, G. and Hall, V. (1994) FE Inc. – business orientation in further education and the introduction of human resource management, *School Organisation*, Vol. 14, no. 1, pp. 3–10.

Ellis, P. (1989) Standards and the outcomes approach, in J. Burke (ed.) *Outcomes, Learning and the Curriculum*, London, Falmer.

Employment Department Group (1993) *Labour Market Needs and Further Education*, London, HMSO.

Employment Department Group (1999) *Labour Market and Skill Trends 1998/99*, Sheffield, Employment Department Group.

European Framework Directive (Council Directive 92/85/EEC)

Farey, P. (1993) Mapping the leader/manager, *Management Education and Development*, Vol. 24, no. 2, pp. 109–21.

FEDA (Further Education Development Agency) (1995) *Mapping the FE Sector*, London, DfEE.

FEFC (Further Education Funding Council) (1996) *College Responsiveness*, Coventry, FEFC.

FEFC (Further Education Funding Council) (1997) *Quality and Standards in Further Education in England, 1996–97*, Coventry, FEFC.

FEFC (Further Education Funding Council) (1998a) *College Accounts 1996-97, Circular 98/43*, Coventry, FEFC.

FEFC (Further Education Funding Council) (1998b) *Main Findings of the Good Practice Guide on Marketing, Circular 98/11*, Coventry, FEFC.

FEFC (Further Education Funding Council) (1998c) *Quality and Standards in Further Education, Chief Inspector's Annual Report*, Coventry, FEFC.

FEFC (Further Education Funding Council) (1998d) *Performance Indicators 1997–98: Further Education Colleges in England*, London, HMSO.

FEFC (Further Education Funding Council) (1998e) *Widening Participation in Further Education Statistical Evidence*, London, HMSO.

FEFC (Further Education Funding Council) (2000) Student numbers at colleges in the further education sector and external institutions in England in 1998–99 (online) *http://www.fefc.cov.net/news/LATEST-MEDIA-RELEASE.html* (accessed 6 January 2000).

FEU (Further Education Unit) (1993) *Management Information Systems and the Curriculum*, London, FEU.

Fidler, B. (1997) Organizational structure and organizational effectiveness, in A. Harris, N. Bennett and M. Preedy (eds) *Organizational effectiveness and improvement in education*, Buckingham, Open University Press.

Field, M. (1993) *APL Developing More Flexible Colleges*, London, Routledge.

Fitz-Gibbon, C. (1996) *Monitoring Education: Indicators, Quality and Effectiveness*, London, Cassell.

Foskett, N. (1996) Introduction, in N. Foskett (ed.) *Markets in Education: Policy, Process and Practice*, Proceedings of an International Symposium organized by the Centre for Research in Education Marketing, University of Southampton, Chilworth Manor Conference Centre, University of Southampton, 4–5 July, 1996.

Foskett, N. (1999) Strategy, external relations and marketing, in J. Lumby and N. Foskett (eds) *Managing External Relations in Schools and Colleges*, London, Paul Chapman.

Foskett, N. and Helmsley-Brown, J. (1999) Communicating the organisation, in J. Lumby and N. Foskett (eds) *Managing External Relations in Schools and Colleges*, London, Paul Chapman.

Fullan, M. (1999) *Change Forces: The Sequel*, London, Falmer.

Gillham, B. (1995) Moving into the open, in D. Thomas (ed.) *Flexible Learning Strategies in Higher and Further Education*, London, Cassell.

Golby, M. (1992) School governors: conceptual and practical problems, *Journal of Philosophy of Education*, Vol. 26, no. 2, pp. 165–72.

Gorringe, R. (1994a) Changing the culture of human resource development in colleges, in G. Brain (ed.) *Managing and Developing People*, Blagdon, The Staff College.

Gorringe, R. (1994b) Devising a new funding methodology for further education – the funding learning approach, in C. Flint and M. Austin (eds) *Going Further*, Blagdon, The Staff College in association with the Association for Colleges.

Goulding, J., Dominey, J. and Gray, M. (1998) *Hard-Nosed Decisions: Planning Human Resources in FE*, London, FEDA.

Gray, L. (1991) *Marketing Education*, Buckingham, Open University Press.

Gray, L. and Warrender, A. (1993) Cost-effective technical education in developing countries, *Coombe Lodge Report*, Vol. 23, no. 5, pp. 359–424.

Greenfield, T. B. (1978) The decline and fall of science in educational administration, *Interchange*, Vol. 17, no. 2, pp. 57–80.

Hall, J. (1999) Partnerships put lid on Pandora's box, *Times Educational Supplement*, 19 November (online) *http://www.tes.co.uk/tp/900000/PRN/teshome.html* (accessed 24 January 2000).

Hall, V. (1994) *Further Education in the United Kingdom*, London, Collins Educational.

Hall, V. (1997) Management roles in education, in T. Bush and M. Middlewood (eds) *Managing People in Education*, London, Paul Chapman.

Handy, C. (1989) *The Age of Unreason*, London, Random House.

Handy, C. (1990) *Understanding Voluntary Organizations*, London, Penguin.

Handy, C. (1993) *Understanding Organizations*, 4th edn, London, Penguin.

Handy, C. (1994) *The Empty Raincoat*, London, Random House.

Hanna, D. (1997) The organization as an open system, in A. Harris, N. Bennett and M. Preedy (eds) *Organizational Effectiveness and Improvement in Education*, Buckingham, Open University Press.

Hargreaves, D. (1996) Teaching as a research-based profession: possibilities and prospects, *The Teacher Training Agency Annual Lecture*, London, TTA.

Harling, P. (1989) The organizational framework for educational leadership, in T. Bush (ed.) *Managing Education: Theory and Practice*, Milton Keynes, Open University Press.

Harper, H. (1997) *Management in Further Education: Theory and Practice*, London, David Fulton.

Hartley, D. (1997) The new managerialism in education: a mission impossible? *Cambridge Journal of Education*, Vol. 27, no. 1, pp. 47–57.

Hatton, A. and Sedgemore, L. (1992) *Marketing for College Managers: A Workbook for the Effective Integration of Marketing into College Planning*, Bristol, The Staff College.

Hedburg, C. and Jonsson, S. (1977) Strategy making as a discontinuous process, *International Studies of Management and Organisation*, Vol. 7, pp. 88–109.

Hesselbein, F. (1999) Managing in a world that is round, in F. Hesselbein and P. Cohen (eds) *Leader to Leader*, San Francisco, Jossey-Bass.

Hewitt, P. and Crawford M. (1997) Introducing new contracts: managing change in the context of an enterprise culture, in R. Levacic and R. Glatter (eds) Managing change in further education, *FEDA Report*, Vol. 1. no. 7, pp. 113–32.

Hofstede, G. (1980) *Culture's Consequences*, Beverley Hills, Sage.

Hofstede, G. (1997) Motivation, leadership and organization: do American theories apply abroad? in D. Pugh (ed.) *Organization Theory*, 4th edn, London, Penguin.

Hopkins, M. (1998) How Effective are the Swindon College Quality Assurance Procedures at assuring quality? Dissertation for the MBA in Education, South Bank University.

Hough, J. (1994) Educational cost-benefit analysis, *Education Economics*, Vol. 2, no. 2, pp. 93–127.

Hoy, W. and Miskel, C. (1989) Schools and their external environments, in R. Glatter (ed.) *Educational Institutions and their Environments: Managing the Boundaries*, Milton Keynes, Open University Press.

Hoyle, E. (1982) Micropolitics of educational organizations, *Educational Management and Administration*, Vol. 10, no. 2, pp. 87–98.

Hughes, C., Taylor, P. and Tight, M. (1996) The ever-changing world of further education: a case for research, *Research in Post-Compulsory Education*, Vol. 1, no. 1, pp. 7–18.

Hughes, M. (1996) *Colleges Working with Industry*, London, FEDA.

Hughes, M. and Kypri, P. (1998) Beyond responsiveness: promoting good practice in economic development, *FEDA Matters*, Vol. 2, no. 5, pp. 5–45.

Imrie, B. (1995) Labour market considerations in Hong Kong, *Industry and Higher Education*, Vol. 9, no. 5, pp. 277–84.

Ishikawa, K. (1985) *What Is Total Quality Control? The Japanese Way*, London, Prentice Hall.

James, S. and Clark, G. (1997) Investing partners: further education, economic development and regional policy, *FEDA Report*, Vol. 2, no. 1, pp. 7–92.

Johnson, G. (1993) Processes of managing strategic change, in C. Mabey and B. Mayon-White (eds) *Managing Change*, 2nd edn, London, Paul Chapman.

Juran, J. M. (1988) *Quality Control Handbook*, New York, McGraw-Hill.

Kanter, R. M. (1989) *When Giants Learn to Dance*, London, Simon and Schuster.

Kennedy, H. (1997) *Learning Works: Widening Participation in Further Education*, Coventry, FEFC.

Kennedy, M. (1997) The connection between research and practice, *Educational Researcher*, Vol. 26, no. 7, October, pp. 4–11.

King, K. (1993) Technical and vocational education and training in an international context, *The Vocational Aspect of Education*, Vol. 45, no. 3, pp. 201–16.

Leney, T., Lucas, N. and Taubaum, D. (1998) *Learning Funding: The Impact of FEFC Funding. Evidence from Twelve Colleges*, London, University of London, Institute of Education and NATFHE.

Lewin, R. (1997) *Complexity: Life on the Edge of Chaos*, London, Phoenix.

Lucas, N. (1998) FEFC Funding: research on 12 colleges, *Journal of Further and Higher Education*, Vol. 22, no. 3, pp. 299–306.

Lumby, J. (1996) Curriculum change in further education, *The Vocational Aspect of Education*, Vol. 48, no. 4, pp. 333–48.

Lumby, J. (1998) Understanding strategic change, in D. Middlewood and J. Lumby (eds) *Managing Strategy in Education*, London, Paul Chapman.

Lumby, J. (1999a) Achieving responsiveness, in J. Lumby, and N. Foskett (eds) *Managing External Relations in Schools and Colleges*, London, Paul Chapman.

Lumby, J. (1999b) Strategic planning in further education: the business of values, *Educational Management and Administration*, Vol. 27, no. 1, pp. 71–83.

Lumby, J. (2000a) Technical colleges in South Africa: planning for the future, *Journal of Vocational Education and Training*, Vol. 52, no. 1, pp. 101–17.

Lumby, J. (2000b) Restructuring vocational education in Hong Kong, *International Journal of Educational Management*, Vol. 14, no. 1, pp. 16–22.

Lumby, J. (2000c) Funding learning in further education, in M. Coleman and L. Anderson (eds) *Managing Finance and Resources in Education*, London, Paul Chapman.

Lumby, J. and Li, Y. (1998) Managing vocational education in China, *Compare*, Vol. 28, no. 2, pp. 197–206.

Lumby, J. and Tomlinson, H. (2000) Principals speaking: managerialism and leadership in further education, *Research in Post-Compulsory Education*, Vol. 5, no. 2, pp. 139–51.

Lundy, O. and Cowling, A. (1996) *Strategic Human Resource Management*, London, Routledge.

Marsh, D. T. (1992) Leadership and its functions in further and higher education, *Mendip Paper 03*, Bristol, The Staff College.

Maslow, A. (1943) A theory of human motivation, *Psychological Review*, Vol. 50, no. 4, pp. 370–96.

McClelland, D. (1961) *The Achieving Society*, Princeton, NJ, Van Nostrand.

McGregor, D. (1970) *The Human Side of Enterprise*, Maidenhead, McGraw-Hill.

Merrick, N. (1996) Deputy posts axed as colleges 'delayer', *13.12.96 Times Educational Supplement* (online) *http://www.tes.co.uk:8484/tp/900000/PRN/network/library/libraryarc.html* (accessed 4 January 2000).

Middlewood, D., Coleman, M. and Lumby, J. (1999) *Practitioner Research in Education*, London, Paul Chapman.

Mintzberg, H. (1996) Ten ideas to rile everyone who cares about management, *Harvard Business Review*, July–August.

Mintzberg, H. and Waters, J. A. (1985) Of strategies deliberate and emergent, *Strategic Management Journal*, Vol. 6, no. 3, pp. 257–72.

Morgan, G. (1986) *Images of Organization*, London, Sage.

Morgan, G. (1997) Imaginization: on spider plants, in D. Pugh (ed.) *Organization Theory*, 4th Edn, London, Penguin.

Nash, I. (1999) Colleges face worst governor shortage, *Times Educational Supplement*, FE Focus, p. 1, 14 January.

O'Neill, J. (1994) Managing human resources, in T. Bush and J. West-Burnham (eds) *Principles of Educational Management*, Harlow, Longman.

Ogawa, R. and Bossert, S. (1997) Leadership as an organizational quality, in M. Crawford, L. Kydd and C. Riches (eds) *Leadership and Teams in Educational Management*, Buckingham, Open University Press.

Parker, S. (1997) Information systems: a strategic approach, *Bulletin*, Vol. 1, no. 14, pp. 1–8, London, FEDA.

Pascale, R. T. (1991) *Managing on the Edge*, London, Penguin.

Perry, A. (1999) Performance indicators: measure for measure or a comedy of errors? Paper given at FEDA Research Conference, Cambridge, 9–10 December.

Peters, T. (1989) *Thriving on Chaos*, London, Pan.

Pfeffer, J. (1993) Understanding power in organizations, in C. Mabey and B. Mayon-White (eds) *Managing Change*, 2nd edn, London, Paul Chapman.

Proctor, J. and Wright, R. (1995) The development of open workshops: how to make it happen, in D. Thomas (ed.) *Flexible Learning Strategies in Higher and Further Education*, London, Cassell.

Quinn, J. B. (1993) Managing strategic change, in C. Mabey and B. Mayon-White (eds) *Managing Change*, 2nd edn, London, Paul Chapman.

Randle, K. and Brady, N. (1997a) Further education and the new managerialism, *Journal of Further and Higher Education*, Vol. 21, no. 2, pp. 229–39.

Randle, K. and Brady, N. (1997b) Managerialism and professionalism in the Cinderella service, *Journal of Vocational Education and Training*, Vol. 49, no. 1, pp. 121–39.

Riches, C. (1994) Communication, in T. Bush and J. West-Burnham (eds) *The Principles of Educational Management*, London, Longman.

Robson, J. (1998) A profession in crisis: status, culture and identity in the further education college, *Journal of Vocational Education and Training*, Vol. 50. no. 4, pp. 585–607.

Rudden, T. (1999) Making sense of statistics, *College Research*, Vol. 3, no. 1, pp. 44–7.

Sallis, E. (1996) *Total Quality Management in Education*, 2nd edn, London, Kogan Page.

Savage, W. W. (1989) Communication: process and problems, in C. Riches and M. Morgan (eds) *Human Resource Management in Education*, Milton Keynes, Open University Press.

Schein, E. H. (1997) *Organizational Culture and Leadership*, 2nd edn, San Francisco, Jossey-Bass.

Scott, P. (1989) Accountability, responsiveness and responsibility, in R. Glatter (ed.) *Educational Institutions and their Environments: Managing the Boundaries*, Milton Keynes, Open University Press.

Scott, P. (1996) Markets in post-compulsory education – rhetoric, policy and structure, in N. Foskett (ed.) *Markets in Education: Policy, Process and Practice*, Proceedings of an International Symposium organized by the Centre for Research in Education Marketing, University of Southampton, Chilworth Manor Conference Centre, University of Southampton, 4–5 July 1996.

Semler, R. (1993) *Maverick! The Success Behind the World's Most Unusual Workplace*, London, Random House.

Senge, P. (1993) *The Fifth Discipline*, London, Century Business.

Sergiovanni, T. (1984) Leadership and excellence in schooling, *Educational Leadership*, February, Vol 41, No 5 pp. 6–13.

Sergiovanni, T. (1990) Adding value to leadership gets extraordinary results, *Educational Leadership*, May, Vol 47, No 8 pp. 23–27.

Shackleton, J. (1988) The professional role of the lecturer, in B. Kedney and D. Parkes (eds) *Planning the Further Education Curriculum: Implications of the 1988 Education Reform Act*, London, FEU.

Shackleton, J. (1989) Planning for the future in further education: beyond a curriculum-led approach, in M. Preedy (ed.) *Approaches to Curriculum Management*, Milton Keynes, Open University Press.

Silverman, D. (2000) *Doing Qualitative Research: A Practical Handbook*, London, Sage.

Simkins, T. (1998) Autonomy, restraint and the strategic management of resources, in D. Middlewood and J. Lumby (eds) *Strategic Management in Schools and Colleges*, London, Paul Chapman.

Skilbeck, M., Connel, H., Lowe, N. and Tait, K. (1994) *The Vocational Quest: New Directions in Education and Training*, London, Routledge.

Smith, D., Scott, P. and Lynch, J. (1995) *The Role of Marketing in the University and College Sector*, Leeds, Heist Publications.

Stead, B., Fletcher, B. and Jones, F. (1995) Relationships between workload, cognitive decision making and psychological wellbeing, in *Proceedings of the British Psychological Society Occupations Psychology Conference*, Eastbourne, January.

Temple, H. (1991) *Open Learning in Industry, Developing Flexibility and Competence in the Workforce*, Harlow, Longman.

Thomas, D. (1995) Learning to be flexible, in D. Thomas (ed.) *Flexible Learning Strategies in Higher and Further Education*, London, Cassell.

Thomas, H. (1999) Managerial implications of adopting formula-based systems of resource allocation, *Educational Management and Administration*, Vol. 27, no. 2, pp. 183–91.

Thorne, P. (1995) Supporting, assessing and accrediting workplace learning, in D. Thomas (ed.) *Flexible Learning Strategies in Higher and Further Education*, London, Cassell.

Tierney, W. G. (1998) *Building the Responsive Campus: Creating High Performance Colleges and Universities*, London, Sage.

Tooley, J. and Darby, D. (1998) *Educational Research: A Critique*, London, Ofsted.

Turner, C. (1990) Organisational culture, *Mendip Paper 007*, Blagdon, The Staff College.

Turner, C. (1991) Structures – fact and fiction, *Mendip Paper 015*, Blagdon, The Staff College.

Wallace, M. (1999) Combining cultural and political perspectives: the best of both conceptual worlds? in T. Bush, L. Bell, R. Bolam, R. Glatter and P. Ribbins (eds) *Education or Management: Redefining Theory, Policy and Practice*, London, Paul Chapman.

Waring, S. (1999) Colleges and customers, in J. Lumby and N. Foskett (eds) *Managing External Relations in Schools and Colleges*, London, Paul Chapman.

Waterhouse, R. (1999) Ten colleges hog the poor grades, *Times Educational Supplement*, FE Focus, p. 1, 26 October.

Weber, M. (1947) *The Theory of Social and Economic Organisation*, New York, Free Press.

Weick, K. (1976) Educational organisations as loosely coupled systems, *Administrative Science Quarterly*, Vol. 21, no. 1, pp. 1–19.

West-Burnham, J. (1994) Inspection, evaluation and quality assurance, in T. Bush and J. West-Burnham (eds) *The Principles of Educational Management*, Harlow, Longman.

West-Burnham, J., Bush, T., O'Neill, J. and Glover, D. (1995) *Leadership and Strategic Management*, London, Pitman.

Wheatley, M. (1999) Good-bye command and control, in F. Hesslebein and P. Cohen (eds) *Leader to Leader*, San Francisco, Jossey-Bass.

Wildavsky, A. (1973) If planning is everything maybe it's nothing, *Policy Sciences*, Vol. 4, no. 2, pp. 127–53.

Wildavsky, A. (1979) *Speaking Truth to Power: The Art and Craft of Policy Analysis*, Boston, MA, Little, Brown.

Yorke, M. (1997) Dynamic hieroglyphic evaluation as confection, in P. Davies (ed.) *Performance Indicators: Evaluating the Student Experience: A BI AIR Compendium*, Blagdon, FEDA.

Young, M. (1993) A curriculum for the 21st century? Towards a new basis for overcoming the academic/vocational division, *British Journal of Educational Studies*, Vol. 41, no. 3, Autumn, pp. 203–22.

INDEX